John Augustine Zahm

Bible, Science, and Faith

John Augustine Zahm

Bible, Science, and Faith

ISBN/EAN: 9783744660525

Printed in Europe, USA, Canada, Australia, Japan

Cover: Foto ©Lupo / pixelio.de

More available books at **www.hansebooks.com**

BIBLE, SCIENCE, AND FAITH.

BY

THE REVEREND J. A. ZAHM, C. S. C.;

PROFESSOR OF PHYSICS IN THE UNIVERSITY OF NOTRE DAME; AUTHOR
OF "SOUND AND MUSIC," "CATHOLIC SCIENCE AND
CATHOLIC SCIENTISTS," ETC.

"'Ἤδη δὲ οὔτε ἡ γνῶσις ἄνευ πίστεως, οὔθ' ἡ πίστις ἄνευ γνώσεως."—
CLEMENT OF ALEXANDRIA.

Behold the star-writ book outspread in space,
Read thou the rock-bound tome the ages trace,
And from them learn that mortal mind nor hand
Of Nature's smallest force hath full command.

Ay, knowledge springs from faith, as bursts the flower
From hidden seed, while in that blossom's dower
Faith lives anew. 'Twas Eden's fateful tree
That shrouded science in dim mystery.

COPYRIGHT, 1894, BY JOHN MURPHY & CO.

TO

THE VERY REVEREND GILBERT FRANÇAIS, C.S.C.,
SUPERIOR-GENERAL OF THE CONGREGATION OF THE HOLY CROSS,

THE CULTURED SCHOLAR

AND

THE SUCCESSFUL EDUCATOR,

THIS BOOK

IS AFFECTIONATELY DEDICATED.

INTRODUCTION.

OURS is pre-eminently an age of intellectual ferment—an age of discovery and discussion and co-ordination. But in nothing is this mental quickening and activity so conspicuous as in questions bearing on science in its relations to religion. Hence the interest aroused by all discoveries—scientific, historical, and archæological—which directly or indirectly affect the Bible, or tend in any way to modify our views of its contents, or throw new light on difficult and disputed passages. Hence also the interest which attaches to what has unfortunately, I think, been called the Higher Criticism, and hence, too, the avidity with which the reading public follows current controversies respecting the origin and age of our race, as well as those regarding other similar topics, which, owing to the results of modern research, we must now, perforce, consider from new points of view. A more extensive acquaintance with the natural and physical sciences, and the accumulation by Egyptologists and Assyriologists of a large mass of new historical facts of far-reaching importance, have thrown a flood of light on many parts of the Bible which previously were ill understood, if at all, and have supplied us with the necessary data for the solution of numerous perplexing problems of a scientifico-scriptural character which before were regarded as mysteries that were simply inexplicable.

Those who still view the Bible as a divinely inspired book, despite the repeated attacks made on its authenticity and inspiration, as well as those who yet hold to the teachings of their faith, notwithstanding the theories of a certain school of scientists, who relegate religion and belief in a personal God to the limbo of idle fancies, are frequently accused of forswearing their liberty of thought, and of voluntarily placing themselves in a condition of intellectual thraldom which incapacitates them from appreciating the true significance of the most important inductions and generalizations of modern science. Groundless as this charge is, there are not a few, even among intelligent people, who believe it to be substantially true.

And yet nothing could be more false or absurd. As well say that the mariner forfeits his freedom of action because, forsooth, he gives heed to the buoys and lighthouses which are stationed along his course, and which signalize reefs and shoals and indicate places where the safety of his vessel would be imperilled or where navigation is impossible. What buoys and lighthouses are to the seafaring man, that expressions of revealed truth and principles of Christian philosophy are to the man of science. They are so many beacons warning him of the hidden rocks of religious error or the treacherous coast-line of a false philosophy. They are lights in the darkness which point out the path which he may travel in safety, and which disclose to him the treacherous shallows where danger is certain and destruction inevitable.

As the master of a ship neither sacrifices his intellectual freedom nor commits an act of unwisdom by following the indications of buoy and lighthouse, so neither does the man of science forfeit his liberty of thought nor violate the dictates of right reason in suffering himself to be guided by the teachings of an infallible faith or by the divinely inspired words of the Book of books. And as the mariner's progress is not impeded by the number of lighthouses along his course, but rather assisted, so likewise is the man of science materially aided in his search after scientific truth by the beacon-lights of faith which point out to him in no unmistakable manner the true and safe realms of science and philosophy.

The truths of faith and the truths of science belong to different categories indeed, but notwithstanding this fact they can never come into conflict. The truths of science are of the natural order, while the truths of faith belong to an order which is supernatural. But both have God for their author, and as He cannot contradict Himself, and as truth cannot be opposed to truth, so the truths of faith never can be at variance with the certain conclusions of science. Whether we study the Bible or the great book of

Nature, we in either case have before us the Almighty's record, and the truths inculcated, if so be that we read aright, will in all cases be in perfect harmony with one another as well as with Truth itself. The testimony, therefore, of Holy Writ and the testimony of the rocks, far from being contradictory, will always, we shall find, be identical in evidence as they are one in origin.

This being the case, the man of science is not only thoroughly untrammelled in his work, but he has absolutely nothing to apprehend, so far as his faith is concerned, from the most searching and the most profound investigations which may be instituted in any of the manifold departments of historical or scientific research and criticism. On the contrary, he welcomes every genuine contribution to science as a precious addition to the already vast store of knowledge, and he encourages the most thorough investigation in every line of human inquiry as something which is sure to issue in results which shall not only be of value to science, but which shall also be of priceless worth in illustrating and corroborating the truths of faith as well.

Should we desire a proof of these assertions, we have it to hand in the life and works of the most eminent representatives of every branch of science and in the positive declarations of the ablest leaders of thought of all time. Copernicus, Mersenne, Linnæus, Champollion, Cuvier, Pascal, Newton, Sir Humphry Davy, Faraday,

Ampère, Cauchy, Descartes, Johann Müller, Schwann, L. Agassiz, Lenormant, Secchi, Leverrier, Dana, Pasteur, Van Beneden, and scores of others equally illustrious, are undying witnesses of the essential oneness of the truth of science and faith, and of the certain conviction, which these great exponents of science always entertained, that the book of Nature and the book of the Spirit, although appealing to us in different tongues, ever voice the same testimony and proclaim the same truth. They both, in words eloquent and sublime, tell us of a God infinite in wisdom and love and perfection, who ordains all things well, and who compasses His ends with infinite knowledge and power.

No, the man of science is not intellectually hampered because he happens to be a man of faith and of strong religious persuasions. His acceptance of the Bible does not handicap him in research nor preclude him from enjoying the completest mental liberty of which mortal man is capable. His faith shields him from danger as the beacon-light protects the mariner from harm, but it in no wise restricts his freedom of thought or action. By hearkening to the gentle voice of religion he escapes the errors of Atheism, Pantheism, Materialism, and Monism, which are at present so rampant, and which have more than anything else obstructed research and retarded the progress of true science.

One may indeed reject the truths of the Bible and

discard the teachings of faith, as the mariner may ignore the saving bell or the friendly pharos, but he does so at his peril. Far from gaining anything by this mad assertion of independence—an independence which means not liberty and life, but rashness and destruction—he inevitably loses, and his loss carries with it the loss and death, it may be, of others besides. There is too much of doubt and uncertainty in the world of science for us to decline the undeniable helps of revelation—too much fog and darkness enveloping many of the problems of philosophy for us to close our eyes to the sun of Truth or for us to make naught of the light of God's inspired word.

Speaking for my single self—and I am sure I but echo the sentiments of all Christian men of science—I can honestly and truly affirm that I have never once felt, during the quarter of a century and more which I have given to the study of religio-scientific questions, that the teachings of faith have in any way embarrassed me, or detracted in the slightest degree from my enjoying the fullest measure of intellectual freedom. And this is not because I have ever been disposed to minimize the force and scope of dogma or sought to explain away the certain declarations of Scripture, for it has never entered my mind to do either the one or the other. No one could be more strenuously opposed to rationalism in matters of religion than I am, and no one could yield more ready and unconditional acquiescence to the teachings of the Church in all matters pertaining to faith and morals.

Rationalism in religion, however, is quite a different thing from a legitimate use of the reason in discussing questions of science and history and archæology which may be incidentally mentioned in Scripture or are indirectly and remotely connected with some teaching of faith. Herein I claim, as every one may claim—and faith and the Church are the first to grant all the lawful demands of the intellect—perfect freedom of investigation according to the principles and methods of science, prescinded from all the restraints of petty dogmatism, and the questionable authority of systems which are obsolete or of schools which have long survived their period of usefulness. Among such questions are those discussed in the following pages, especially the questions concerning the Mosaic Hexaëmeron, the Noachian Deluge, the origin and antiquity of the human race, and the biblical chronology, not to mention a number of correlative topics of similar purport.

Parts I. and II. of this work are composed of articles, revised and annotated, which have appeared in the *American Ecclesiastical Review*, while Part III. embraces a series of papers which were printed in the *American Catholic Quarterly Review*. The articles cover substantially the same ground as a course of lectures which I gave last year before the Catholic Summer School at Plattsburgh, N. Y.—lectures which excited widespread interest, and which for some time furnished both the religious and the secular press with special material for comment and criticism. With few exceptions I have more than reason to be gratified with the complimentary notices given of the lectures, especially by the secular press, and for the friendly spirit which it displayed on all occasions, as well as for the extreme interest it manifested in the questions discussed. It is in consequence of these kindly notices, as well as of my desire to comply with repeated requests from all parts of the United States and Europe to have the lectures published, that I now give this volume to the public, trusting that it will prove an acceptable contribution to a subject which is daily growing in interest and importance.

For the benefit of readers who may wish to pursue further the questions of which this book treats I have endeavored to indicate in the footnotes the chief authorities I have followed, and to give volume and page for the quotations and extracts I have reproduced. In attempting to discuss several great and comprehensive questions within the compass of a single small volume I have been necessarily brief, but, I trust, not obscure. For all shortcomings which may be detected—and no one is more conscious of their existence than myself—I crave in advance the reader's benignity and indulgence.

J. A. ZAHM, C. S. C.

NOTRE DAME UNIVERSITY,
  May 22, 1894.

CONTENTS.

PART I.

THE MOSAIC HEXAËMERON IN THE LIGHT OF EXEGESIS AND MODERN SCIENCE.

CHAPTER I.

MOSES AND SCIENCE.

Systems of cosmogony and geogony.—The world-egg of the Polynesians and Hindus.—Hindu view of the earth.—Natural history of the Hindus.—Cosmogonies of Homer and of the Ionic School.—Theories of Pythagoras and Ptolemy.—Opinion of Plato.—The cosmogony of Moses.—Declarations of modern scholars respecting the Mosaic cosmogony.—Dillman and Donoso Cortes on the Genesiac narrative of creation.—Chief lessons taught by the cosmogony of Moses.—Statement of Cuvier.—Genesis and science.—Words of Linnæus.—Difficulties of Genesis.—Exploded theories.—Liberty of thought enjoyed by children of the Church.—The Bible not a text-book of science.—Declarations of Cardinal Newman and Father Ryder.—Faith and science always at one 23

CHAPTER II.

ALLEGORISM AND LITERALISM.

The Alexandrine School as represented by Clement of Alexandria and Origen.—Allegorical, mystical, or ideal systems of interpretation.—The Syrian School and the literal system of exegesis.—The theory of intervals or restitution.—The period or concordistic system.—The eclectic system of St. Gregory of Nyssa and St. Augustine.—Philo Judæus.—Views of Clement of Alexandria.—Genius and achievements of Origen.—His erudition and love of science.—Opinion of St. Athanasius.—The Alexandrine theory in the light of geology and palæontology.—Schools of Antioch, Edessa, and Cæsarea.—Teachings of St. Ephrem.—Views of St. John Chrysostom.—The *Hexaëmeron* of St. Basil.—Gnostics and Neo-Platonists.—Mistakes of St. John Chrysostom and Cosmas Indicopleustes.—Defects of extreme literalism and allegorism.—A *via media* 44

CHAPTER III.

ST. GREGORY OF NYSSA AND THE NEBULAR HYPOTHESIS.

Cæsarea, "the metropolis of the arts and sciences."—Objections of the Manichæans and of Julian the Apostate.—Love of science manifested by the Cappadocian Doctors.—Learning and brilliancy of St. Gregory of Nyssa.—Erroneous views entertained by the earlier students of science.—Philosophic method of St. Gregory.—He avoids the excessive allegorism of the Alexandrine and the exaggerated literalism of the Syrian Schools.—Gregory's system of cosmogony explained.—Meaning of the words "void and empty"—*inanis et vacua*—as used in the first chapter of Genesis.—Marvellous intuitions of St. Gregory.—The primitive nebulous matter according to Gregory, and his views regarding the origin of the solar and stellar systems.—Realization of difficulties which could not be solved until a much later period.—St. Gregory of Nyssa the father and founder of the modern school of scriptural interpretation, and the originator of the nebular hypothesis as subsequently developed and explained by Laplace 60

CHAPTER IV.

ST. AUGUSTINE AND EVOLUTION.

St. Augustine's knowledge of profane science.—His keen intellect, critical acumen, and logical method.—Eminent as philosopher, theologian, and exegetist.—Founder and chief representative of the eclectic school of interpretation.—His doubts and difficulties.—Various systems adopted and rejected.—His most important works on cosmogony. The meaning of the word "day" as employed in the Mosaic account of creation.—St. Augustine's views regarding the government of the universe by law.—His ideas concerning miracles and specific creations.—His interest in Hebrew cosmogony.—The six days of creation and their explanation.—Creation—*ex nihilo*—

of primordial matter, and evolution of worlds from primitive nebulous matter.—Precursor and prophet of the modern school of exegesis.—Creation by secondary causes, or derivative creation.—St. Augustine anticipates the teachings of modern evolutionists.—His *causales rationes*.—The *opus creationis* and the *opus formationis*.—Animals and plants created potentially, not as they now appear.—The saint's exuberance of language and wealth of illustration.—Formless matter.—Theory of creation as held by the Fathers and St. Thomas Aquinas.—The laws of nature.—Principles of exegesis.—Value of science and philosophy in the service of faith.—Invariability of the principles of exegesis, and changeableness of scientific theories.—St. Gregory's views on the transformation of matter—on the nature of light.—Modern theories respecting the nature of light.—Nothing in modern science to impair the truthfulness of the Mosaic cosmogony.—Perfect harmony between Genesis and science . . . 70

CHAPTER V.

MODERN THEORIES OF COSMOGONY AND INTERPRETATION.

The restitution or interval theory, a link between the literal and period theories.—Proposed by Buckland and favored by Chalmers and Cardinal Wiseman.—The period or concordistic theory, proposed by Cuvier, and the one most favored at present. -According to this theory the word "day," as used in the Genesiac narrative of creation, signifies an indeterminate period of time.—The Mosaic days metaphorical, not only as to their signification, but also as to their number.—Creation of organized beings according to Genesis.—Barrande and Cuvier on Genesis and geology.—The concordistic theory but provisional.—The theory of Bishop Clifford, who regards the first chapter of Genesis not as an historical narrative, but as a ritual hymn.—Reasons in support of this view.—Intellectual freedom of the Fathers and Doctors of the Church.—St. Augustine on the interpretation of the Genesiac account of creation.—Inspiration of the biblical writers.—Father Faber on religion and science.—No possible antagonism between science and faith, and none between science and Genesis.—Recapitulation and conclusion 92

PART II.

THE NOACHIAN DELUGE.

CHAPTER I.

THE GEOGRAPHICAL AND ZOOLOGICAL UNIVERSALITY OF THE DELUGE.

PAGE

Interest attaching to the subject.—Notions of early geologists regarding fossils as *reliquiæ Diluvianæ*.—Voltaire's opinions.—Views of Buckland and Moigno.—When and by whom the geographical universality of the Deluge was first called in question.—Teaching of fossil remains.—Number of species of animals.—Divers centres of creation and distribution.—Multiplication of miracles.—The water of the Deluge.—Universal terms employed in the narrative of the Deluge; their significance.—Illustrations.—Teaching of Fathers and Doctors.—Statements of Pallavicini, St. Thomas, Patrizzi, and Fessler.—Exceptions noted.—Views of Franzelin and Suarez.—Not of faith that the Deluge was universal, either as to the earth's surface or as to the animals which inhabit it.—An open question to be settled by science 119

CHAPTER II.

THE ANTHROPOLOGICAL UNIVERSALITY OF THE DELUGE.

Novelty of the question.—Broached but recently. The Church has never taught that the universal destruction of mankind is of faith.—Restricted meaning of universal terms.—Objections on the part of science against the ethnographical universality of the Deluge.—The teachings of geology, archæology, ethnology, physiology, and linguistics.—The Deluge in the light of scriptural exegesis.—Opinion of Canon Motais.—" Sons of God and daughters of men."—Who were the Cainites?—Prophecy of Balaam.—Advocates of the theory of a restricted deluge.—Résumé of the question by Abbé Motais.—Opinion of Cardinal Gonzalez.—Liberty of thought in controverted questions.—Words of Leo XIII.—Testimony of St. Augustine and St. Thomas Aquinas 152

PART III.

THE AGE OF THE HUMAN RACE ACCORDING TO MODERN SCIENCE AND BIBLICAL CHRONOLOGY.

CHAPTER I.

THE ANTIQUITY OF MAN ACCORDING TO ASTRONOMY AND HISTORY.

PAGE

Imaginary antagonism between the teachings of Scripture and the findings of modern science.—Prevalence of Rationalism during the first centuries of the Church's history, during the Middle Ages, and in modern times.—English Deists, French Infidels, German Rationalists.—The work of Voltaire, Reimarus, Lessing, Strauss.—Modern Materialism and Atheism.—Dogmatism of science.—Hindu astronomy.—Zodiacs of Esneh and Denderah.—Champollion's discoveries.—Chronology of India.—Researches of Sir William Jones, Klaproth, and Heeren.—Opinions of Max Müller, Mgr. Laouënan, and Barthélemy Saint-Hilaire.—Boasted antiquity of the Chinese without foundation.—Monuments, papyri, and inscriptions of Egypt respecting the antiquity of man.—Dynasties of Manetho.—Views of Brugsch, Mariette, De Rougé, and Vigouroux.—Cuneiform inscriptions of Western Asia.—History of Berosus.—Discoveries of Niebuhr, Grotefend, Burnouf, Lassen, and Sir Henry Rawlinson.—Investigations of Botta, Layard, and Smith.—Library of Assurbanipal.—Chaldean astronomy.—Researches of Strassmaier and Epping.—Assyrian chronology, its trustworthiness.—The age of our race according to Egyptology and Assyriology 177

CHAPTER II.

THE ANTIQUITY OF MAN ACCORDING TO GEOLOGY AND CLIMATOLOGY.

The Golden Age of the pagan poets.—The teachings of certain modern scientists regarding primitive man.—Views of Häckel.—His twenty-two types in the genealogy of man.—*Bathybius Hackelii.*—*Alalus* and Lemuria.—Scientific Atheism.—Declarations of Häckel, Vogt, Royer, Virchow, Büchner, and Flourens.—Principles of

Monism.—Tertiary man.—Investigations of Abbé Bourgeois and Abbé Delaunay.—M. Mortillet's *Anthropopithecus*.—Lyell's Uniformitarianism.—Alluvial deposits.—Rate of growths of peat-bogs. —Formation of stalagmites.—De Lapparent on the Quaternary Epoch.—Was Europe inhabited in antediluvian times?—Evidences of cataclysmic action.—Destructive effects of earthquakes and volcanoes.—Causes of the Ice Age.—Theories of Lyell, Croll, and Geike.—Observations of Prestwich and Wright.—Views of Howorth and the Duke of Argyll.—Ancient Greek and Roman authors on the climate of Europe.—Declaration of M. Fuster.—The mammoth, reindeer, cave-bear, cave-lion, hyena, and Irish elk.— Animals which have become extinct within historic times 219

CHAPTER III.

THE ANTIQUITY OF MAN ACCORDING TO PREHISTORIC ARCHÆOLOGY.—GEOLOGICAL CHRONOMETERS.

Evolution of the industrial arts.—Views of Hesiod as compared with those of modern scientists concerning early man.—The ages of Stone, Bronze, and Iron.—No fixed period of time for the Stone Age.—No Age of Bronze in Italy or Gaul.—The succession of the ages not general nor absolute.—Implements found in Chaldean tombs and Assyrian ruins.—The Iron Age in Africa.—Statement of Dr. Livingstone.—Schliemann's excavations at Hissarlik and Mycenæ.—Declarations of Percy and Tschering.—Meaning of the term *prehistoric*. Phœnician bronze.—The "ships of Tarshish."—Observations of M. Kerviler.—Remains of primitive man. —Skulls of Canstatt and Neanderthal.—Kitchen-middings.—Lake-dwellings of Switzerland and elsewhere.—Geological chronometers. —The Falls of Niagara and St. Anthony.—The age of the world and the duration of life on its surface.—Conclusions of various scientists.—Building theories on trifles.—Evidences of early man in the Trenton gravels.—Declaration of Goethe 266

CHAPTER IV.

THE ANTIQUITY OF MAN ACCORDING TO THE BIBLE.

Difficulty and uncertainty of biblical chronology.—Declarations of Abbé le Hir and Sylvestre de Sacy.—Des Vignoles' "Chronology of

Sacred History."—*L'Art de Vérifier les Dates*, by the Benedictines of St. Maur.—The Hebrew and Samaritan texts of the Scriptures.—The Greek version of the Septuagint.—Variants of the divers texts and versions.—Estimates of various chronologists.—The labors of Scaliger, Lepsius, and Usher.—Genealogical lists of the patriarchs —*Lacunæ* in these lists.—Oriental systems of genealogy.—Illustrations from the Old and New Testaments —Probable mnemotechnic reasons for incomplete genealogical tables —Views of Fathers Bellynck and Brucker.—Value of the chronological statements of the Sacred Text.—Opinions of Abbé de Foville and Abbé Bourgeois.—Fabre d'Envieu and Valroger on Preadamites.—Sundry estimates respecting the antiquity of man.—Declaration of Vigouroux.—Author's opinion regarding the age of our race.—The question to be settled by history rather than by science.—The certain conclusions of science in harmony with the teachings of Holy Writ.—Vagaries of modern science and scientists.—Indications of a return to a more conservative *régime* 293

PART I.

The Mosaic Hexaëmeron in the Light of Exegesis and Modern Science.

"Hæc autem de Scriptura pauca posuimus ut congruere nostra cum philosophis doceremus."

"We have alleged these few things from Scripture, so to show that our doctrines agree with those of the philosophers."
—St Jerome, *Adversus Jovinianum.*

BIBLE, SCIENCE, AND FAITH.

PART I.

The Mosaic Hexaëmeron in the Light of Exegesis and Modern Science.

CHAPTER I.

MOSES AND SCIENCE.

Cosmogonies of Polynesians and Hindus.

PROMINENT, if not chief, among the questions that from time immemorial have engaged the attention of mankind are those pertaining to the origin and constitution of this world of ours. All nations and all peoples, with the exception of those in the lowest scale of intelligence, have had their peculiar theories regarding geogony and cosmogony, to which they have clung with greater or less tenacity. Some of these theories were very elaborately worked out and contained many elements of truth; others, on the contrary, were absurd and ridiculous in the extreme, and afford us the most striking evidence possible regarding the simplicity of the people who accepted them, and their utter ignorance of the commonest laws and phenomena of nature.

According to the Sandwich Islanders, all was originally a vast ocean. It was then that an immense bird deposited on the waters an egg from which arose the islands of Hawaii. But this idea of a world-egg is not peculiar to the Hawaiians. It obtains among the Polynesians generally, and has prevailed among many peoples of the Old World as well. We find special prominence given to it in the Ordinances of Menu, wherein the Hindu cosmogony is developed at length. Brahma, the progenitor of all the worlds, was, we are informed, born from a golden egg. In this egg the supreme power remained for a divine year. Each one of the three hundred and sixty days of this divine year was equal to 12,000,000 of our years. After this long period the cosmic egg broke, and from its fragments were formed the heavens and the earth, the atmosphere and the abyss of waters.

The earth, according to the *Shastras*, "is a circular plain, resembling a water-lily. Its circumference is four hundred millions of miles. It is borne upon the backs of eight huge elephants; the elephants stand upon the back of an immense tortoise, and the tortoise upon a thousand-headed serpent. Whenever the serpent becomes drowsy and nods, an earthquake is produced. . . . The earth consists of seven concentric oceans and as many continents. They are arranged in regard to each other like the waves produced by throwing a pebble into water. The first ocean, the one nearest the centre, is filled with salt water, the second with milk, the third with the curds of milk, the fourth with melted butter, the fifth with the juice of the sugar-cane, the sixth with wine, and the seventh with fresh water. Beyond the seventh ocean is a land of pure gold, but inaccessible to man; and far beyond that extends the land of darkness, containing places of torment for the wicked.

"The continent at the centre of the earth is 250,000 miles in diameter. From its centre Mount Meru, composed entirely of gold and precious stones, rises to a height of 600,000 miles. Unlike all other mountains, it is much the largest at the top. It is crowned with three golden summits, which are the favorite residences of Brahma, Vishnu, and Shiva. Near these summits are the heavens of many of the inferior gods. One of them is described as being 800 miles in circumference and 40 miles in height. Its dome is supported by pillars composed of diamonds, its numerous palaces are of pure gold, and it is so ornamented with brilliant gems that its splendor exceeds the brightness of twelve suns."[1]

On the western slope of Mount Meru are found beautiful stretches of country, in which men who are of the color of gold live to the age of 10,000 or 12,000 years.

According to the Mahabharata, "The beings on the earth are divided into two classes—the animate and the inanimate. The animals constitute fourteen species, seven of which—monkeys, bears, elephants, buffaloes, wild boars, tigers, and lions—are wild in the forests; whilst seven others—men, sheep, goats, cows, horses, asses, and mules—live with men in towns. Man is the first of domestic animals; the lion is the first of savage animals. There are five species of plants."[2]

[1] *Historic Incidents and Life in India*, by Caleb Wright and J. A. Brainerd, pp. 26, 27.
[2] Barthelémy Saint-Hilaire, in the *Journal des Savants*, Jan., 1868, pp. 33, 34.

Greek Cosmogonies.

In the time of Homer, about 900 B. C., it was believed that the earth, surrounded by the river Oceanus, filled the lower half of the sphere of the world, while its upper half extended aloft—that Helios, the sun, quenched his fires every evening and relighted them the following morning, after having immersed himself in the deep waters of the ocean.

Thales and the Stoics and those of their school, we are informed by Plutarch, taught that the earth is spherical, like a ball; Anaximander maintained that it was in the form of a stone column. Many fancied it to have the form of a cube, and to be attached by its four corners to the vault of the firmament. Others, among them Leucippus, imagined it to have the shape of a drum, while others still declared it to be a disk, protected by the river Oceanus or guarded by a serpent which encircled it. Epicurus, who accepted the popular belief, taught that the stars were extinguished when they set, and relighted when they rose again—that the earth is held in place by cords or ligaments, just as the head is connected with the neck or trunk. To explain the revolution of the heavenly bodies, Anaximander taught that they were fixed in crystal spheres. Anaximenes, a disciple of Anaximander, maintained that the earth is flat like a table. He likewise held the same view regarding the sun. In accordance with the generally accepted opinion of his age, he thought that the stars were fixed like nails in a solid revolving sphere, which was invisible by reason of its transparency. In order to account for the peculiar motions of the sun, moon, and planets, Pythagoras devised his famous theory of *eccentrics and epicycles*[1]—a theory that, at a later date, was adopted and developed by Ptolemy, and accepted as the true explanation of planetary movements until the time of Copernicus. To meet new difficulties presented by the peculiar motions of the sun, moon, and planets, Eudoxus of Cnidus increased the number of crystal spheres to twenty-six. But these spheres, which were regarded as so many heavens arranged one inside the other, were not yet sufficiently numerous to account for the many and varied motions of the planets. The number was therefore augmented until astronomers recognized no fewer than fifty-six of these solid, revolving, invisible, transparent spheres.

Plato regarded the heavenly bodies as animated beings. The world, according to him, was but an animal, and its spherical form was the type of perfection. "The Creator," he tells us in the *Timæus*, "gave to the world the figure which was suitable and also natural. Now, to the animal which was to comprehend all animals that figure was suitable which comprehends within itself all other figures. Wherefore he made the world in the form of a globe, round as from a lathe, having its extremes in every direction equidistant from the centre, the most perfect and the most like itself of all figures; for he considered that the like is infinitely fairer than the unlike. This he finished off, making the surface smooth all round for many reasons: in the first place, because the living being had no need of eyes when there was nothing remaining outside him to be seen, nor of ears when

[1] Cf. *Histoire de l'Astronomie*, par Ferdinand Hoefer, p. 107.

there was nothing to be heard; and there was no surrounding atmosphere to be breathed; nor would there have been any use of organs by the help of which he might receive his food or get rid of what he had already digested, since there was nothing which went from him or came into him; for there was nothing besides him. Of design he was created thus, his own waste providing his own food, and all that he did or suffered taking place in and by himself. For the Creator conceived that a being which was self-sufficient would be far more excellent than one which lacked anything; and, as he had no need to take anything or defend himself against any one, the Creator did not think it necessary to bestow upon him hands; nor had he any need of feet nor of the whole apparatus of walking; but the movement suited to his spherical form was assigned to him, being of all the seven that which is most appropriate to mind and intelligence; and he was made to move in the same manner and on the same spot, within his own limits revolving in a circle. All the other six motions were taken away from him, and he was made not to partake of their deviations. And as this circular movement required no feet, the universe was created without legs and without feet." [1]

The foregoing theories of geogony and cosmogony are sufficient to show how hopelessly at sea even the greatest philosophers have been regarding the origin and constitution of the world. It were easy to adduce numerous other similar theories, but space forbids. We look upon them all as childish and absurd, and justly so. Nothing could be more preposterous,

[1] Jowett's translation.

according to our views of nature, than some of the cosmogonic notions entertained by the philosophers of Greece and India. Even the "divine Plato" did not, as we have seen, escape falling into the most ridiculous conceptions of the universe. True it is that most of the theories mentioned were formulated in the infancy of science. Their authors had not at their disposal the delicate instruments of precision which now enable the physicist and astronomer to solve with ease many of the problems which the sages of antiquity attacked in vain. Being deprived of the geographical knowledge which is now ours, we need not be surprised that they accepted the most erroneous and foolish ideas respecting the form and size of the earth and the creatures which inhabit it. Chemistry was then unknown, and geology was not thought of until some thousands of years later. Fancy was substituted for fact, and the most extravagant vagaries were seriously offered in lieu of sober truth.

Cosmogony of Moses.

Contrast we now the cosmogonal fantasies and speculations of even the most eminent exponents of ancient Hindu and Greek thought with a system of cosmogony which dates back as far as—if not farther than—any of those of which I have spoken.

"In the beginning," says Moses, "God created heaven and earth." How simple, and yet how sublime! By a *fiat* of omnipotence, by a mere act of His will—not with *a thought*, as the Hindus taught—God created the world and all that is in it from nothing.

The first chapter of Genesis so impressed the great

pagan rhetorician Longinus that he declared: "The legislator of the Jews, who was not an ordinary man, having strongly conceived the greatness and power of God, expressed it in all its dignity at the beginning of his laws in these words: God said, Let light be, and it was; Let the earth be made, and the earth was made." Reflecting on the same sublime declarations of Genesis, the illustrious scientist and scholar Ampère did not hesitate to affirm: "Either Moses possessed as extensive a knowledge of the sciences as we now have, or he was inspired." "The first pages of the Mosaic account of creation," declares Jean Paul, "is of greater import than all the ponderous tomes of naturalists and philosophers." It gives us the first clear statement of creation by an almighty and self-existent Being, and furnishes us views of God and His creatures that are quite different from those which are at the foundation of the mythologies and false philosophical systems of the ancient world.

But the "Mosaic idea of creation—an idea to which the sages of India, Greece, and Rome never attained—is something with which we have been familiar from our infancy, and for this reason we do not attach the importance we otherwise should to the inspired words of Genesis." If, however, we give but a cursory examination to the pagan ideas which prevailed on the subject of creation among the peoples of Egypt, Phœnicia, and Babylon at the time of Moses and even long afterward—for the religion of Brahma still affords us a striking instance in point—"we shall," says Haneberg, "realize the full importance of the Mosaic dogma regarding God, the world, and man." In Genesis is an entire suppression "of that irrational theory, so generally accepted in antiquity, of a divine being who was a slave to fate, and who acted only through necessity or caprice. In it is banished the terrible apprehension of a blind tyranny of chance; of a maleficent power, the enemy of man; or of other similar phantoms that weighed down upon paganism like a mountain. Delivered from these vain fears, man may look at creation and heaven with confidence, because he knows that a personal God, living and powerful, is the Creator of the Universe." [1]

"The Mosaic cosmogony alone," declares Delitzsch in his *Commentary on Genesis*,[2] "proposes to us the idea of a creation from nothing, without eternal matter and without the intervention of any intermediate being or demiurge. Paganism, it is true, permits us to catch a glimpse of this idea, but it is much obscured. Pagan cosmogonies either suppose pre-existing matter—that is, dualism—or they substitute emanation for creation, and then fall into pantheism."

Even such a rationalist as Dillman when speaking of the cosmogony of Genesis is forced to confess that "it does not contain a single word which is unworthy of the thought of God. From the moment an attempt was made to portray, in language intelligible to man, the work of creation, something that will ever remain a mystery to us, it has been impossible to outline a picture which is grander or more worthy. With reason, then, does one see in it a proof of its revealed character. Only there where God had manifested

[1] *Geschichte der bibl. Offenbarung*, p. 12.   [2] P. 71.

Himself could He be delineated. It is the work of the Spirit of Revelation."[1]

Contrasting the cosmogonies of the ancient pagan world with that of Genesis, the illustrious Donoso Cortes truthfully observes that "in spite of marked differences they all have this in common, that they exhibit an infinite disproportion between the principle, the mean, and the end; between the agent, the act, and the work; between the Creator, the act; His creation, and the creature. In all of them the universe . . . is superior in dignity and beauty to the Creator who made it by His will—to the agent of which it was the work and the principle which gave it being. This should not surprise us when we consider that the universe is a creation of God, whilst its Creator, according to all these cosmogonic systems, was a creation of men. What wonder, then, if the work of the Creator was superior to the work of the creature! . . . Where shall we find a man who, being part of the universe, is able to form a conception of a God who is greater than the universe, if he be not inspired by God? . . . Who can such an one be if it is not Moses?"[2]

But Moses is not satisfied with the simple declaration that God in the beginning created heaven and earth. He descends to details. He tells us that all that exists, all that we can see, all creatures, the sun, the moon, and the stars, the fishes of the sea, the birds of the air, the animals that roam the earth, the flowers that delight the eye, the fruits that are grateful to the

[1] *Genesis*, p. 9.
[2] Quoted by Padre Mir in his learned work, *La Creacion*, p. 29.

taste, man, the lord of creation, are the works of God. And because they are the works of God he also tells us that "God saw that it was good."

Prime Object of the Genesiac Narrative.

The reason for these detailed and explicit declarations is manifest. The Hebrew people had lived among idolaters and were surrounded by people who gave divine worship to many of God's creatures. Moses wished to impress upon their minds that neither the sun, nor the moon, nor the stars, neither any animal, nor the earth which affords its nourishment, nor any of the elements, are God, as was supposed by the Sabianism of the Orient, especially of Chaldea; by the worship of animals in Egypt; by the divine honors paid to the earth by the Romans, Pelasgians, and Germans; and by the cult of the fire-worshippers of Greece and Persia. All these things, the objects of the adoration of the heathen, are the works of God. There is no power opposed to God which is equal to Him. Neither is matter, as such, according to the later opinions of the Platonists, the seat of evil. Everything is the work of God, and everything, therefore, is good.[1]

From the foregoing it is manifest that the prime object of the Mosaic narrative, like that of all revelation, was a religious one. "The Gospels," says St. Augustine, "do not tell us that our Lord said, 'I will send you the Holy Ghost to teach you the course of the sun and moon;' we should endeavor to become Christians, and not astronomers." So it is with the

[1] Cf. Hettinger's *Apologie des Christenthums*, chap. iv. vol. iii.

Mosaic account of creation. Its purport is not to teach geology, physics, zoology, or astronomy, but to affirm in the most simple and direct manner the creative act of God and His sovereignty over all creatures. Its object is not to anticipate any of the truths of science or philosophy, but to guard the chosen people of God against the pernicious errors and idolatrous practices which were then everywhere prevalent.

The Holy Father, in his recent admirable Encyclical on the Study of the Holy Scriptures, clearly brings out this idea when he says: "It must be borne in mind, first of all, that the sacred writers—or rather the Spirit of God, which spoke through them—deemed it inadvisable to teach men these things—that is, the inner constitution of visible objects—since this conduces in no wise to salvation; and accordingly these writers, instead of entering into an investigation of nature, sometimes described and explained things in a certain figurative style or in ordinary language, such as is employed among men, even of deep learning, at the present day."

All the cosmogonies of the ancient world—that of Moses excepted—were, as we have seen, erroneous not only in the false views they gave of God, but also in the notions which they displayed of Nature and her laws. One and all, they have long since been rejected by science as ridiculous and absurd. Not so, however, with the cosmogony of Genesis. The more closely it has been examined in the light of the science of these latter days, the more has it been found to harmonize in the most remarkable manner with the latest results of scientific investigation. The words of the great Cuvier, who wrote in the early part of the century, are as true now as when they were first penned. "Moses has left us," says the illustrious naturalist, "a cosmogony the exactitude of which is daily verified in the most admirable manner. Recent geological observations are in perfect accord with Genesis regarding the order of appearance of the various forms of organized beings."

Genesis and Modern Science.

Again, God not only created the world out of nothing, but He gave it its present form during a succession of epochs. According to Genesis, as well as according to science, He first created primitive, nebulous matter, and after a long, indefinite period of time He fashioned from this matter "without form" all the myriad forms of the organic and inorganic worlds. And, according to Genesis as well as according to science, the Creator proceeded from the simpler to the more complex. He first created light, without which organic development, as we know it, is impossible. He then separated the earth from the waters of the ocean and prepared it for the abode of terrestrial life. Plant life precedes animal life in the scheme of creation, and the waters of the deep are peopled before the dry land is inhabited. In both the vegetable and animal kingdoms the lower forms of life precede the higher. The culmination of the work of creation was man, whose apparition, according to both revelation and science, was posterior to that of all other creatures.

Here we have in a few lines a résumé of some of the most important conclusions of modern science respecting the origin of the earth and its inhabitants. And the Mosaic account, be it remembered, was written long before any attention was given to the natural or physical sciences, and many thousand years before geology, palæontology, and astronomy had achieved those triumphs which will render this nineteenth century of ours for ever memorable.

And not only this. Moses makes statements in his narrative that were for many long ages regarded as contrary to science and philosophy—declares truths which, humanly speaking, could not have been known before an exhaustive study had been made of the past life of our globe, and before the telescope and the spectroscope had given us the knowledge we now possess concerning the origin and constitution of the material universe.

What Moses declared in the infancy of our race, and what science now affirms, not only was not accepted as true in the earlier ages of the world, but was rejected as positively erroneous. The various profane cosmogonies that obtained from time to time among divers peoples were against it. Philosophers decried it as contrary to the teachings of science, and rationalists and unbelievers fancied they discovered in its supposed contradictions an argument against the inspiration and authenticity of the Sacred Record. But as Genesis was more carefully scrutinized and as science advanced it was found that a remarkable harmony existed between the two, and that, far from being contradictory, they both told the same story, although in different languages. The conclusion, therefore, is inevitable. There is something in Genesis above man—something supernatural, something divine. In a word, Moses was inspired. In the words of Linnaeus: "It is materially demonstrated that he did not write and could not write except under the inspiration of the Author of nature—*neutiquam suo ingenio sed altiori ductu.*"

Difficulties of Genesis.

I would not, however, have it inferred from what has been said that there are no difficulties in Genesis, or that I am disposed to underrate their magnitude. Far from it. What I do maintain and insist on is that there is nothing in the Mosaic cosmogony that is contrary to any of the certain truths of science. Scientific theories without number have been formulated which were contrary to the teachings of the Mosaic narrative, but theories are not science. In the last century especially, as well as during the present one, many of these hostile theories were based on geology and palæontology. "From the time of Buffon," wrote Cardinal Wiseman more than fifty years ago, "system rose beside system, like the moving pillars of the desert, advancing in threatening array; but, like them, they were fabrics of sand; and though in 1806 the French Institute could count more than eighty such theories hostile to Scripture, not one of them has stood still or deserves to be recorded."[1]

And more than this. All sorts of extravagant interpretations have been given to the first chapter of Genesis, some of which were even more absurd than the scientific speculations of which I have just spoken. But such commentaries are no more to be accepted as the last word on the Mosaic narrative than are the hypotheses and fantasies of scientists to be regarded as veritable science. That such theories and interpreta-

[1] *Science and Revealed Religion*, vol. i. p. 268.

tions are discordant and contradictory is no evidence whatever of any discrepancy between the Mosaic cosmogony and the logical deductions from the known facts of science. Theories and conjectures may be at variance with one another, but science and the word of God never.

I have said that I have no disposition to minimize the difficulties of the Mosaic narrative of creation, nor have I. I think one may safely assert that no one chapter in the Bible contains so many and so great difficulties as does the first chapter of Genesis. On no single chapter, probably, have the Fathers and schoolmen and commentators expended more time and learning, and in no instance have they exhibited a wider divergence of views than when endeavoring to explain this self-same chapter, and reconcile certain of its declarations with the known or supposed teachings of profane science.

Scientific Freedom of Catholics.

And just here it may be observed that we could have no better illustration of the perfect liberty of thought enjoyed by the children of the Church in all matters outside of positive dogma than that afforded by the diversity of views entertained by saints and doctors respecting the true meaning of many controverted passages of the Mosaic cosmogony. Commentators have endeavored to accommodate the declarations of the Hebrew lawgiver to the scientific notions of their time, and, as a consequence, we have in their interpretations a faithful reflex of all the speculations and vagaries that have at one time or another been put forth as genuine science. We often hear it said that believers in dogma and the Bible—especially Catholics —are so hampered by restrictions of all kinds that they are ever in a condition of intellectual thraldom. We are told that there are many questions in science that we, as Catholics, may not investigate, much less discuss, and that our religious beliefs forbid us to accept many of the demonstrated truths of science. I wish here and now to record in the most emphatic manner possible a formal and explicit denial of each and every one of these imputations, and to declare that they are utterly without foundation in fact. The example of the Fathers and the Schoolmen and the commentators of every age of the Church gives the lie to such foolish declarations. In everything outside of revealed truth and the doctrinal teaching of the Church they have shown us that they were ever permitted the greatest degree of latitude in exegesis, and that they always enjoyed the greatest possible measure of intellectual freedom. They recognized all along that the prime object of the Bible is to save souls, and not to teach science—that its main purpose is, in the language of Cardinal Baronius, "to teach us how to go to heaven, and not how the heavens go." The learned Catholic historian and Orientalist, François Lenormant, expresses the same idea when he declares that the object of Scripture is not to inform us as to "how the things of earth go and what vicissitudes follow one another here below. The Holy Spirit has not been concerned with the revelation of scientific truths or with universal history. In such matters 'He has abandoned the world to the disputes of men'—*tradidit mundum disputationibus eorum.*"[1] In questions, then,

[1] *The Beginnings of History*, Preface.

of chronology, biology, astronomy, geology, ethnology, and anthropology we must have recourse to reason and research, to observation and experiment. Induction, and not revelation, must be our guide in all such matters, except—and this is very rarely the case—when a certain and incontrovertible statement of fact in matters of science is made by the Sacred Text itself. The specific unity of the human race taught both by the Bible and the Church is a case in point.

It is a grave mistake, therefore, to regard the Bible, especially the first two chapters of Genesis, as a compendium of science, as so many have done. For, as Cardinal Newman observes, "it seems unworthy of the divine greatness that the Almighty should, in the revelation of Himself to us, undertake mere secular duties, and assume the office of a narrator, as such, or an historian, or geographer, except in so far as the secular matters bear directly upon the revealed truth."

Catholics who have a correct knowledge of the teachings of their faith will not admit that they are in any way hampered in the pursuit of science by the exigencies of dogma. On the contrary, they claim and enjoy, in the truest sense of the word, the greatest mental freedom—a freedom that truth alone can give; a freedom that those who are outside the pale of the Church know not of—the freedom of the children of God.

In the case of a Catholic "it is not," as Very Rev. Father Ryder truthfully remarks, "so much his freedom of investigation as his freedom from investigation that is controlled. He is bound to be rigid and exacting in his scientific method, to maintain cautiously all the reserves of doubt. He is precluded from that facile abandonment to the prevailing wind of doctrine which is so characteristic of our modern scientific world. . . . A Catholic man of science may be a specialist, but he is bound to be—nay, he can hardly fail to be—something more. He must know something of all the territories of science—their outlines at least—for he has a theology which is more than coextensive with them all, and which has a word to say of each, though it be only, as is commonly the case, to assure the student that here he is within his right and that his way is clear." [1]

The faith of Catholics, consequently, far from restricting their liberty of research, gives it a vivifying principle which it could not otherwise possess. And far from circumscribing their views of nature or giving them false notions of the laws and phenomena of the material world, it extends their horizon, and illumines the field of their investigation with a brilliance all its own. The mistake made by many in denying to Catholics liberty of thought in the study of science is that they confound liberty with license. Revealed truth and dogma never do and never can conflict with science; neither are they incompatible with the most perfect intellectual freedom. They are, however, incompatible with intellectual license. They save the Catholic scientist from many errors into which those who are not guided by religious truth inevitably fall; they shield him from the blasts of false doctrine which the Eolus of error is ever sending forth from his cave, and enable him to steer clear both of the Scylla of ignorance and superstition on the one

"The Proper Attitude of Catholics toward Modern Bible Criticism," in the *Catholic World*, June, 1893, pp. 405 et seq.

hand and the Charybdis of agnosticism and materialism on the other. They protect him from flighty speculations which always issue in discomfiture. They hold him to the *terra firma* of true science, and thus, like Hercules, he is able to vanquish the Antæus of fallacy and hallucination with comparative ease.

But let us now turn our attention to the teaching of the various schools of exegesis that have existed in diverse periods of the Church's history. A brief résumé of what they have severally taught will be not only interesting, but instructive from several points of view. It will confirm what has been said concerning the liberty of thought accorded the children of the Church respecting matters outside of faith and dogma. It will show that while entertaining diverse and even contradictory opinions in matters of science, the Fathers and Doctors were always of one mind in everything that appertained to faith and revealed truth. And more than this: it will prove conclusively something that is generally ignored, if not entirely unknown, and that is that some of the grandest conceptions and generalizations attributed to modern scientists are in reality due to the early Greek and Latin Fathers. Most people are wont to credit to contemporary science much that belongs to Tradition and the School, and this because they have been taught to believe that all the ideas of the earlier commentators of Genesis were fantastical and contrary to the results of modern scientific researches. Even the cursory examination that we shall be able to make of the cosmogonic views of some of the Church's Doctors, especially St. Gregory and St. Augustine, will, I trust, effectively dispel these erroneous notions—notions which have so long obtained, even among those who should know better—and demonstrate beyond any possibility of doubt that we have in some of the Fathers, especially the two just named, the precursors of the most illustrious exponents of a true theory of the visible universe and of evolution of the various forms of terrestrial life. We shall find that they have anticipated the noble conceptions of Descartes, Laplace, and Herschel, and expressed them in words that cannot be misunderstood. And we shall likewise learn that they have laid down principles which are in perfect accord with the latest and most approved theories regarding the origin and constitution of the universe and the development of the manifold forms of animal and vegetable life. I do not mean by this to assert that they had anything approaching the knowledge we now possess of the natural and physical sciences, because they had not. But what I do affirm—and this I shall insist on, because it is capable of the completest demonstration—is, that they had a clear conception of the nature of some of the most profound problems of science with which the human mind has ever grappled, and which even now cannot be said to have received a complete solution. But more of this as we proceed.

CHAPTER II.

ALLEGORISM AND LITERALISM.

DIVERS SCHOOLS OF INTERPRETATION.

ONE of the greatest difficulties in the interpretation of the Mosaic account of creation turns on the meaning to be assigned to the word *day*. This is a difficulty which has been recognized from the earliest ages of the Church and has given rise to divers systems or schools of interpretation. Of these various schools it will be sufficient for our purpose to review briefly the teachings of the four principal ones.

The Alexandrine School, of which the illustrious Origen was the most distinguished representative, favored what is known as the *allegorical, mystical*, or *ideal* system of interpreting the Genesiac days. The Syrian School stoutly opposed the teachings of the Alexandrines, and advocated what is called the *literal* system. The most eminent exponents of this system were St. Ephrem and St. John Chrysostom and the great Cappadocian, St. Basil. The third system, adopted by Cardinal Wiseman, Buckland, Chalmers, and other distinguished scientists of their time, defends what is known as the theory of *intervals* or *restitution*. The fourth system, which is the one now generally preferred, is called the *period* or *concordistic* system. The last two systems are quite modern and do not antedate the present century. They are based on the discoveries of geology and palæontology, and are an attempt to reconcile the teachings of science with those of revelation. The period or concordistic system is due to the great Cuvier, who gave the first exposition of it in 1821.

Besides these four systems of interpretation I must direct attention to a fifth, known as the *eclectic* system —championed by St. Gregory of Nyssa and St. Augustine. It has had many followers, and has, probably, wielded a greater influence in exegesis, and that, too, for a longer time, than any other system of interpretation.

Christian School of Alexandria.

According to the Alexandrian School, the Mosaic narrative of creation is to be interpreted as a simple allegory. The six days are not to be understood in a literal, but in a mystical, sense. The work of creation was not distributed over a period of six days of twenty-four hours each, but all things in the material universe—the cosmos—were created instantly and simultaneously. The words of Moses are to be understood not in their natural and ordinary acceptation, but are to be interpreted in a figurative sense. And more than this: by this method of procedure the text was forced to disclose divers moral and dogmatic teachings which are entirely excluded by the literal and common meaning of the words.

The allegorical method of interpretation, which exercised such a profound influence on scriptural exegesis in the earlier ages of the Church, was introduced by the rabbinical schools of Palestine long anterior to the Christian era. It, however, found its strongest advocates in the Judæo-Alexandrine School, of which Aristobulus and Philo Judæus were the chief representatives. The former lived about one hundred and fifty years B. C., whilst the latter was a contemporary of our Lord. Philo was an ardent admirer of the Greek philosophy, especially that of Plato. Of him it was said: "Either Plato philonizes, or Philo platonizes." He endeavored to reconcile the teachings of Plato with those of the Hebrew lawgiver, and when he could not do so by interpreting Moses literally, he had recourse to allegory. According to him, the narrative of the creation of the world and of man, and likewise the account of the Garden of Eden, are but figures and symbols. "When," says Philo, "Moses declares that God completed His work on the sixth day, you must not imagine that there is a question of an interval of days, but of the perfect number[1] six." This is the number of perfection, because it contains six unities, three dualities, and two trinities. When, therefore, the words of Genesis declare that the world was created in six days, we must understand that this is nothing more than a metaphorical declaration of the perfect order that reigns in the universe. "It would be the height of simplicity to think," affirms the Jewish philosopher, "that the world was created in six days, or indeed that any time whatever was required." [2]

The Christian School of Alexandria followed closely

---

[1] A perfect number is one that is equal to all its divisors or aliquot parts. The first in the order of numbers is $6 = 1 + 2 + 3$; the second is $28 = 1 + 2 + 4 + 7 + 14$.

[2] Εὔηθες πάνυ τὸ οἴεσθαι ἐξ ἡμέραις, ἢ καθόλου χρόνῳ κόσμον γεγονέναι. — *Sacræ Legis Allegor.*, lib. i. p. 41, edit. Turnebe.

the allegorism of Philo. Its exponents, like the Jewish philosopher, reduced the narrative of Moses to a beautiful allegory, and contended that God created all things visible, the heavens, the earth, and all that it contains, plants, animals, man, in an instant of time. They imagined that they thereby attributed to the Creator an action more in harmony with His power and immutability. And the accomplishment of this action, which they conceived to be unique and general, is, they declared, plainly indicated in the first words of Genesis: "In the beginning God created heaven and earth."

The first representative of this school whose opinions on the cosmogony of Moses have been preserved to our time is Clement of Alexandria, who died in the early part of the third century. He expressly declares that all creatures were created simultaneously, ὁμοῦ—that the distinction in the Mosaic narrative of the six days does not indicate a real succession of time, but is a manner of speaking by which the inspired author accommodates himself to our intelligence and to our habit of conceiving things. This is Philonism pure and simple.

Teachings of Origen.

But it is in Origen, a pupil of Clement, that we find the most ardent advocate of allegorism. He was unquestionably the most learned man of his time. His knowledge was truly encyclopedic in character. He was not only a master of all branches of sacred knowledge, but was profoundly versed in all the departments of profane science as well. Besides this he had a capacity for work that was simply stupendous.

Living in the greatest intellectual centre of the world—"in the Babel of profane erudition," as Villemain calls Alexandria—surrounded by Gnostics and Neo-Platonists, whose intellects were as acute as their hatred of Christianity was intense, he soon perceived the necessity of making an effort to reconcile the teachings of faith with those of science and philosophy, and to show that the truths of revelation were in perfect accord with the certain principles of knowledge taught by Plato and Aristotle. He wished, in the language of Mgr. Freppel,[1] that "letters, the arts, and the sciences should form the propylæa of a temple of which philosophy should be the base and of which theology should be its summit and crown." He studied the Sacred Scriptures from every point of view, and wrote numerous and exhaustive commentaries on them. He established a school which was famous throughout the Orient, and introduced a system of exegesis that left its impress on all subsequent systems.

Unfortunately, a great portion of Origen's voluminous works have been lost. Enough, however, is left of his writings to enable one to know his mind regarding the Genesiac days of creation.

Like his predecessors, Philo and Clement, Origen believed in the simultaneous creation of the universe. His reason for holding this opinion was because he found it impossible to conceive of days, like the first three days of Genesis, with evenings and mornings, without sun and moon. "What man," he asks, "possessed of ordinary common sense will believe that there could have been a first, a second, and a third day, an evening and a morning, without sun, or moon, or

---

[1] *Cours d'Éloquence Sacrée, Origène*, tome i. p. 46.

stars?"[1] For this reason he does not hesitate to declare that the word "days" is to be interpreted figuratively—that it means not divisions of time or duration, but refers rather to the order or gradation of God's works. The opinion of the celebrated bishop of Alexandria, St. Athanasius, respecting simultaneous creation was essentially the same as that of Origen: "No creature is older than another. All species were created at the same time by a single fiat of the Divine will."[2]

But Origen's teaching regarding the days of creation is negative rather than positive. He does not so much formulate a theory concerning the nature of these days as he demonstrates the inadequacy of six days to explain the facts detailed in the narrative of the inspired writer. His opinion regarding the simultaniety of creation is rather a provisional conjecture than a clearly conceived hypothesis to be advocated to the exclusion of every other explanation. A careful examination of his works discloses this fact, and evinces beyond cavil that it was not *succession* in the divine works that he objected to, nor the *idea of time* as implied in the cosmogonic days. Neither did he combat the idea of *days* understood in a vague sense as synonymous for indefinite periods of time. It was the theory that the Mosaic days were days of twenty-four hours each that he repudiated, and which he found impossible to reconcile with either the facts of nature

[1] Τίς γοῦν ἔχων νοῦν οἰήσεται πρώτην καὶ δεύτεραν καὶ τρίτην ἡμέραν, ἑσπέραν τε καὶ πρωίαν χωρὶς ἡλίου γεγονεται, καὶ σελήνης καὶ ἀστρων. Περὶ ἀρχῶν, lib. iv. 16.

[2] Τῶν κτίσματων οὐδὲν ἕτερον τοῦ ἑτέρου προγέγονεν, ἀλλ' ἀθρόως ἅμα πάντα, τὰ γένη ἑνί καὶ τῷ αὐτῷ προστάγματι ὑπέστη, Orat. ii., Contra Arian, n. 60.

or the words of the Sacred Text. We may therefore say of Origen what the Abbé Motais affirms of the school of which the erudite Alexandrine was the most illustrious representative: "It is then undeniable that the School of Alexandria taught in reality but one thing—the inadequateness of days of twenty-four hours for the interpretation of Moses."[1]

The Alexandrine theory, as we now know, is contrary to the teachings of science. Geology establishes the fact that the creation, or at least the ordering of the world, was not simultaneous, but gradual and progressive. The earth did not at once appear, as we behold it to-day, divided into seas and continents, adorned with its garment of verdure, and animated by the presence of man and a multitude of animals of every species. Life was manifested only by degrees, as in the creation described by Moses, with whom geologists are in essential accord.

"The error of the Alexandrines proceeded from the defects of the science of the time. Philo attempted to reconcile Hellenism with the teachings of Moses. Clement and Origen endeavored to apply the philosophical spirit to the data of a Christian revelation, and to demonstrate that Plato and his pagan compeers were one in their doctrines, and that, furthermore, in so far as they were true, they were one with the Bible. They essayed, therefore, to fathom the dogmas of revelation, and cause them to be respected by reason, by corroborating them by the authority of the most venerable sages of antiquity, and by making all human sciences ancillary to theology. The end was

[1] *Origine du Monde d'apres la Tradition*, ouvrage posthume du Chanoine Al. Motais, de l'Oratoire de Rennes, p. 127.

grand and noble, but the undertaking was difficult, and even the genius of Origen bent under the load. The masters of the Christian School falsely imagined that there were passages in Scripture which it was impossible to defend by taking them literally, and, hence, in order to explain them, they, after the example of Philo, had recourse to allegory."[1]

They fancied, among other things, that it was impossible to accept as literally true the biblical narrative of creation. How could one, for instance, believe that God was obliged to interrupt His work six different times before completing it? How reconcile this with His almighty power? The naturalists of that period never suspected that our globe had assumed its actual form only after a long series of revolutions. Ignorant of the truth and persuaded that the literal sense of the biblical narrative was irreconcilable with the philosophy of their epoch, Clement and Origen concluded that the first chapter of Moses was but an allegory, and they interpreted it accordingly. Such is the explanation of their exegetical system. But suppose their environment to have been different—suppose them to be living in our day. We may be certain that the Clements and the Origens would hail with gladness the discoveries of geology, because they would not be obliged to change any of their fundamental principles regarding the accordance of science and faith. All that would be necessary would be to give these principles a different application.[2]

[1] *La Cosmogonie mosaique*, par l'Abbé Vigouroux, pp. 35, 36.
[2] Op. cit., p. 37.

The Literalism of the Syrian Schools.

The allegorism of the Alexandrine School—an allegorism that was frequently of the most extravagant character—was not long in provoking opposition. A reaction was inevitable, and it came from the schools of Edessa, Antioch, and Cæsarea, the most distinguished exponents of which were respectively St. Ephrem, St. John Chrysostom, and St. Basil.

St. Ephrem, who wrote in Syriac, and whose writings exercised for many centuries a profound influence on the thought of Western Asia, rejects in the most positive manner the Alexandrine teaching respecting simultaneous creation. "In the beginning," he declares, "God created the substance of heaven and earth; that is, of a heaven and an earth truly existing in nature. Let no one, therefore, presume to look for allegories in the work of the six days. It is not permitted to affirm that those things were created instantly which the Scripture informs us appeared successively and on separate and distinct days. It is equally forbidden to imagine that the words of Scripture are names which do not designate things, or which designate things other than those that the words themselves signify. In the same manner, then, in which we understand by the heaven and earth which were at first created a true heaven and a true earth, and do not suppose that the two terms signify something else, so likewise should we be on our guard against holding to be without meaning the terms which express the arrangement of other substances and the sequence of divers works, and should boldly confess that the nature of these divers beings is very accurately represented by the different terms by which they are denominated."[1] According to him, the days of Genesis are ordinary days of twenty-four hours each.

But a very remarkable fact in St. Ephrem's view of creation is that he maintains that the first verse of Genesis teaches the creation *ex nihilo* of elementary matter, from which all the bodies of the material universe, earth, sun, moon, stars, were subsequently formed. We shall see in the sequel how this idea was at a later period developed by St. Gregory of Nyssa, and how it forestalled the general conception of Kant and Laplace concerning the nebular hypothesis.

St. John Chrysostom, like the illustrious deacon of Edessa, formally repudiates the teaching of Origen and his school regarding simultaneous creation. God could, he is willing to concede, have created the universe in the twinkling of an eye, but He did not choose to do so. On the contrary, He deigned to conform, in a measure, with our way of acting, in order that we might the more readily comprehend His work. He wished, moreover, to teach us that this world is not the result of chance, but the work of an all-wise Providence, who "ordained all things in measure and number and weight."

Severien, bishop of Gabales in Syria, a contemporary of St. John Chrysostom, expresses with even greater precision than the golden-mouthed orator his views regarding the Hexaëmeron. At the same time he distinctly enunciates the opinion of St. Ephrem respecting the creation from nothing of the primitive matter from which all things visible were afterward

[1] Quoted by Motais, op. cit., p. 131 et seq.

fashioned. "God," he tells us, "made all things in the space of six days. The first day, however, differs from those which followed. On the first day God produced from nothing—ἐκ μή ὄντων—and, starting from the second day, He did not create from nothing, but transformed according to His pleasure that which He created the first day. . . . God, then," he concludes, "created primal matter—ὕλας τῶν κτισμάτων—on the first day, and during the subsequent days He did no more than give form and beauty to what He had already called from nothing." [1]

[1] Τήν μόρφωσιν καί τήν διακόσμησιν τῶν κτίσματων, Orat. I. n. 3, De Mundi Creat. It is a significant fact that in the narrative of creation given in the first chapter of Genesis the word בָּרָא (bârâ), to create from nothing, occurs only three times—viz. in vs. 1, 21, and 27. In the first instance the inspired writer speaks of the creation of the inorganic world; that is, of the elementary matter from which, according to St. Ephrem and his school, the universe is evolved. In the other two cases there is question of the creation of animal life and of man.

Not only in the record of creation, however, but in almost every passage of Scripture in which the term is found, the word בָּרָא (bârâ) signifies creation *ex nihilo*. It is the consecrated term, therefore, to designate, so far as human language can express such an idea, the creation of substance from nothingness, and its creation, furthermore, by the sole act of the Almighty's will.

On examining the first two chapters of Genesis we shall find that there are no less than four different words to express the creative action of the Deity. Besides בָּרָא (bârâ), to create from nothing—creation strictly so called—we have also the words עָשָׂה (âsâh), to make; יָצַר (yâsâr), to form; and בָּנָה (bânâh), to build. With the exception of the three cases signalized above —viz. the creation of matter, the creation of life, and the creation of man—God does not, properly speaking, create, but merely fashions, His creatures from pre-existing material. Thus, He did not *create*, but "made, a firmament" from mate-

What St. Ephrem taught at Edessa and Nisibus—because he was alternately the head of both these schools—and what St. John Chrysostom maintained at Antioch, St. Basil defended at Cæsarea. The master of the Schools of Edessa and Nisibus had laid down the canons of literalism, and the chief representatives of the Schools of Antioch and Cæsarea accepted them with but slight modifications. The basis of St. Ephrem's system of interpretation may be summed up in two propositions: First, that the things named by Moses have a real existence; and, secondly, that the Genesiac days are ordinary days of twenty-four hours.

To these canons of St. Ephrem, St. Basil cordially subscribes. Nay more: in his defence of literalism he is disposed to go even farther than had any of his predecessors. Origen had pushed allegorism to its extreme limit. He saw a hidden meaning in the simplest declarations of Scripture. According to his method of interpretation, what he called the spiritual or mystical sense came first; the literal sense—he named it the "corporeal sense"—was in most cases but secondary.

rial which He had already brought from nothingness; similarly, He did not create, but "He *made*, two great lights," and "He made the beasts of the field according to their kinds;" He "*formed* out of the ground all the beasts of the earth;" and He "*built* the rib which He took from Adam into a woman."

It is interesting to observe in this connection that the prophet Isaias uses the first three of the above words in a single verse. In chapter xliii. v. 7 it is written: "And every one that calleth upon my name, I have *created* him for my glory, I have *formed* him and *made* him."

For a full exposition of בָּרָא (bârâ), as meaning to create in the strict acceptation of the term, see Gesenius's *Thesaurus Philologicus*, pp. 235, 236.

But if Origen erred by carrying allegorism too far, St. Basil, in his efforts to counteract the tendency of the illustrious Alexandrine's teachings, fell into an analogous error by laying too much stress on the literal method. In his zeal to conserve the true meaning of the words of the Sacred Text he rejected allegory entirely, and thus often confounded the proper sense, in which the words are to be taken *ut sonant*, with their figurative sense, which, in the mind of the author, gives their true literal meaning. In his ninth homily on the Hexaëmeron he enunciates distinctly the principles of exegesis by which he is guided. "I know," he tells us, "the laws of allegory, although I am not their author, but have found them in the works of others. Those who do not follow the common interpretation of the Scriptures do not call 'water' water. They see in this word something entirely different. And in like manner they give a fantastical meaning to the words 'plants' and 'fishes.' And yet more. The generation of reptiles and other creatures becomes, according to their arbitrary teaching, a subject of allegory. In this they resemble those who give to the objects of their dreams a signification which is in accordance with their tastes or desires. As for myself, I call 'a plant' a plant, and I interpret the words 'plant,' 'fish,' 'wild animals,' and 'flocks' as I find them in the Scripture." He gives to these words their proper, literal meaning, because Moses employs the words ordinarily used for designating these objects. In a similar manner, because the inspired writer employs the word "day" in his narrative, he insists on attributing to it the primary signification of a period of twenty-four hours. In a word, he concludes, though falsely and illogically, that because some of the words are to be understood in their plain, obvious sense, they are all to be so interpreted. What he found reprehensible in Origen—the application of a figurative sense to a whole narrative because some of the words of this narrative were figurative—is precisely similar to what we find fault with in his too close adherence to literalism. Because some of the words of the Genesiac narrative are undoubtedly to be taken in their proper and simple signification, he infers that all are to be thus understood—that all figures are to be rejected even when the words of the context plainly indicate, as in some of the passages of the first chapter of Genesis, that the figurative sense of the words is in reality the only one which can truly give the literal sense of their author.

The Syrian Schools, therefore, as distinguished from the School of Alexandria, contend that the true sense of Holy Writ is to be found by a strict interpretation of the letter of the text, without, however, excluding entirely all allegory. But with them, as we have seen, the figurative sense is always secondary. They escaped, indeed, the reefs encountered by Origen and his followers, but they ran foul of other obstacles equally perilous. In their anxiety to preserve intact the word of God they fell into numerous errors in matters of science from which the Alexandrine School escaped. But we need not go far to seek the reason for such lapses into error. The natural and physical sciences did not receive the attention in Syria that was given them in Egypt's brilliant capital. The Doctors of Edessa and Nisibus and Antioch did not have to meet the objections proposed to the masters of the

Christian School of Alexandria by the keenest exponents of Neo-Platonism and Gnosticism. They had not to ward off shafts of sarcasm and ridicule like those which were so persistently directed against Origen by that precursor and prototype of Voltaire—Celsus, one of the bitterest and keenest opponents of the Christian name. And it was because they were thus free from the attacks of anti-Christian philosophy that they were guilty of blunders in science which they would not otherwise have committed. Literalism, no doubt, rendered good service to the cause of exegesis, but its too exclusive adoption was the source of many errors that were prejudicial to the cause of both Scripture and science.

A couple of instances in point will make my meaning clearer.

St. John Chrysostom, interpreting literally the words of the Psalmist, "Who established the earth above the waters," maintains that the earth actually reposes on the waters. He fails to distinguish the metaphorical from the proper sense of the words, and mistakes a figurative statement for a positive declaration of science.

Again, by a forced interpretation of the words of Isaias, "He that stretcheth out the heavens as nothing, and spreadeth them out as a tent to dwell in," the Egyptian monk, Cosmas Indicopleustes, imagined that the universe had the form of a tent or of the tabernacle built by Moses in the wilderness, and that the earth is a rectangular plane twice as long as it is broad and enveloped on all sides by the heavens or firmament.

No better example could be cited of the danger of insisting on a too literal interpretation of Scripture, especially in matters that evidently come within the purview of science. If allegorism is fraught with danger when pushed too far, literalism is equally so when accepted as the chief, if not sole, norm of biblical interpretation.

CHAPTER III.

ST. GREGORY OF NYSSA AND THE NEBULAR HYPOTHESIS.

Via Media of St. Gregory of Nyssa.

AS a consequence of the failure of literalism and allegorism to satisfy the demands of critics and explain numerous difficulties in the Mosaic account of creation—not to speak of other parts of the Bible—it soon became apparent that some other system of interpretation was required that would not be open to the defects inherent in the systems of Alexandria and Syria. A compromise was needed—a sort of *via media*—which would evade what was objectionable in the older schools, while it retained all that was good and consonant with the requirements of science and biblical criticism.

The first one to broach this compromise and to pave the way for a *via media* was the illustrious brother of St. Basil, St. Gregory of Nyssa. St. Basil, by the very brilliance and ardor of his defence of the literal school, had precipitated a reaction which was as inevitable as was that which followed the allegorism of Origen. For Cæsarea, where the great bishop gave his exposition of the Hexaëmeron, like Alexandria, was, as St. Gregory Nazianzen tells us, "a metropolis of arts and sciences." In Cæsarea, as in Alexandria, the Bible and the dogmas of Christianity were the objects of the constant attacks of pagan philosophy and Manichæan dualism. But no question, probably, excited greater interest or provoked more discussion than that respecting the origin of the world. To the Genesiac account of the unity of origin of all things the Manichæans opposed their system of dualism, while Julian the Apostate labored with demoniac zeal and persistency to prove that the cosmogony of Plato was superior to that of Moses. All the resources of Greek science were marshalled against the Christian citadel; every species of stratagem was resorted to and every form of assault tried, but in vain. The Christian defences remained impregnable, and the soldiers of the Crucified came forth from the conflict not only unscathed, but stronger than they had ever been before, and better prepared to fight new battles and achieve other and more glorious triumphs.

A characteristic of the great Cappadocian Doctors that we must not lose sight of was their great love of science. They were eminent not only for their vast knowledge of the Sacred Scriptures, but also for their accurate acquaintance with all the branches of profane science as taught in the best schools of their time. Indeed, in the Hexaëmeron of St. Basil we have, according to the Abbé Bayle, a résumé of all that was known in the illustrious prelate's day respecting astronomy, physics, and natural history. While studying at Athens he devoted special attention to profane science, and made a critical examination of the diverse systems of cosmogony as taught by the various schools of Greek philosophy. According to all accounts, he was one of the most learned men of his century, and if we detect errors of science in his exegesis, we must attribute them to the defective knowledge of his age—when all the inductive sciences were still in an inchoate state—rather than to an ignorance on his part of any of the positive knowledge possessed by his contemporaries. For we must not forget that in the time of the great bishop of Cæsarea *a-priori* reasoning, rather than observation and experiment, was appealed to to explain the origin and nature of the visible universe. Theory and speculation, as a consequence, often took the place of real science, and errors innumerable were the inevitable result.

Such being the case, far from finding fault with the mistakes in science which we observe in the works of the early Christian exegetists, we should rather be surprised that the errors are so few. They were certainly not more numerous, nor more serious, than those found in the works of the ablest of the professional exponents of the profane science of the period. It were foolish to expect them to know more about geography than Eratosthenes and Strabo and Pomponius Mela, who had made a life-study of the subject; or to demand of them a more accurate knowledge of astronomy than was possessed by Hipparchus or Ptolemy; or to suppose that they should have a more precise and a more extended acquaintance with physics and natural history than had Aristotle or Pliny. Such an exaction would be the height of unreason. As well might we find fault with them for not being so well versed in physics as Ampère or Maxwell, or reproach them for knowing less of astronomy than Leverrier or Father Secchi, and less of geography than Humboldt, Malte-Brun, or Carl Ritter—men whose science was based on the experiments

THE MOSAIC HEXAËMERON. 63

and observations of thousands of investigators and on the accumulated knowledge of wellnigh twenty centuries.

Nebular Hypothesis of St. Gregory.

But we may go yet further. Not only were the exegetists I have named, especially those of Alexandria and Cæsarea, imbued with a love of science and fully abreast with every advance of scientific research, but they were the first to propose and develop a true theory of the origin of the world, and to lay the foundations of cosmogonic doctrines that are usually credited to investigators of a much later epoch. A most striking illustration of the truth of this statement is found in that marvel of exegesis—the *Hexaëmeron* of St. Gregory of Nyssa—wherein is developed, in unequivocal terms, the same hypothesis that has so long been regarded as the special glory of the *Système du Monde* of Laplace.

St. Gregory of Nyssa, who was the youngest brother of St. Basil, was induced to write his great work by an elder brother, Peter, the bishop of Sebaste, who became alarmed at the criticisms that were constantly made on the cosmogonic views of the eloquent bishop of Cæsarea. Gregory was inferior to Basil in eloquence and erudition, but surpassed him in scientific method and philosophic spirit. His prime, if not his sole, intention, when he took up his pen and engaged in the controversy was to defend his brother from the attacks of his critics. But he soon found himself, almost unconsciously and against his own will, forced to abandon this idea. He discovered that the cosmogonal views of Basil could no longer withstand the onslaughts of the critical Greeks, who had carefully followed them from beginning to end.

But he would never admit that there was any fundamental difference between his teaching and that of his distinguished brother. He maintained that Basil, speaking in a large church to a numerous audience, was obliged to adapt his language to the intelligence of his hearers, but that in spite of his precautions he was often misunderstood. Gregory's purpose, then, was to explain the views of his brother, and not to contradict them or proclaim them untenable. But, although he disavows any intention of advocating aught that was different from what his brother had taught, and although he explicitly declares that his sole purpose is to graft a small shoot on the noble tree of his master, he does, as a matter of fact, teach doctrines essentially different, and promulgates a theory of cosmogony that not only makes him the founder of a new school of exegesis, but which evinces that he was one of the clearest and boldest thinkers that the world has ever known.

St. Gregory of Nyssa, like his brother St. Basil and his illustrious friend St. Gregory Nazianzen, accepted the Alexandrine doctrine of simultaneous creation. But he succeeded better than either his brother or his friend in keeping to the *via media* between the Alexandrines on the one hand and the Syrians on the other. He avoids the excessive allegorism of the former as well as the exaggerated literalism of the latter. Like Origen and Athanasius, he admits the name and idea of simultaneous creation, but rejects the purely symbolic explanation of the first chapter of

Genesis which was given such vogue by Philo. With the Syrians he distinguishes six real days in the work of creation, but, unlike them, he is not a slave to the letter of the Sacred Text. His method is more critical, and he acknowledges on all occasions the service that profane science may render to scriptural exegesis.[1]

According to St. Gregory of Nyssa, the words "In the beginning God created heaven and earth" do not refer to the creation of the heavens and the earth as we now behold them, and still less do they signify the creation of the creatures—plants, animals, and man—that inhabit the earth. They refer rather to the creation from nothing of the primitive cosmic matter, from which all forms of matter, organic and inorganic, were subsequently fashioned. In modern phraseology all the material universe was at first in a gaseous or nebulous condition, and from this nebulous matter all the heavenly bodies, sun, moon, stars, planets, were in course of time evolved. The saint finds a warrant for this intrepretation in the words of Genesis itself, for, according to the inspired writer, the earth after the first creative act was "void and empty," or, as the Septuagint has it, "invisible and discomposed."[2]

[1] Cf. F. Vigouroux, op. cit., p. 88.
[2] The words of the Vulgate are *inanis et vacua*. The Septuagint, however, employs terms that are more expressive, and which are at the same time in perfect accord with the teaching of modern science regarding the origin of the world. The words used by The Seventy are ἀόρατος καὶ ἀκατασκεύτος—*invisibilis et incomposita*—and indicate a condition of things implied by the word *chaos* of the Greek philosophers, the "*rudis indigestaque moles*" of the Roman poet, and by the Hebrew words הֹהוּ וָבֹהוּ, *tôhou vâbôhou*, which are often rendered by the words *solitudo et inanitas*.

In the beginning, then, all things were created potentially rather than in act; they were contained naturally or in germ in the invisible and unformed matter that came forth from nothing in response to the divine fiat. The first sentence of Genesis tells us of creation properly so called—the *opus creationis*. That which follows refers to the formation, from pre-existing matter, of all the bodies of the universe. This is what theologians call the *opus formationis*, and what modern scientists denominate development, or evolution.

In the beginning, therefore, according to St. Gregory of Nyssa, all was in a chaotic or nebulous state. But it did not remain so, because the Almighty put it under the action of certain physical laws by virtue of which it was to go through that long cycle of changes of which science speaks, and about the existence of which there can, it seems, no longer be any reasonable doubt.

The manner in which the saint expresses himself when treating of this subject is, considering the scientific knowledge of his time, simply marvellous. He seems to have had an intuitive knowledge of what could not then be demonstrated, and of what could be known only after the revelations of modern geology and astronomy. In this respect he often reminds one of Aristotle, who had intuitions of certain of the laws and processes of nature of which there was no experimental evidence until more than two thousand years after he had given expression to his opinions.

After the primitive nebulous matter of the cosmos was created, certain molecules, St. Gregory teaches, began, under the influence of attraction, to unite with other molecules and to form separate masses of matter.

In the course of time these masses of matter, rotating on their axes, gave off similar masses, which assumed a spherical form. In this wise were produced the sun and moon, stars and planets.

The various heavenly bodies resulting from the condensation of the primitive nebulæ that filled all space exhibited, as St. Gregory declares, many and striking differences. They differed in size, weight, luminosity, in their relative distances from their centres of attraction, and in the orbits which they describe with such unerring precision and harmony.

But in this brilliant conception, in which he could but divine what Laplace and his compeers have made all but certain, St. Gregory recognized the existence of laws which he was unable to detect, much less comprehend. These were the laws made known long ages afterward by the investigations of Kepler, Newton, and Plateau, and the laws of chemical affinity which have thrown such a flood of light on the secret operations of nature. But in spite of its many defects, due to the ignorance of the age in which he lived, his *Hexaëmeron* will ever remain a noble specimen of learning and philosophical acumen, and his theory of the formation of the world must always be regarded as a marvel of scientific divination that is unsurpassed by even the boldest conceptions of that master-intellect of the world—Aristotle. No exegetist has ever been more happy in the employment of the scientific method; no one has ever had a keener appreciation of the reign of law and order which obtains in the universe; no one has ever realized more thoroughly that the cosmos, as we now see it, far from being the work of chance or the result of a series of divine interventions, is the outcome of a gradual evolution of that primordial matter which God created in the beginning, which He then put under what we call the laws of nature, and which He still conserves by His providence. Excepting unimportant details, the general tenor of his cosmogony is to-day as consonant with the teachings of Scripture and the latest conclusions of science as is that of an interpreter of our own century. He is conscious of the difficulty of making the days of Genesis days of twenty-four hours, as did his brother and the exponents of the literal school generally, but out of respect for those whom he held in such great reverence he appears to have been unwilling to grapple with the difficulty directly, much less to propound a theory that could be construed as a contradiction of the doctrine of St. Basil, whom he had it in purpose to explain and defend. But, notwithstanding his deep reverence for his brother and the delicacy of feeling he exhibits toward him throughout his masterly work on Genesis, one cannot but recognize that he considered the teachings of the literal school inadequate to explain the declarations of Moses, and that a new interpretation—the one he himself so modestly suggests—is the only one which can afford a logical answer to the difficulties raised, and which at the same time harmonizes with both the words of the Sacred Text and with the teachings of profane science. His teaching regarding the evolution of the universe under the action of physical laws, and the gradual formation of the earth, and the successive production and development of the various creatures which inhabit it, leaves us in no doubt as to his theory of cosmogony, nor as to the fact that he is in all justice to be regarded as the father and founder of the modern school of scriptural interpretation, as well as the real originator of the nebular hypothesis[1] that is so exclusively attributed to modern thinkers, particularly Kant, Herschel, and Laplace.

[1] The materialistic cosmologists of the Ionic Schools, especially Thales, Anaximander, and Anaximenes, who are sometimes credited with originating the nebular hypothesis, had but a vague perception of its truth.

CHAPTER IV.

ST. AUGUSTINE AND EVOLUTION.

EXEGESIS, OLD AND NEW.—ST. AUGUSTINE AND ECLECTICISM.

BUT wonderful as were the scientific intuitions of St. Gregory of Nyssa, they were eclipsed by those of the illustrious Latin Doctor, St. Augustine. Both men were remarkable for the keenness of their perceptions and for the logical manner in which they treated every question that was presented them for discussion. Both had a complete acquaintance with the profane sciences as taught in their day, and recognized the assistance a knowledge of science may render the student of Scripture. Both, too, excelled in the scientific and philosophic method, which they employed with singular success in the elucidation of controverted biblical topics, and possessed a critical faculty which was far superior to that observable in any of their contemporaries. But, distinguished as he was among the exegetists of his day, and notwithstanding the fact that he was *facile princeps* among the intellectual giants of his time and race, the bishop of Nyssa had neither the genius nor the erudition nor the comprehensiveness of view that we admire in the prelate of Hippo. In the great African doctor we seem to have combined the searching and potent dialectics of Plato, the profound scientific conceptions of Aristotle, the learning and versatility of Origen, the grace and eloquence of Basil and Chrysostom. Whether we regard him as philosopher, theologian, or exegetist; as confuting Arians, Pelagians, and Manichæans; or as vindicating the faith of the Gospel against paganism; or grappling with the difficult and obscure questions of Mosaic cosmogony; or fixing, with long and steadfast gaze, his eagle eye on the mystery of the Trinity,—the Doctor of Grace is ever admirable, at once the glory of the Church and the master of the ages.

In scriptural exegesis he is the author of the system usually known as *eclecticism*, a system that was based in some measure on the teachings both of the Alexandrine and Syrian Schools. Like St. Gregory of Nyssa, he saw the necessity of a *via media* between the systems advocated by Origen and Ephrem, but, unlike him, he was more positive in his repudiation of the insufficiency of literalism and in his condemnation of the extravagances of allegorism. He scrutinized both systems closely, and exhibited in the most luminous manner the merits and defects of each. At one time he was disposed to take refuge in the simultaneity of the Alexandrines; at another he sought light in the interpretations of their opponents at Edessa and Cæsarea. He critically examined, one by one, the theories of his predecessors and found them wanting. He evolved theories of his own until they numbered more than half a score, but without any satisfactory result. Indeed, the Mosaic Hexaëmeron seemed to possess a special fascination for him, and the problems which it raised appeared to haunt him from the time of his conversion until the end of his life. He returns to them over and over, and takes them up repeatedly as if for the first time. He rejects methods that he had once approved, and casts aside as untenable theories which he himself had most strongly supported. At one time he appears to be a disciple of Origen and Clement, at another a pupil of Ephrem and Basil. His is the intellect of genius groping in darkness and essaying the impossible in the region of mystery. We see this whenever the question of creation is mooted—in his "Confessions" and in his "City of God;" in his unfinished work on Genesis, and in his "Retractions," and his crowning treatise on the subject—the most complete antiquity has left us on creation—the twelve books entitled *De Genesi ad Litteram.*

Meaning of the Word "Day."

During the twenty-five best years of his life the first two chapters of Genesis were continually before the saint's mind. What did Moses mean by the words "days"? he asks again and again in accents of mingled pathos and despair. How could there be days in the ordinary acceptation of the word before the sun was created on the fourth day? Were not the first three days mentioned by Moses periods of time rather than ordinary days of twenty-four hours each? And what about the seventh day—a day that had no evening—a day, therefore, that still endures? And yet another difficulty: How explain, according to the laws of nature, which are the laws of God, the production and development of the various forms of plant and animal life in the short period of six ordinary days?

The idea that God during the Genesiac days operated in a manner different from that which subsequently characterized His providence; that the laws which governed the material universe were not the same then as they were afterward; that the Hexaëmeron was distinguished by a series of miracles and a succession of specific creations, rather than by the reign of law that the Creator Himself had imposed on matter, and by which it was endowed with the power of gradual evolution and differentiation,—seemed so repugnant to the keen and logical intellect of Augustine that he could never bring himself to adopt it, much less give it his support.

That the Almighty should interrupt his work after having commenced it, that He should take it up six several times before completing it, was to his mind as inconsistent with just ideas of divine power and wisdom as it was to that of Origen. What he knew of the uniformity of the laws of nature contradicted such an interpretation, and the more he studied the Sacred Text the less warrant there seemed to be for it in the words of the inspired writer. He does not deny the miraculous. Far from it. But he does not favor the invoking the aid of miracles without necessity or appealing to them in every difficulty of interpretation, and thus making them serve the purpose of a *Deus ex machinâ*.

In his "Confessions"[1] St. Augustine gives us an idea of the special attraction which the Hebrew cosmogony always possessed for him. "Let me hear and understand," he prays, "how in the beginning Thou didst make the heaven and the earth. Moses wrote

[1] Book xi. cap. iii.

this; he wrote and departed—passed hence from Thee to Thee. Nor now is he before me, for if he were I would hold him and ask him, and would adjure him by Thee that he would open unto me these things, and I would lend the ears of my body to the sounds bursting from his mouth. . . . As, then, I cannot inquire of him, I beseech Thee—Thee, O Truth, full of whom he spoke truth—Thee, my God, I beseech, forgive my sins; and do Thou, who didst give to that Thy servant to speak these things, grant to me also to understand them."

The meaning of the word "day" was as great an enigma to him as it was to Origen and his school. His reason revolts at the idea of regarding the days of Genesis as ordinary days of twenty-four hours. He is convinced that they cannot be true "solar days"—that they are not produced by the revolution of the heavenly bodies. They must, therefore, be "entirely different from the days that compose our weeks"—"of a character quite extraordinary and to us unknown."

"What are these days?" he inquires in his great work *De Civitate Dei*.[1] "It is very difficult, if not impossible, to conceive, much less to declare in words.[2] The days which we know have an evening when the sun sets and a morning when the sun rises. But the first three days were without a sun, which, according to Scripture, was created only on the fourth day."

"If," he writes elsewhere, "in the six other days the words *evening* and *morning* characterize a succession of time analogous to that with which we are

---

[1] Lib. xi. cap. vi.

[2] "Qui dies cujusmodi sint, aut perdifficile nobis, aut etiam impossibile est cogitare, quanto magis dicere."

familiar in the daily alternations of evening and morning, I fail to see why the seventh day did not have an evening, and why it was not followed by another morning. I look in vain for a reason why it is not said of this day as of the others, 'And the evening and the morning were the seventh day.' In the hypothesis of ordinary days it is one of the seven which constitute the week, the repetition of which gives us months and years and centuries. It should, consequently, have had an evening, and been followed by the morning of the eighth day. Then, and then only, would Moses have completed his enumeration and returned to the first day named. It is, then, more than probable that the seven days of Genesis were entirely different in their duration from those which now mark the succession of time. Nothing of which we are now cognizant can give us any information regarding the first six days of the earth's formation. The evening and the morning, the light and darkness, called day and night, were not, then, the same as we now understand by solar days. Regarding the three days which preceded the formation of the sun this may be accepted as certain."[1]

But if the Genesiac days are not solar days, what are they? The saint has told us what they are not. Had he any conception of what they were? A close study of his latest works will leave no doubt about this matter.

The word "days," according to the illustrious doctor, are not to be taken in a literal, but in a figurative, sense. They mean, not ordinary days, but the works of creation which were unfolded in time by

[1] *De Genesi ad Litteram*, lib. iv. cap. 18.

a series of progressive transformations. For a similar reason the words evening and morning are to be interpreted metaphorically as meaning not dusk and dawn, but the beginning and end of the divine works.[1]

God, according to St. Augustine as well as according to St. Gregory of Nyssa, first created matter in an elementary or nebulous state. From this primordial matter—created *ex nihilo*—was evolved, by the action of physical laws imposed on it by the Creator, all the various forms of terrestrial life that subsequently appeared. In this process of evolution there was succession, but no division of time. The Almighty completed the work He had begun, not intermittently and by a series of special creations, but through the agency of secondary causes—by the operation of natural laws and forces—*causales rationes*—of which He was the Author.

The seventh day, which has no evening, still endures. It means, therefore, a period of time, as do also the other six days, for they are and must be identical. The divine week spoken of in Genesis is consequently unlike the human week. The days in the two cases, far from being analogous, are widely dissimilar and express ideas totally different.

The great doctor of Hippo was not, it is true, able to demonstrate the truth of his theory, but he showed that it was more reasonable and more probable than any others that had been advanced, and at the same

---

[1] "Restat ergo ut intelligamus, in ipsa quidem mora temporis ipsas distinctiones operum sic appellatas, vesparam propter transactionem consummati operis, et mane propter inchoationem futuri operis."—*De Genesi contra Manichæos*, lib. i. cap. 14.

time more conformable both with the words of the Sacred Text and with the declarations of science. He blazed out the road to be travelled by those who came after him, and established principles which served as the basis of all future exegesis.

"Unable to enter the port himself, he avoided mistaking a moving island for the main land. If he cast anchor, it was but *en passant* and during the night only. His stops, while his vessel was riding at anchor, were but so many halts in his voyage. For twenty-five years he sailed the high seas without being able to touch land. Less fortunate than Columbus, he never reached the world which was the object of his quest. The voyage was too long for a mariner without a compass. But it prepared the way for discovery. He signalized all the shoals, he pointed out the route, erected lighthouses, and indicated the direction to be taken. Unable to be the author of modern exegesis, he was its precursor and prophet. Prevented from establishing it on a firm basis, he did what was probably better. In the name of Moses he demonstrated its necessity." [1]

A little geology, a view of the fossiliferous strata of the earth's crust in the light of palæontology, an inkling of the theory of cosmogony as based on the discoveries of modern physics and astronomy, were all that the saint required to place his system of interpretation on the solid foundation on which it now reposes.

He was conscious of his ignorance of certain data, which he did not possess and of which he could not divine the character. But he looked to the future to

[1] *Origine du Monde*, par Al. Motais, p. 220.

remove difficulties which to him were insuperable. And when, long centuries afterward, geology and astronomy achieved their glorious triumphs, exegetists had nothing more to do than apply the inductions of science to the principles which the great Doctor had laid down, and lo! Moses became his own interpreter and the Bible and Science were one.

Derivative Creation.

The most remarkable feature of St. Augustine's system of exegesis—a feature that has been only incidentally alluded to in what precedes—is the special stress he lays on the operation of natural laws, and the observations he makes concerning derivative creation or creation through the agency of secondary causes. In this respect he is unique among the Fathers, and far in advance of any of his predecessors. Indeed, it is only now that the world is beginning to awaken to a realization of the far-reaching character of the principles which the saint established, and of their complete harmony with both the teachings of science and the truths of revelation. This is especially the case in respect of the bearing of his doctrines on the modern theory of evolution.

It may seem strange to some of my readers to be told that St. Augustine was the father of theistic evolution, and yet, paradoxical as it may appear, the statement is substantially true. Of course it is quite evident that he knew nothing about evolution as it is now taught. When nothing more was known of the sciences of botany, physiology, and zoology than the little that had been taught by Aristotle, Galen, and Pliny; when only a few species of animals and plants had been studied, and those but imperfectly; when geology and palæontology were unknown, and when the few fossils that were occasionally met with attracted either no attention or were regarded as mere *lusus naturæ* or evidences of the plastic power of the earth; when the microscope was undreamed of, and when the world of microscopic life, the world "of the infinitely little," was still hidden from the gaze of the investigator; when the telescope and the spectroscope were not available for researches regarding the origin and constitution of the physical universe,—it could not be expected that even a genius like that of St. Augustine, marvellous as it was for its intuitions and for its grasp of scientific principles, would be able to take the same comprehensive view of the vast field of nature as one may now take fifteen hundred years later, or as the illustrious Doctor would himself take if he were now living.

And if the saint could have had no knowledge of evolution in the sense in which it is now understood, still less could he have been an evolutionist like unto Darwin, Romanes, or Herbert Spencer, or like Schmidt, Vogt, or Ernst Haeckel. The faith he professed, the philosophy by which he was guided, and the revelation which illumined an intellect naturally perspicacious and open to truth made this impossible. In what sense, then, was he an evolutionist, and how may he be considered as the precursor or father of modern evolution? Let us see.

We have already remarked that St. Augustine seems to have been the first of the Fathers to have a distinct conception of the fact that the world is under the reign of law, and that God in the government of the physical universe acts not directly or immediately, but indirectly and through the agency of secondary causes, or what we are pleased to denominate "the laws and forces of nature." His language on this subject is so explicit that it cannot be mistaken. In his commentaries on Genesis, in his "City of God," as well as in his other works, he is continually speaking of the laws of nature—*leges naturæ*—by which created things are governed; the ordinary course of nature—*usitatum cursum ordinemque naturæ;* the causal reasons of things—*causales rationes*—which God gave to the world when He created all things, and in virtue of which inorganic matter became capable of transformation and organic matter acquired the power of development. He insists on it that we should explain the phenomena of the physical world in conformity with the nature of things—*naturas rerum*—and not by the constant intervention of miracles, and emphasizes the fact that the Almighty has "ordained all things in measure and number and weight."

St. Augustine, as we have seen, clearly distinguishes between creation properly so called—*opus creationis*—and the work of formation or development—*opus formationis*. The former was direct and simultaneous, for God, the saint declares, created *omnia simul*, while the latter, he contends, was gradual and progressive and conformable to the laws of nature which now obtain. He tells us distinctly that animals and plants were produced not as they now appear, but virtually and in germ—*in semine* or *ex seminibus*—and that the Creator gave to the earth the power of evolving from itself by the operation of natural laws the various forms of animal and vegetable life.

"As there is invisibly in the seed," he affirms, "all that which in the course of time constitutes the tree, so also are we to view the world when it was created by God—*cum simul omnia creavit*—as containing all that which was subsequently manifested, not only the heavens with the sun and moon and stars, . . . but also those things which He produced potentially and causally—*potentialiter atque causaliter*—from the waters and the earth before they appeared as we now know them."[1] Again, he affirms that all things were in the beginning created in an elementary condition—*in quadam textura elementorum*—and received their development subsequently, *acceptis opportunitatibus*.

In order that he may not be misunderstood the saint expressed himself in manifold ways. He has an exuberance of language to make his meaning clear, and a wealth of illustration which is as beautiful as it is simple and apposite. In commenting on the words, "Let the earth bring forth the green herb," he states explicitly that plants were created not directly, but potentially—*in fieri, in causa*—that the earth produced herb and tree causally—*causaliter*—and in virtue of a power it had received from the Creator—*producendi accepisse virtutem*.[2]

He insists on it that Moses in the first chapter of Genesis teaches that creation was successive, *secundum intervalla temporum;* that the works of creation were not disconnected, but that, on the con-

---
[1] *De Genesi ad Litt.*, lib. v. cap. xxiii.
[2] "Causaliter ergo tunc dictum est produxisse terram herbam et lignum, id est producendi accepisse virtutem."—Op. cit., lib. v. cap. v.

trary, they were continuous and dovetailed, so to speak, into one another; that there was a *permixtio dierum;* that all things, plants, trees, and animals, appear, multiply, and develop according to the special laws of their nature—*ut agant temporales numeros suos naturis propriis distributos;* that their development is normal, according to laws ordained for each individual; that it was the same in the beginning as it is now; that then, as now, it was effected not within a few ordinary solar days, but during a period of time which is indeterminate—*per volumina sæculorum.*

"In the beginning," he declares in his great work against the Manichæans,[1] "God created heaven and earth. By the words heaven and earth are meant all creatures made by God. They are thus denominated by the name of visible things in order that weak human minds may more readily comprehend them. Matter then as just created was invisible and formless, and in the condition which the Greeks designated by the word *chaos*. From this individual beings—those having form—were produced."

This formless matter, which God created from nothing, was first called heaven and earth, and it is written that "In the beginning God created heaven and earth," not because it was forthwith heaven and earth, but because it was destined to become heaven and earth.[2] When we consider the seed of a tree, we say that it contains the roots, the trunk, the branches, the fruits, and the leaves, not because they are already there, but because they shall be produced from it. It is

[1] *De Genesi contra Manicheos*, lib. i. cap. v.
[2] "Non quia jam hoc erat, sed quia jam hoc esse poterat."

in this sense that it is declared that "In the beginning God created heaven and earth ; that is to say, the seed of the heaven and the earth when the matter of the heaven and the earth was yet in a confused state. Because heaven and earth were to be produced from this matter, it is thus called by anticipation, as it were, heaven and earth."[1] Verily, in reading these words we can fancy that we are perusing some modern scientific treatise on cosmogony instead of an exposition of Genesis written by a Father of the Church fifteen centuries ago.

The theory of creation, therefore, as held by the Fathers, does not, contrary to what is so often supposed in our day, "necessitate the perpetual search after manifestations of miraculous powers and perpetual catastrophes. Creation is not a miraculous interference with the laws of nature, but the very institution of those laws. Law and regularity, not arbitrary intervention, was the patristic ideal of creation. With this notion they admitted without difficulty the most surprising origin of living creatures, provided it took place by *law*. They held that when God said, 'Let the waters produce, let the earth produce,' He conferred forces on the elements of earth and water which enabled them naturally to produce the various species of organic beings. This power, they thought, remains attached to the elements throughout all time."

St. Thomas Aquinas brings out this idea clearly when, in quoting St. Augustine, he declares that "in the institution of nature we do not look for miracles,

---

[1] Loc. cit., lib. i. cap. vii.

but for the laws of nature."[1] The same Angel of the Schools, in comparing the literal interpretation of St. Basil with that advocated by St. Augustine, asserts that the former is more conformable to the text, but that the latter is more reasonable and better adapted to defend the Sacred Scriptures against the attacks of unbelievers.[2]

Principles of Exegesis Unchangeable.

From the foregoing it will be seen how ill founded is the charge that Catholic exegesis is continually changing in order to make way for the new. So far is this from being the case that it in many cases rejects the new and holds on to the old. This is particularly true of the theories of St. Gregory of Nyssa and St. Augustine regarding the origin of the world, and it were easy to show that it is equally true of other views which they maintained. In details, in matters of minor importance, no one denies or can deny that there have been changes, or that Catholic exegetists have modified their expositions of the Scriptures so as to make them harmonize with the latest results of scientific research.

But changes in matters of detail in biblical interpretation, changes in points of view regarding the Mosaic cosmogony, are quite different from changes of principles in questions of exegesis. The principles that have guided theologians and commentators have ever remained the same, however great may have been the

[1] "In prima autem institutione naturæ non quæritur miraculum, sed quid natura rerum habeat, ut Augustinus dicit. Lib. ii. sup. *Gen. ad Litt.*, cap. i." Sum. Iae, lxvii. 4 ad 3.
[2] *Ibid.*

mutations of profane science, and however much scientific investigation may have caused us to revise our views of nature.

Catholic exegetists have always regarded the Bible as the word of God, but one of the principles of interpretation which they never lose sight of, and which it is important for us to bear in mind here, is that we must submit certain questions of Scripture to the examination of both reason and science. This is especially true of topics like the cosmogony of Moses, which refers to many things that come within the purview of science, and which science alone can explain.

Origen attached so much importance to a knowledge of profane science that, as St. Gregory Thaumaturgus relates, he taught his students physics and astronomy before he introduced them to the study of Sacred Scripture. St. Augustine is no less positive in affirming the necessity on the part of the commentator of making his interpretation accord with the dictates of reason and the certain data of science—*certissima ratione vel experientia.* He asserts expressly that the human sciences raise the mind to divine things—*disciplinæ liberales afferent intellectum ad divina;* that philosophy, which is the chief among the sciences—*omnium disciplinarum excogitatrix*—is of special service in begetting, defending, nourishing, and strengthening the faith: *Fides, quæ per scientiam gignitur, nutritur, defenditur, corroboratur.*

One of the reasons that moved the Alexandrine School to adopt the theory of simultaneous creation was, as we have seen, that it harmonized better than any other theory with the philosophical systems then in vogue. And the reason why, at various subsequent epochs, divers other views were held was because such views were considered to be more in consonance with the deductions of science and the declarations of the Sacred Text.

The theories, then, of exegetists have changed because science—or what was called science—has changed, and not because there has been any change in, much less repudiation of, the principles of scriptural interpretation. The principles of exegesis that Origen taught, that Basil followed, that Augustine proclaimed were ever the same, and one with the principles that Catholic theologians now employ.

Cardinal Franzelin, in his learned tractate on Sacred Scripture, expressly declares that "the interpretation of questions of Scripture which treat of natural things may be materially aided by the natural sciences."[1] This view of the erudite cardinal, to which Leo XIII. gives renewed and emphatic expression in his late Encyclical *Providentissimus Deus*, is the one universally held by contemporary theologians, and it was the one, and the only one, which found acceptance with the Fathers and Doctors of the early Church. No, I repeat it, the principles of exegesis have not changed, but science has progressed, and theories that were once considered as so much veritable science have been discarded for others which for the nonce are looked upon as being more tenable.

If scientists themselves modify their views to suit the latest advance of science, can they, with any show of reason, find fault with theologians and exegetists

---

[1] Interpretatio in locis Scripturæ quæ agunt de rebus naturalibus, multum juvari potest per scientias naturales.—*Tractatus de Trad. et Script.*, p. 731.

for doing the same? Surely not. The Fathers and Doctors of the Church were fully abreast with the science of their time, and it were folly to expect more than this of them—to exact of them a knowledge which those who made the pursuit of science a specialty did not possess, or to imagine that they should be as far advanced in the inductive sciences as those who have had the benefit of long centuries of observation and experiment.[1]

So far, I have directed attention to the interpretation by the Fathers of the Genesiac word "day"—to the theory of St. Gregory of Nyssa regarding the primitive matter from which the universe was formed, and to the still more remarkable theory of St. Augustine concerning organic evolution. It would not be a difficult matter to point out other points of resemblance —some of them almost equally striking—between the views of the early Fathers in matters of science and the current teachings of some of the most competent exponents of contemporary thought.

Matter and Light.

Thus, St. Gregory of Nyssa tells us that in nature there is transformation, but no annihilation, of matter. "Everything is transformed; nothing is lost." All things move, as it were, in a circle. There are, indeed, changes innumerable, but all things, sooner or later, return to their original condition. Under the influence of the sun clouds are formed from the sea; the clouds produce rain, and the rain eventually

[1] See also, in this connection, the statement of Leo XIII. in the above-mentioned Encyclical.

returns again to the sea whence it came. So it is with the phenomena of combustion and decay, in the burning of oil, in the disintegration of the human body. There is a continuous and uninterrupted cycle of changes, chemical and physical, but no destruction of matter. How like a paragraph from a modern treatise on chemistry are those words of the Hexaëmeron of the illustrious Greek exegetist of fifteen centuries ago!

Again: How wonderfully the views of the acute Greek Doctor regarding the nature of light are corroborated by the results of modern physical research! It has been objected to the Mosaic cosmogony that it must be false because it represents light as having been created before the sun and moon and stars. Light, according to the narrative of Genesis, was created on the first day, whereas the heavenly bodies were not called into existence until the fourth day. These statements, rationalists and superficial unbelievers have declared, are irreconcilable with the known conclusions of science, but so far is this from being the case that, paradoxical as it may appear, they are in perfect accord with the latest available knowledge regarding the nature of light. But St. Gregory of Nyssa finds no difficulty in admitting the existence of light before the formation of the sun and other celestial luminaries. Anticipating the corpuscular theory of Newton, he imagined that light was a special kind of matter of which the luminous orbs of heaven were composed; that the light-giving molecules which compose the sun and moon and stars were originally disseminated throughout the primordial nebulous mass, and came together in virtue of certain laws of affinity and attraction to which they were subject. His theory was wrong, we now say, and so was Newton's wrong, although there are not wanting certain contemporary scientists who still aver that it is more tenable than any other theory yet advanced. But be that as it may, the fact remains that light, whatever its nature, could and undoubtedly did exist before the creation of the "two great lights" that Genesis speaks of as the work of the fourth day. Whether or not we accept the Huyhenian hypothesis that light is due to the vibration of a medium filling all space, known as the ether, the undulations of which are capable of producing an impression on the retina, it still remains an incontestable fact, according to Laplace's beautiful theory, that "the sun is born of light, rather than light of the sun." For, long before the nebulous mass from which the sun was evolved was sufficiently condensed to form the brilliant luminary which we now behold, the revolving cosmic mass had, in virtue of its condensation and contraction, begun to emit light and dissipate the darkness that before had enveloped the immensity of chaos. Not only this. The principle of light, whatever it be, is, as all physicists are aware, ever latent round about us, and requires only special excitants to develop it and make us conscious of its existence. It is disclosed in the lightning's flash, in the aurora borealis and aurora australis, and in various phenomena of chemical and mechanical action and phosphorescence.

If, however, we interrogate scientists regarding the nature of light, the only response which we shall receive is, "We do not know." We can but study its properties, and these lead us to believe that it is most probably a mode of motion excited in the ether by what are called luminous bodies. It is the undulatory movements of this ether which, by means of the eye give rise to the sensation of sight. But of the true nature of light we are absolutely ignorant.

"At what period in the development of the universe the emission of light began science is unable to say. It can, however, assert that light existed long prior to the separation of matter or the formation of distinct luminous bodies. For this reason there can, therefore, be no question of a contradiction between the Genesiac narrative and the declarations of science regarding the origin of light."[1]

There is certainly nothing in modern science that can impair in the least the truthfulness of the Mosaic cosmogony, much less discredit the Genesiac narrative. We may to-day have truer conceptions of the nature of light than had St. Gregory and St. Augustine, but the enemies of the Bible are no more able now to show any discrepancy between the certain data of science and the words of Genesis regarding the creation of light than were the impugners of the Inspired Record in the first ages of the Church's existence.

And so I might continue giving illustrations of the perfect harmony that exists, and must exist, between Genesis and science. But my object is not to write a treatise on the subject, but only to exhibit, in a few of the more controverted points, the fact that there is no ground whatever for the statements that are so often made regarding the hopelessly irreconcilable

[1] Pfaff: *Schoepfungsgeschichte*, p. 746.

conflict which a certain class of scientists would have us believe exists between revelation and science—between the declarations of Moses and the legitimate conclusions of the Higher Criticism or the indisputable inductions of geology and astronomy.

CHAPTER V.

MODERN THEORIES OF COSMOGONY AND INTERPRETATION.

THE RESTITUTION OR INTERVAL THEORY.

REGARDING the *Restitution* and *Period* theories, of which mention has already been made, a brief account will be sufficient.

The *Restitution* or *Interval* theory, as it is sometimes called, is a kind of link between the literal and period theories. Like the former, it interprets the word "day" literally, but at the same time it postulates an indefinite lapse of time between the first act of creation and the six days of Genesis. In this wise it aims to harmonize the assumptions of the two theories and to blend them into one.

According to the interval theory, the creation of the earth, of animals, and of plants was slow and successive, as is evidenced by the facts of geology. But a great cataclysm supervened which destroyed all forms of terrestrial life—whence the fossiliferous deposits of the earth's crust—and reduced everything to chaos. This, we are told, is what is signified by the words, "And the earth was void and empty, and darkness was upon the face of the deep."

If, however, the first creation, indicated by the words, "In the beginning God created heaven and earth," was slow and successive, the second creation, or restoration, following the great catastrophe, was accomplished in such a short space of time—six ordinary days—that there is left no trace of it for scientific investigation. But this system, proposed by Buckland and favored by Chalmers, Cardinal Wiseman, and other distinguished scholars, has now but few if any defenders, as it is manifestly at variance with some of the simplest facts of geology.

"A careful study of the earth's crust and the fossils which it contains," says a well-known French writer, "proves that the cataclysms which were formerly admitted never had any existence in fact—that between the flora and fauna of any given period and those of the period following there was never any solution of continuity. The species of one epoch overlap those of the next epoch. Among the mollusks at present existing in our seas, and even among contemporary mammals, there are many which antedate man's apparition on earth by centuries, and even many thousands of years. For this reason it is impossible to suppose that these animals were created only a few days before the advent of man."[1]

The Period Theory.

According to the *period* theory, which at present has more defenders than any other, the "days" of Genesis were not ordinary days of twenty-four hours, but indeterminate periods of time. It is also known as the *concordistic* theory, because its advocates contend that it exhibits a perfect accord between the teachings of

[1] Lavaud de Lestrade: *Accord de la Science avec le Premier Chapitre de la Genèse*, pp. 30 et seq.

science and the declarations of Genesis, in opposition to various *non-concordistic* theories, which deny any possible reconciliation between geology and Moses.

The Genesiac days, concordists claim, were not ordinary solar days, but indefinite periods of time. The possibility of attaching any other meaning to the word is, they assure us, precluded, not only by science, which utterly repudiates days of twenty-four hours, but also by the Sacred Text itself.

As all the readers of the Bible are aware, there are many passages in the Old Testament, not to speak of the New, in which the Hebrew word יוֹם, *yôm*—day—signifies an indeterminate period of time. Indeed, one may find a striking instance in point without going outside of the Mosaic narrative of creation. In Genesis ii. 4 we read the words: " These are the generations of the heaven and the earth, when they were created, in the day that the Lord made the heaven and the earth." Here the word "day" obviously signifies not any ordinary day, but an indefinite period of time.

Again, as Abbé Vigouroux well observes, " Moses was obliged to employ the word יוֹם, *yôm*—day—to signify period or epoch, as there is no special word in Hebrew to express this idea. This fact, generally unknown, deserves serious consideration. The repugnance that many have to admitting day-epochs arises from the fact that they make our word day absolutely identical with the word יוֹם, *yôm*, which is not the case. We have the word "day" distinct from the word "epoch," whereas in Hebrew there is but one expression for these two ideas. The Hebrew tongue is not so rich in its vocabulary as our own, and hence it is obliged to make a metaphorical use of the word יוֹם,

THE MOSAIC HEXAËMERON. 95

yôm, to express the idea that we attribute to the word epoch."[1]

But more than this. The Mosaic days, as the writer just quoted remarks, are metaphorical, not only as to their signification, but also as to their number. The figure six in Genesis is not to be taken in a rigorous and absolute sense. It does not mean that there were only six epochs in the work of creation, but simply that there were several successive periods of development. The number six was chosen in order that the divine might correspond with the human week, in which six days are given to work, and the seventh, the Sabbath, is consecrated to repose. Furthermore, it must be noted that the cosmogony of Moses supplies only the chief outlines of the work of creation; the details, which are of less importance to the generality of men, are neglected.[2]

Again, Genesis, be it remembered, was not intended by its author to serve as a treatise on natural or physical science. Moses was neither a geologist nor an astronomer, and the scope of his narrative did not require of him either an exact or a profound knowledge of science. All attempts, therefore, to find in his account of creation an anticipation of the results of modern geologic and astronomic discovery, and to exhibit a detailed and exact correspondence between

[1] *Manuel biblique*, tome i. p. 444. It is scarcely necessary to observe here that the words "evening" and "morning," עֶרֶב ('ereb) and בֹּקֶר (bôker), employed in the Mosaic story of creation, are likewise to be understood in a metaphorical sense. Cf. St. Augustine, *ut supra*, p. 199.

[2] Cf. *Les Livres Saints et la Critique rationaliste*, par Abbé Vigouroux, tome iii. p. 262.

the days of Genesis and the different geological epochs, are as unwarranted as they are sure to prove nugatory. We cannot, as is so often imagined, draw a line of demarkation between any one geological age and that which precedes or follows it. The fauna and flora of one period frequently overlap those of proximate periods. Throughout the whole of geologic time—from the Cambrian to the Quaternary Period—we observe a dovetailing of the various forms of life into one another, and have exhibited in the most striking manner that *permixtio dierum* of which St. Augustine speaks, but of which he could have had no knowledge in the sense in which, since his day, it has been disclosed by geology. Both science and Genesis tell us of a gradation from the lower to the higher forms of life, and in this respect their testimony is as consonant as it is remarkable.

M. Barrande, the most eminent of modern palæontologists, and one most competent to interpret the facts we are now considering, declares, in speaking of the subject, that—

"As regards the creation of organized beings the whole Genesiac narrative may be reduced to the establishing of three main facts, in reference to which it is in perfect harmony with the information which we have thus far gained by a study of geology. These facts are as follows: 1. Vegetable preceded animal life both in the sea and on land. 2. Animal life was at first represented by animals living in the sea and by birds. 3. As a consequence animal life appeared on the land at a subsequent period, and man's advent postdates that of all other creatures. . . .

"From this we infer that the inspired writer had it

in purpose to fix only the relative dates of apparition of plants and of marine and terrestrial animals, without entering into any historic detail relative to the subsequent development of animal and vegetable life. This development took place in the course of time, either in virtue of new and repeated acts of the Creator Himself, or as the result of laws originally established by Him, and of which He has not been pleased to reveal the nature.

"In studying from this point of view the history of the creation of the vegetable and animal kingdoms as given by Moses, we find that it is in perfect harmony with that which geology has gleaned from the observation of facts; that is, from a study of stratigraphic rocks and organic remains—vegetable and animal—which they contain."[1]

These words of the distinguished French geologist are corroborated by a similar declaration of the illustrious Cuvier, who does not hesitate to affirm that "the successive evolutions of creation, as they are traced for us by the first book of the Pentateuch, harmonize in a remarkable manner with the deductions we have been able to make from the discoveries of geology, zoology, and other sciences of our time."

It must not, however, be forgotten that the concordist theory, like all other theories having for their object the reconciliation of science and Genesis, is but a theory and nothing more. Just now it is more generally accepted than any other theory, and has, no doubt, much to recommend it. But even it does not explain numerous difficulties that still puzzle exegetists. There are yet many problems to be solved—

[1] Quoted by Vigouroux, op. cit., p. 261.

problems of physical and natural science, problems of philosophy, problems of higher criticism—which baffle all present efforts, and whose solution we must leave to the future. Judging from what has already been achieved, we can have no doubt about what remains to be accomplished. The result is foreshadowed by the triumphs of modern exegesis, which give a positive assurance that in God's own time all mysteries will be cleared up, and that both science and Genesis will eventually render the same testimony, and in language as clear as it shall be unmistakable.

Bishop Clifford's Theory.

Before closing our review of the most prominent theories that have obtained regarding the interpretation of the Mosaic Hexaëmeron it will be well to say a few words of the now famous theory advanced a few years ago by the late English bishop, Clifford of Clifton. According to this theory, which is intermediate in character between the theories advocated by the Schools of Alexandria and those of Edessa and Cæsarea, between the allegorism of Origen, Clement, and Athanasius and the literalism of Ephrem, Chrysostom, and Basil, the first chapter of Genesis is not to be construed as an historical narrative, but as a ritual hymn. To quote the bishop's own words: "The first thirty-four verses of the Bible, although they stand foremost in the collection of the writings of Moses, form no portion of the book of Genesis which immediately follows them. They constitute a composition complete in itself. They are a sacred hymn recording the consecration of each day of the week to the memory of one or other of the works done by the true God, Creator of heaven and earth, in opposition to a custom established by the Egyptian priests of referring the days of the week to the sun, moon, and planets, and of consecrating each day of the month to the memory of the actions of false deities. The hymn, when examined by the light which the knowledge of the customs of Egypt, such as may at the present day be derived from the monuments and records of that country, throws upon it, shows how carefully its detail has been arranged for the purpose of guarding against those special dangers of idolatry to which the Isaaelites were exposed at the time of their delivery from Egyptian bondage, thus affording an indirect but valuable confirmation of the fact that Moses was its author. This hymn not being a history of the creation, but a ritual work, the statement in it must be interpreted in the sense in which similar statements are understood when they occur in writings of a ritual character. When it is said that certain works are performed on certain days of the week, nothing more is implied than that those days are consecrated to the memory of the work referred to. Subject to this proviso, the works of Moses are to be understood in their usual sense and present no special difficulty. A *day* means the space of twenty-four hours in this as in other portions of the writings of the same author. By seven days are meant the days of the week, which are simply referred to as the first, second, instead of Sunday, Monday, Tuesday, and so on, because, all reference to the planets being forbidden, there remains but the numerical order by which to cite them. Words descriptive of natural objects and phenomena, such as the firmament, the deep, the waters above the firmament, and such like, mean nothing more or less than what was implied by the same words when used by the wise men of Egypt in the days of Moses. The notions of these men were wrong on many points of natural philosophy, but their error lay in the interpretation they gave to the phenomena; the phenomena themselves had a real existence. The language of Moses refers to the phenomena independently of any interpretation which may be given the same. At the present day we speak of the stars shining in the sky, the rain pouring down from the sky, the rainbow appearing in the sky, though we are all well aware that the stars are removed far above the atmosphere in which the rain gathers which reflects the rainbow. Thus understood, the words of Moses present no manner of opposition to scientific facts. In this hymn he records two things: First, that God created all things. This is a truth which no scientific fact can invalidate. Secondly, that each of the first six days of the week is consecrated to some special work performed by God, and that the seventh is consecrated to the rest of God and must be kept holy. . . . As to the order in which the various parts of the creation came into existence, and whether a longer or shorter period of time elapsed before our earth and its furniture assumed the appearance they now present, these are matters which form no part of Moses' task to explain. They enter not into his subject, and he does not allude to them, and therefore, whatever be the conclusions which scientific men may come to on these points, they meet neither with approval nor with opposition from the words of Moses. The records of the stages of the existence of our globe form, no doubt, a subject of great interest to inquirers, but beyond the fact that in the beginning God created heaven and earth no revelation has been given to men concerning them. They belong exclusively to the province of science. They are a part of that *travail which God hath given to the sons of men to be exercised in it. He hath made all things good in their time*, and *hath delivered the world to their consideration* (Eccles. iii. 10, 11)."[1]

Science and Patristic Exegesis.

But it may be asked, What is the use of all this discussion where there are so many elements of uncertainty? "What," inquires St. Augustine, "is the net result of all this winnowing? Where is the good wheat that was to come of it? You raise questions without giving answers. Give us something positive, something conclusive."

The response of the saint shall be also mine. I have done all that in the present state of science and exegesis it is possible to do. "I have shown that there is not a single declaration of science that is contrary to the teachings of Moses."[2] For us this is sufficient.

[1] *Dublin Review*, April, 1881, pp. 330–332. See also same *Review*, Oct., 1881, and Jan. and April, 1883.

[2] "Dicet aliquis: Quid tu tanta tritura dissertationis hujus, quid granorum, exuisti? Quid eventilasti? Cur propemodum in quæstionibus adhuc latent omnia? Affirma aliquid eorum quæ multa posse intelligi disputasti. Cui respondeo, ad eum ipsum me cibum suaviter pervenisse, quo didici non hærere homini in respondendo secundum fidem, quod respondendum est hominibus qui calumniari libris nostræ salutis effectant, ut aliquid ipsi de natura rerum veracitus documentis

There have, it is true, been theories innumerable which their authors fondly imagined were subversive of the Hexaëmeron of Moses, and antagonistic, consequently, to the integrity of Scripture; but there is not to-day, any more than there was in the time of St. Augustine, a single fact of science that can justly be construed as contravening the system of cosmogony contained in Genesis or as opposed to the clear and explicit teachings of the inspired writer.

I might here conclude, but there are a few other facts disclosed by this long discussion, which deserve at least a passing notice.

The first of these facts is the perfect intellectual freedom that the Fathers and Doctors of the Church have always claimed and enjoyed in matters outside of positive dogma. This is particularly observable in the discussion and interpretation of such questions as the one we have been considering, where science rather than revelation must be appealed to for a solution of the difficulties encountered.

We have a striking illustration of this liberty of thought in St. John Damascene, the last of the great theologians of the Oriental Church. In matters of cosmogony he chooses freely between the doctrines of the Syrian and Cappadocian Schools. At one time he declares for St. Ephrem, at another for St. Basil, and at still another for St. Gregory of Nyssa. He feels that he is treading on safe ground, and that he is perfectly free to select such opinions as, according to his judgment, are most conformable to fact and truth.

And St. Gregory of Nyssa not only shows that he

demonstrare potuerint, ostendamus nostris Litteris non esse contrarium."—*De Genesi ad Litteram*, lib. i. cap. 21.

enjoyed perfect intellectual freedom himself, but also that he respected the opinions of others and allowed them equal liberty of thought. He does not, for instance, in the disputed questions of Mosaic cosmogony insist on the acceptance of his own views, but modestly declares "I think" this is so or may be so.

St. Augustine, in referring to the divers interpretations which the Genesiac record admits, says: "Let each one choose according to the best of his power; only let him not rashly put forward as known that which is unknown, and let him not fail to remember that he is but a man searching, as far as may be, into the works of God."[1] In another place he declares that "in the obscurities of natural things our investigations should be characterized by hypothesis rather than by positive declarations—*magis præstemus diligentiam inquirendi, quam affirmandi temeritatem,*" and does not hesitate to affirm that "rash and inconsiderate assertations in uncertain and doubtful passages of Scripture may easily degenerate into sacrilege." On every page of his works he inculcates both by precept and example the caution and reserve that should be exercised in the discussion of disputed questions, and is ever ready to admit in problems of cosmogony the necessarily provisional character of many of his explanations. Thus, regarding one of his theories of the days of Genesis, he tells us frankly that it is but an attempt to explain a difficult problem, and that he may sooner or later reject it for another theory. But he is the first to recognize the inadequateness of some of his hypotheses, and wishes better success to others.[2]

[1] *De Genesi Liber Imperfectus*, cap. ix. n. 80.
[2] Fieri enim potest ut etiam ego aliam (sententiam) his

Science, Scripture, and Religion.

Another fact, often lost sight of, is that when the inspired writers of the Sacred Books make incidental reference to natural phenomena while teaching religious truth, they accommodate themselves to the prevailing ideas regarding such phenomena. "Many things in the Sacred Scriptures," says St. Jerome, "are expressed according to the opinion of the times in which they were written, and not according to the truth."[1]

"The biblical writers," says Reusch, "received supernatural enlightenment from God, but the object of this enlightenment and of the divine revelation altogether was only to impart *religious* truths, not profane knowledge; and we may therefore, without detracting from the respect due to the holy writers or in any way weakening the doctrine of inspiration, safely allow that the biblical writers were not in advance of their age in the matter of profane knowledge, and consequently of natural science. The praises given by certain French savants to the genius or scientific knowledge of the Jewish lawgiver because of the supposed anticipation in Genesis of modern scientific discoveries are, therefore, not to the purpose. As regards profane knowledge Moses was not raised above his contemporaries by divine revelation, and there is no

---

divinæ Scripturæ verbis congruentiorem fortassis inveniam. Neque enim ita hanc confirmo ut aliam quæ proponenda sit inveniri non posse contendam.—*De Genesi ad Litt.*, lib. iv. cap. 28.

[1] "Multa in Scripturis Sanctis dicuntur juxta opinionem illius temporis, quo gesta referuntur, et non juxta quod rei veritas continebat."—Jer. xxviii. 10, 11.

proof whatever of his being in a position to raise himself above them by his own thought and inquiry."[1]

"It might, indeed," declares Cardinal Newman, "have pleased the Almighty to have superseded physical inquiry by revealing the truths which are its object, but He has not done so." And yet, notwithstanding this lack of revelation in matters of science, there is, and can, I repeat it, be no discrepancy between Genesis and science. For, "in Holy Scripture," as Kurtz has well expressed it, "all future science can find a place; it has made no mistake; no new science can cry out, '*si tacuisses.*' It is by this means that it shows its divine character in dealing with questions of natural science."

"'Theology itself," Father Faber happily observes, "will be found to fit all discoveries as they come. It is only the individual theologians who may sometimes have to humor their own private ideas."[2]

If, then, there is nothing, and can be nothing, in science that is antagonistic to faith, still less is there anything about it, as some have absurdly fancied, that is irreligious. On the contrary, "to a religious mind," as the charming writer just quoted remarks, "physical science is an intensely religious thing."

"No sight," he avers, "can be more grateful to a true theologian than to behold the giant strides of scientific discovery and the bold methods of scientific research. He has nothing to fear for his faith, except an embarrassment arising from the very riches of its demonstration which these discoveries are continually supplying. Nothing can be more narrow, vulgar, or

---

[1] *Bibel und Natur*, English translation, p. 32.
[2] *The Blessed Sacrament*, p. 331.

stupid than the idea of an antithesis between science and religion. It is true that some of the sciences, in the earlier periods of their construction, turned the heads of those who drank at their fountains, and crude theories, incompatible with the dogmas of faith, were the result. Yet these only changed, at last, to fresh and more striking proofs of the divine and unalterable truth of our holy faith; for further discovery and a larger induction led, in every case, to an abandonment of the irreligious theory." . . .

"Geology, which is the history of nature, has been regarded as a science the cultivation of which is especially dangerous to religious habits of mind. If it be so, it is the mind that is at fault, and not the science. The whole series of controversies ending in the admission of the extreme modernness of the present surface of the globe and the novelty of man in creation is nothing else but a long chain of proof of the Mosaic narrative." [1]

But if there is, and can be, no antagonism between Genesis and science—if, on the contrary, the two, as far as understood, are found to be in perfect accord—there are difficulties yet unsolved. Darkness is still upon the deep mysteries of many problems of Mosaic cosmogony. The future, I am convinced, will do much toward dissipating this darkness. The past history and present condition of both science and exegesis warrant such a view. But the perfect exhibition of all the hidden harmonies that we know to exist between science and revelation; the complete reconciliation of the Inspired Record and the record of the rocks; the *fiat lux* that shall dispel all the mists of

[1] Op. cit., pp. 324–326.

error and the clouds of misinterpretation which now prevent our seeing things as they are,—may indeed be "a consummation devoutly to be wished," but something, most likely, that shall be vouchsafed us only in that world where all is knowledge and light, where the mysteries of creation shall be revealed in the effulgence of God's glory.

Summary and Conclusion.

But notwithstanding the difficulties presented by the first two chapters of Genesis, the cosmogony of Moses is the only one which antiquity has left us that can claim our assent or challenge the investigation of science. There may be passages in it which do not at present admit of a satisfactory explanation, but there is nothing involving contradiction, and still less is there aught that can be pronounced an absurdity. Compared with the other cosmogonies of the ancient world, it is absolutely peerless, and is as far above them as history is above fiction, as truth above falsehood. Science may not unravel the knotty problems which still abound, but it cannot gainsay what Moses declares. Where there is apparent discord we are, from the very nature of the case, certain that there is perfect harmony.

It is only when we contrast the Mosaic account of creation with the cosmogonies of the more advanced nations of antiquity that we can realize how remarkable the declarations of the Hebrew lawgiver really are, and how he has answered questions before which pagan philosophy stood mute and impotent.

The Aryans of early India surprise us by their

achievements in literature, science, and art. Since their discovery, in the last century, the Vedas and codes of laws of the ancient Hindu have been the subjects of wonder and enthusiastic comment by scholars the world over. But Hindu philosophy never arose to a true conception of the one God. The Brahmin, wherever found, meditating on the banks of the Indus or the Jumna, or officiating in the temples of Delhi and Benares, was an idolater who entertained the most grotesque notions regarding the origin and configuration of the world.

The geogonies and cosmogonies of Assyria and Babylonia were scarcely less extravagant and absurd than were those of India. Recent discoveries have shown that the peoples of Mesopotamia had attained a degree of civilization that would not have been credited a few decades ago. The arts and sciences were cultivated with ardor, and libraries were found in all the principal cities of Mesopotamia. Her philosophers were famed for their wisdom, and the astronomers of Nineveh and Babylon could predict eclipses and determine the courses of the heavenly bodies with a degree of precision that, considering the rude instruments at their disposal, is nothing short of marvellous. But the gods of Assyria and Babylonia were but blocks of clay and stone variously fashioned by the hand of man, and the peoples inhabiting the valleys of the Tigris and the Euphrates were as far from a knowledge of the true God, the Creator of all things out of nothing, as were the philosophical Brahmins who taught and speculated beyond the Himalayas.

What has been said of India and Mesopotamia may be iterated with even greater truth of the land of the

Pharaohs. To Egypt even the greatest of the philosophers of Greece went in quest of knowledge, and many of the doctrines which they afterward taught their disciples were learned from the priests in the temples of Memphis and Heliopolis.

Her ruins, scattered all along the Nile Valley from Ipsambul to Alexandria, are even now, after the lapse of thousands of years, the admiration of all who behold them. Philæ, Thebes, and Abydos, great in decay, are, like the Pyramids of Gizeh, the best evidence of the greatness and genius of the people who could plan and execute such marvels. But the builders of Cheops and the designers and constructors of the Ramesseum and the Serapeum of Memphis, and the teachers of the sages of Greece, deified the river that brought fertility to their land, and worshipped not only the animals that grazed in the valley of the Nile, but even the reptiles that crawled in its slime and the leeks and onions which grew in its gardens.

> "Crocodilon adorat
> Pars hæc, illa pavet saturam serpentibus ibin.
> Effigies sacri nitet aurea cercopitheci,
> . . . .
> Illic æluros, hic piscem fluminis, illic
> Oppida tota canem venerantur, nemo Dianam.
> Porrum et cepe nefas violare et frangere morsu:
> O sanctas gentes, quibus hæc nascuntur in hortis
> Numina!"[1]

---

[1] "The snake-devouring ibis these enshrine,
Those think the crocodile alone divine;
Others . . . .
Set up a glittering brute of uncouth shape
And bow before the image of an ape!
Thousands regard the hound with holy fear,
Not one, Diana; and 'tis dangerous here

Nor was Greece, immortal Greece, the home of art, eloquence, poesy, of science, history, and philosophy, exempt from the errors and vagaries which were so characteristic of the great nations of the Orient. For thousands of years her art has been the art of the world, her literature the literature of the world, her philosophy the philosophy of the world. The culture of the world, the taste of the world, the æstheticism of the world, come to us from the land of Plato and Aristotle, Phidias and Sophocles, Pericles and Demosthenes. For thousands of years she has been the inspiration of scholars in every clime, and has contributed to the advancement of knowledge in every department of human research. From the Academy and the Lyceum human genius winged its loftiest flight, and while soaring aloft in the blue empyrean surveyed the fairest domains of human thought. For thirty centuries the Greek mind has directed the meditations of the philosopher and controlled the speculations of the man of science. Her sculptured marbles have been the despair of all subsequent artists, as the Parthenon, although in ruins, still remains a dream of unsurpassed loveliness. But the noblest productions of this great land, from the matchless poems of her sightless bard to the most exquisite carving that ever graced the Acropolis, were tinctured with false views of God, and were designed to perpetuate a system of religion and foster a form of idolatry that would for

> To violate an onion, or to stain
> The sanctity of leeks with tooth profane.
> O holy nations! sacro-sanct abodes!
> Where every garden propagates its gods."
> JUVENAL, *Sat.* xv., vers. 2 et seq.

ever preclude man from having just notions of the Creator of the universe or of His relations toward His creatures. Polytheism of the most ridiculous character dominated in Greece, and systems of cosmogony the most fantastical contended for supremacy in the greatest schools of an otherwise enlightened people.

And so it was with Rome, imperial Rome, the conqueror of the world. The architectural wonders of Athens are reproduced in the City of the Seven Hills; the golden eloquence of Cicero recalls the burning philippics of Demosthenes; in the noble epic of Virgil we recognize the sublime inspiration of the Muse of Homer. But the gods of the Pantheon are the gods of Greece, reinforced by countless accessions from the temples of all the lands in which the Roman eagle had been carried and in which Roman legions had been triumphant. Lucretius embalms in elegant verse the teachings of Epicurus; the myths of Hesiod are repeated by the author of the *Metamorphoses*, and all the errors of Greek philosophy are rehearsed in patrician villas and in the palaces of the Cæsars.

How different the doctrines of the legislator of Israel! With a few bold strokes he gives us a picture of the history of creation, and in a few simple words he tells us how *in the beginning God created heaven and earth*. There is no doubt, no vacillation, in the mind of the author of Genesis, no obscurity in his statements regarding the creative acts of Jehovah. In a single sentence he condemns the dualism of the Eastern sage and the doctrine of the eternity of matter of the Greek Sophist. At the same time he brushes aside numberless other errors in philosophy and theology, and prepares the mind for a conception of the

Deity that even the greatest of the pagan philosophers never attained.

In the cosmogony of Moses we have manifested in every line the spirit of revelation. Moses answers questions that the wise men of the ancient Gentile world had essayed in vain, because he is inspired. He declares the truth, because he is preserved from error by the Spirit of God. Only in his history of creation does reason find a satisfactory response to the queries suggested by the very existence of the visible universe, and in Genesis alone have we a cosmogony that is in accord with all the certain declarations of science. Infidel sciolism may reject the Mosaic account of creation, and endeavor to offer a substitute, but all such attempts are sure to prove futile and to issue in contradictions and absurdities. Physical science cannot tell us anything about creation, cannot tell us anything about the beginning of things. Neither can it clear up the mystery enveloping the origin of life, nor show us matter, as the great Cuvier happily expresses it, *s'organisant.* Before Moses atheistic materialism and pantheistic idealism, so characteristic of pagan philosophy and pagan religion, go down as the pigmy before the giant, and the deification of nature is seen in all its hideousness and inconsistency.

And the declarations of Moses remain the same whatever theories we may have regarding the inspiration of Genesis or the sources from which the history of creation was drawn. Is Genesis, as we now have it, revealed or inspired?—that is, is the narrative a direct revelation in its entirety or is it simply a human tradition, the most ancient of our race, collected and used by writers who were inspired by the Spirit of

Truth? Is the inspiration verbal, or does it extend only to the subject-matter of the text? Does it include all the *obiter dicta* of the narrative, or does it embrace only objects of faith and morals, and obtain, to use the words of the Council of Trent regarding the true sense of the Sacred Scriptures, only "*in rebus fidei et morum, ad ædificationem doctrinæ Christianæ pertinentium*"? Did Moses make use of traditions that were the common property of all the peoples of Western Asia, and was the inspiration under which he wrote limited to inerrancy only in the employment of the materials at hand and in the elimination from them of the imperfections with which they abounded? Did he have at his disposal a primitive tradition, integral and unaltered, brought by Abraham from Ur of the Chaldees? or did he avail himself of other, it may be older, traditions—or legends even—that were current among the Accadians and Sumerians, who were the precursors of the Chaldeans and Assyrians in the valleys and on the plains of Mesopotamia? And if he used human documents, were they then encumbered with the exuberant polytheism of Chaldea, and vitiated by the clumsy anthropomorphism that was so prevalent among all the pagan nations of antiquity? Are we to understand that in such an event inspiration meant simply the action of the Holy Ghost whereby Moses was able to substitute monotheism for polytheism, and convert a narrative replete with the grossest natural notions into a compendium of moral and dogmatic verities of the most exalted spiritual character?[1]

---

[1] I have purposely abstained, as beside my purpose, from any reference to the discussion which has so long obtained regarding

Such are a few of the questions asked by modern science and the Higher Criticism, and suggested by the Assyrio-Chaldean investigations of these latter days. So far as the contention of this paper is concerned the answers are immaterial. Affirmative or negative, the statements of the author of the Hexaëmeron convey the same meaning and proclaim the same truths. Whatever the responses eventually given to the questions propounded, it will ever remain an incontestable fact that the "theodicy of the Chaldean tablets is as far from that of the Pentateuch as the theodicy of

the composite character of the Genesiac narrative of creation. Whether the first two chapters of Genesis were written by Moses or by some one else—whether the date of their composition corresponds to that assigned by the traditional view or whether it is much later—matters not so far as my thesis is concerned. Neither does it matter whether there are two accounts—the Jehovistic and Elohistic—incorporated into the narrative, as critics contend, or whether the story is the production, not compilation, of but a single author. The words Elohim and Yahveh may have all the significance the Higher Criticism claims for them; Genesis may have been written at a far later date than has usually been believed; it may have been the joint work of several writers; but, even if these assumptions be granted, they in no wise militate against the conclusions I have drawn respecting the character of the cosmogony which a vague tradition ascribes to Moses. Other writers as well as the Hebrew lawgiver wrote under the inspiration of the Holy Spirit, and even if Moses had no part whatever in the authorship of the Pentateuch—which is to be proven—the position I have taken respecting the cosmogony of Genesis would remain unchanged. It would still be all that I have asserted for it, and its author or authors, whoever they were, would still be entitled to all the encomiums bestowed on Moses, and the first two chapters of Genesis would still be as manifestly as ever the product of Divine inspiration.

the Mahabharata or of the Theogony of Hesiod is from that of the Gospel.

The Mosaic Hexaëmeron is, then, proof against all attacks that may be directed against it in the name of modern science, Assyriology, or the Higher Criticism. It alone of all the cosmogonies of the ancient world has withstood the onslaughts of flippant skeptics and blatant Rationalists, because it alone has fully satisfied the demands of the intellect and the aspirations of the soul. What pagan philosophy ever failed to do, what modern science, of itself, is incompetent to achieve, the author of Genesis has realized in his simple yet magnificent portrayal of God as *Deum unum, Deum omnipotentem, Deum creatorem omnium visibilium et invisibilium.*

PART II.

The Noachian Deluge.

PART II.

The Noachian Deluge.

CHAPTER I.

*THE GEOGRAPHICAL AND ZOOLOGICAL UNIVERSAL-
ITY OF THE DELUGE.*

WIDESPREAD INTEREST IN THE QUESTION.

BARRING the creation of the world and of man, it may be questioned if any event recorded in the Old Testament has given rise to more commentaries and provoked more discussion than the terrible cataclysm recorded with such minuteness of detail in the seventh chapter of Genesis. The Fathers in their interpretations of the inspired volume, and the Schoolmen in their ponderous tomes, devoted entire treatises to the consideration of the subject. The exegetists who succeeded the Schoolmen found the question of the Deluge no less interesting, and, judging from the space they gave to the discussion of the subject, they considered its elucidation of prime importance. With scarcely a dissenting voice the Fathers, the Schoolmen, and the exegetists who immediately followed them were at one regarding the universality of the catastrophe of which the Sacred Text gives such a vivid record.

The words of the Bible were taken literally, and the almost general consensus of opinion among theologians and commentators was that the Deluge was universal, not only in relation to mankind, but also in reference to the earth's surface. The words describing the great cataclysm seemed to be so clear and so explicit as to preclude the possibility of doubt, and among all classes, as well as with theologians and commentators, it was the generally received opinion—an opinion that with many differed but little from an article of faith—an opinion that could not be called in question by any consistent believer in the divine inspiration of the Scriptures without seemingly going counter to the teachings of the Church—that the Flood prevailed over the whole earth and destroyed all the human race except the eight persons who were in the ark with Noah.

Fossils as Witnesses of the Universality of the Deluge.

Fossil shells found on plain and mountain were appealed to as certain evidences of the extent and magnitude of the Deluge. Fossils found imbedded in the solid rock, in marl-beds, and in gravel-pits gave strength to the argument derived from shells scattered over the earth's surface.

Woodward, an English geologist who wrote in the latter part of the seventeenth century, imagined "the whole terrestrial globe to have been taken to pieces and dissolved at the Flood, and the strata to have settled down from this promiscuous mass as any earthy sediment from a fluid." And to bolster up his fanciful hypothesis he went so far as to declare, contrary to all the facts in the case, that "marine bodies are lodged in the strata according to the order of their gravity, the heavier shells in stone, the lighter in chalk, and so of the rest."

Thomas Burnet, a contemporary of Woodward, entertained still more extravagant views. In his *Telluris Theoria Sacra*, or "Sacred Theory of the Earth"—a work which attracted widespread attention at the time—he explained why the primeval earth enjoyed a perpetual spring before the Flood, showed how the crust of the globe was fissured by the sun's rays, so that it burst, and thus the diluvial waters were let loose from a supposed central abyss.

At the same time, William Whiston, at first the deputy and subsequently the successor of Sir Isaac Newton in the chair of mathematics at Cambridge, published his *New Theory of the Earth*, wherein he discussed the universal Deluge from a new standpoint. He attributed the Flood to the near approach to the earth of a comet, "and the condensation of the vapor of its tail into water." Having ascribed an increase of the waters to this source, he adopted Woodward's theory, supposing all stratified deposits to have resulted from the "chaotic sediment of the Flood."[1]

These physico-theological systems of the English cosmologists were refuted and ridiculed by Vallisneri, Moro, and the Carmelite friar Generelli, who are justly regarded as the ablest exponents of the science of geology during the first decades of the eighteenth century.

But, notwithstanding the researches and discoveries

[1] Cf. Lyell's *Principles of Geology*, vol. i. chap. iii.

of the Italian school of geologists, so prevalent was the notion that fossils, wherever found, were the result of Noah's Deluge that Voltaire, "in his anxiety to shake the popular belief in the universal Deluge, endeavored to inculcate scepticism as to the real nature of fossil shells, and to recall from contempt the exploded dogma of the sixteenth century that they were sports of nature."

To Voltaire, Bernard Palissy, who was the first one in France to promulgate true notions respecting the nature of fossil shells, was but a visionary whose theories were both ridiculous and absurd. The views of the Italian geologists, as well as those of Palissy, he dismissed with a sneer or a simple expression of undisguised contempt. At best they gave him but little concern. It was against the popular views advocated by Woodward, Burnet, Whiston, and their school—views which obtained not only in England, but also in France and Germany as well—that he directed all the resources of his genius and all the force of his sarcastic and sophistical pen.

"The Scriptures," says the "Sage of Ferney," "tell us that there was a Deluge, but there is apparently no other monument of it on the earth but the memory of a terrible prodigy which warns us, but in vain, to be just." In his estimation it is but a fable, like the deluges of Deucalion and Ogyges, and this, forsooth, because there is no record of such an inundation in the writings of Herodotus or Thucydides.

Rather than give credence to the Bible, and rather than accept the scriptural narrative of the Deluge as then interpreted, the great infidel had recourse to the silliest and most puerile explanations of the nature and occurrence of those countless and widespread witnesses (as was currently taught) of a great catastrophe —the fossils which were everywhere so abundant.

He did not hesitate to revive the exploded view that fossils were but *lusus naturæ*—mere sports of nature [1] due to the plastic power of the earth itself. He was ready even to credit a story which was circulated about fossil shells having been experimentally produced in a certain soft stone—*dans une pierre tendre*—or to believe that marine shells were produced in fresh-water lakes of the existence of which there was not a scintilla of evidence.

His views regarding ammonites are as amusing as they are far-fetched. "Reptiles," he informs us, "almost always form a spiral when not in motion; and it is not surprising that when they petrify they should assume the form of a volute. More natural still is it to conceive that certain stones spontaneously assume a spiral form. The Alps and the Vosges are full of them. These are what naturalists denominate *cornua Ammonis*." [2]

---

[1] In his *Dictionaire philosophique*, article "Coquilles," he asks: "Est on bien sûr que le sol de la terre ne peut enfanter ces fossiles? La formation des agates arborisées ne doit-elle pas nous faire suspendre notre jugement? Un arbre n'a point produit l'agate qui represente parfaitement un arbre; la mer peut aussi n'avoir point produit ces coquilles fossiles qui ressemblent à des habitations de petits animaux marins."

[2] Les reptiles forment presque toujours une spirale, lorsqu'ils ne sont pas en mouvement; et il n'est pas surprenant que quand ils se petrifient, la pierre prenne la figure informe d'une volute. Il est encore plus naturel qu'il y ait des pierres formés d'elles mêmes en spirales: les Alpes, les Vosges en sont pleines. Il a plu aux naturalistes d'appeler ces pierres des

The fossil remains of a reindeer and a hippopotamus which were discovered near Étampes, and which excited a great deal of discussion at the time, found a simple explanation at the hands of Voltaire. They were simply specimens which had strayed from the collection of some naturalist—skeletons "*qu'un curieux avait eu autrefois dan son cabinet.*"

As a result of his examination of the faluns of Touraine, situated over a hundred miles from the sea, Palissy proved that the marl there found was composed of pulverized marine shells. This indicated that the site now occupied by the faluns was formerly under the ocean. This to Voltaire was absurd. He sent for a box of the marl in order that he might examine it personally. As a result of his inspection he declares: "It is certain, as far as my eyes can give certitude, that this marl is a species of earth, and not a conglomeration of marine animals numbering more than a hundred thousand milliard milliard." [1]

The fossil oyster-shells found in the Alps were, according to Voltaire, but the shells of fresh-water mussels. He was positive in maintaining, in the face of innumerable facts to the contrary, that marine shells are always found near the ocean or on level plans but little above sea-level, but never at high altitudes, especially on the top of high mountains.

When he was told that petrified fish had been found

---

cornes d'Ammon.—Dissertation sur les Changements arrivés dans Notre Globe, Envoyée à l'Académie de Boulogne. Œuvres complètes de M. de Voltaire, Paris, Sanson et Cie., 1792, vol. 43, p. 131.

[1] Op. cit., vol. 55, p. 330.

in the mountains of Germany and Switzerland, he answered at once that their presence there could easily be accounted for. They were but fish which a traveller had taken with him, which, becoming spoiled, were thrown away and were subsequently petrified."[1]

New difficulties, however, multiplied in rapid succession. Countless shells were found in Italy and France and round about Mont Cenis, which, it was claimed, resembled those occurring in the eastern Mediterranean. But, nothing daunted, Voltaire, as usual, had an answer to his hand, but such an answer as only one reduced to the narrowest straits would ever think of giving.

The great infidel was leading a forlorn hope in his attack on geology and the Bible: the teachings of the two were one as then understood, but this he would never admit. He was intent on discrediting the Bible, on relegating to the domain of fable the Genesiac narrative of the Flood, and to attain his end he employed arguments that were as ludicrous as they were irrational.

His attempts at explaining the occurrence of marine shells resembling those found in the Syrian sea in the neighborhood of the Alps are so characteristic of the methods of Voltaire, and his style of argumentation generally, that I give at length what he says on this topic.

"There have," he says, "been found in the provinces of Italy, France, and elsewhere small shells which, we are assured, originally came from the sea of Syria. I do not wish to call their origin in question; but should we not bear in mind that those count-

[1] Op. cit., vol. 43, p. 331.

less hosts of pilgrims and Crusaders who carried their money to the Holy Land brought back shells on their return? Or should we prefer to believe that the sea of Jaffa and Sidon at one time overflowed Burgundy and Milan?"[1]

Elsewhere he expresses himself as follows: "Is it altogether a fantastical idea to reflect on the immense crowds of pilgrims who travelled afoot from St. James in Galicia, and from all the provinces, to Rome by way of Mont Cenis, carrying shells on their caps? They came from Syria, from Egypt, from Greece, as well as from Poland and Austria. The number of those who thus went to Rome was a thousand times greater than was that of those who visited Mecca and Medina, because the roads to Rome are better and the travellers were not forced to go in caravans. In a word, an oyster near Mont Cenis does not prove that the Indian Ocean has enveloped all the lands of our hemisphere."[2]

But when, later on, the bones of man were discovered in many of the caverns of Europe, it was thought,

[1] Op. cit., vol. 43, p. 132.
[2] This is such a typical specimen of Voltairean reasoning that I reproduce the original: "Est-ce d'ailleurs une idée tout-a-fait romanesque de faire réflexion à la foule innombrable de pélerins qui partaient à pied de St. Jacques en Galice et de toutes les provinces pour aller à Rome par le Mont Cenis, chargées de coquilles à leur bonnets? Il en venait de Syrie, d'Égypte, de Grèce, comme de Polonge et d'Autriche. Le nombre de Romipètes a été mille fois plus considérable que celui des hagi qui ont visité la Mecque et Médine, parce que les chemins de Rome sont plus faciles, et qu'on n'était pas forcé d'aller par caravanes. En un mot, une huitre près de Mont Cenis ne prouve pas que l'océan Indien ait enveloppé toutes les terres de notre hemisphère."—Op. cit., vol. 55, p. 312.

by those who argued that the Deluge was universal, that the question was put beyond further discussion. Even such a distinguished geologist as Buckland saw in these remains of early man the relics of a universal Deluge—*reliquiæ Diluvianæ*—and the majority of scientific men of his day were disposed to accept his conclusions as correct, and to consider the universality of the biblical Deluge as one of the demonstrated facts of geology. Indeed, so anxious were some of those who were interested in making the Sacred Text square with their preconceived notions regarding the nature and extent of the Flood that they saw a witness of the Deluge—*testis diluvia*—in a fossil that long passed as the skeleton of a man, but which more exact investigation proved to be the remains of an extinct salamander. The *Andrias Scheuchzeri*—such was the name given this relic of an extinct form of animal life—will always remain a monument to the credulity and the unguarded zeal of those who were too hasty in jumping at conclusions that were not justified by the facts on which they were made to repose.

Whether there are now any geological traces of the Noachian Deluge is doubtful.[1] Even granting that the Flood covered the whole earth, as some still contend, it is highly improbable that the changes effected on the earth's surface would have been of such a character as to be recognized so many ages after the event.

[1] See, however, *The Origin of the World*, p. 256 and *Modern Science and Bible Lands*, chapters iii. and iv., by Sir J. W. Dawson. Compare also Howorth's two masterly works—*The Mammoth and the Flood* and *The Glacial Nightmare and the Flood*. See also Professor Prestwich on the same topic in *The Bulletin of the Victoria Institute*, April, 1894.

The late Abbé Moigno, who defended to the last day of his life the geographical universality of the Deluge, in referring to this matter expresses himself as follows: "We refuse to accept as evidence of the Deluge not only the ancient deposits of shells which existed before it, and which it could not have produced, but also the presence in our part of the world of animal remains which are supposed to have belonged to other climates. We likewise decline to regard as witnesses of the Deluge a certain number of rhinoceroses and elephants which have been preserved in ice-beds; the countless boulders scattered over the soil, far from the mountains from which they were detached; the organic débris found in caves and alluvial deposits; in a word, almost all that which the illustrious Buckland, in what was probably an excess of orthodoxy, pronounced the relics of the Deluge—*reliquiæ Diluvianæ.*"[1]

DOUBTS AND DIFFICULTIES REGARDING A UNIVERSAL DELUGE.

One of the first seriously to controvert the theory of the geographical universality of the Deluge was Isaac Voss, a Protestant theologian, in 1659, in his *Dissertatio de Vera Mundi Ætate*. He maintained that not more than the one-hundredth part of the earth was submerged by the Flood. The distinguished Benedictine Dom Mabillon having, at the request of the Congregation of the Index, examined the work of

---

[1] *Les Livres Saints et La Science.* See also *Splendeurs de la Foi*, tome iii. chap. xi. For an interesting review of the question consult *Bibel und Natur*, by Dr. F. Reusch, cap. xx., xxi., xxii., and xxiii.

Voss, gave it as his opinion that the teaching of Voss regarding the non-universality of the Deluge was neither against faith nor morals, and could therefore be tolerated.[1]

Among English-speaking geologists, besides Charles Lyell, the first to call in question the universality of the Deluge were the famous Scotch geologist, Hugh Miller,[2] and the scarcely less eminent American geologist, Prof. Edward Hitchcock.[3] Both, following Poole and Stillingfleet, directed attention to the fact that the words of the Mosaic account of the Flood did not necessarily imply that the Deluge was universal as to the earth's surface. They argued that it was universal only in so far as man was concerned, and showed that this interpretation was in accordance with both Scripture and the teachings of science.

At the time the two last-mentioned authors wrote, over a third of a century ago, the difficulties that had presented themselves to their predecessors against the acceptance of the opinion that the Deluge was universal had so increased that they seemed wellnigh inexplicable. And as the question was more closely examined and the knowledge of nature became more extensive new difficulties arose, whilst the older ones, instead of disappearing or dwindling in size, rapidly assumed larger proportions. So great, indeed, was the impetus given to the development of the natural sciences, and so numerous and important were the

---

[1] "*Hæc opinio*," says Mabillon, "*nullum continet errorem capitalem neque contra fidem neque contra bonos mores; itaque tolerari potest et criticorum disputationi permitti.*"
[2] *Testimony of the Rocks*, lectures vii. and viii.
[3] *Religion and Geology*, lecture iv.

contributions made by zoology and geology, that it soon became evident to every thinking man that the time had come for subjecting the older theories regarding the Deluge to thorough revision.

In the first place, no one could any longer seriously maintain that the fossils found in the various strata of the earth's crust were deposited there by the Deluge of Noah. Such a view was now regarded as simply untenable, if not absurd. It contravened the most elementary principles of geological science—principles about the truth of which there could no longer be any doubt.

Again; owing to the active researches of naturalists the world over, it was discovered that the number of species of animals was far in excess of what had previously been imagined. Indeed, when the number came to be computed, it was found to be far too great to find lodgment, not to speak of subsistence, in such an ark as Moses describes. The older interpreters were called upon to make provision for a few hundred species at most. These were all that were then known. But the number had risen to thousands, yea, to tens of thousands, and additions of new species were being made daily to the already formidable list. Whether, then, the exegetist measured the ark by the Hebraic or the Egyptian cubit, it still remained too small to accommodate such a multitude of living creatures and contain the food necessary for them during their enforced confinement therein. According to the most liberal calculations, the vessel built by Noah could not have been much larger than—if indeed it was so large as—the Great Eastern. Such a vessel might have been sufficiently capacious for the few hundred species that the Fathers and Schoolmen had in mind, but it was totally inadequate to supply lodgment for the vast multitude that was known at the date at which Miller, Hitchcock, and their compeers wrote.

And then a new difficulty presented itself that the earlier commentators could take no note of, and one, too, that could not be ignored. The advocates of a universal Deluge had taken it for granted, apparently, that all the different species of animal, not to speak of vegetable, life might be found in one place on the earth's surface. Contrary to what Linnæus had taught, Cuvier and others pointed out the fact that there are several distinct foci or centres of animal life—that certain species and classes of animals are found in one part of the world, while other species have their habitat in another part. Thus Australia is peculiarly the land of marsupials; Borneo, Java, and Sumatra, the habitat of the gibbon and the orang-outang; the giraffe, the zebra, and the chimpanzee are indigenous only in Africa; while in America alone are found armadillos, ant-eaters, peccaries, bisons, llamas, and a large group of tailed monkeys entirely different from any ever seen in the Old World. And what holds good for the fauna and flora of to-day in these different countries obtains for the fossil remains of the remote geologic past.

It seems unreasonable, therefore, to suppose, even if the ark had been large enough, that the representatives of the different species of animals of these various distant countries of the world came or were brought to the ark. And yet, according to the theory of those who interpret literally the story of the

Deluge, there were in the ark polar bears from Alaska, wapiti from Canada, tapirs and jaguars, sloths and condors from South America, lions, gorillas, and ostriches from Africa, elephants and tigers from India and Siam, lemurs from Madagascar, kangaroos, ornithorhynchi, and emus from Australia.

But, granting that all these animals, together with representatives of all the other species found in the various parts of the world, were in the ark; that there was room and food for them there for a year, the question arises, How did they get there? How were they transported from their distant homes and conveyed across the broad oceans that separated them from the spot where the ark awaited them? And where did this multitude of animals, many of them carnivorous, find food after leaving the ark? The earth then was deserted and desolate. Not a living creature, according to the theory we are now considering, then inhabited it; nothing that could appease the hunger of the thousands of voracious beasts that could subsist only on the flesh of other animals.

More than this. How were the representatives of all the various faunæ of distant continents and far-off isles of the ocean returned to the places whence they came? One difficulty suggests another, and the more closely the question is investigated, the more numerous and the more formidable the difficulties become.

MIRACLES.

The advocates of a universal Deluge have a very simple way of disposing of all objections to their theory. "All things," they argue, "are possible with

God; therefore a universal Deluge was possible." They admit Divine intervention wherever a difficulty presents itself, and tell us it is as easy for God to work a hundred thousand or a million miracles as it is for Him to perform one. With them a miracle is the sure and final answer to every objection.

But these good people are assuming what is to be proved. They assume that the Bible teaches the universality of the Deluge, and on the assumption that it was universal they proceed at once to call in the aid of Divine interposition to account for everything that cannot be explained by the operation of purely natural agencies. They forget one of the first laws of sound hermeneutics, which forbids the arbitrary introduction of the miraculous in commenting on disputed or even difficult passages of Scripture. They lose sight of the fact that neither the example of the Fathers nor that of approved exegetists will permit them to invoke the aid of miracles simply to remove a difficulty or explain a vexed question of Scripture, especially when the words of the Sacred Text do not warrant one in assuming the fact of a providential intervention. St. Augustine in his *De Genesi ad Litteram*, and St. Gregory of Nyssa in his *Hexaëmeron*, are very explicit on this point. The substance of their teaching in this matter, briefly stated, is that miracles are not to be multiplied without reason, and that they are not to be introduced except when the text demands them or when it is otherwise inexplicable.

Another difficulty that precluded the acceptance of the geographical universality of the Deluge was the impossibility of explaining the source of such an immense volume of water as the biblical inundation, if the Mosaic account was to be taken literally, would presuppose. In Genesis we read that "all the fountains of the great deep were broken up and the floodgates of heaven were opened;" "and the waters prevailed beyond measure upon the earth; and all the high mountains under the whole heaven were covered. The water was fifteen cubits higher than the mountains which it covered." But what do these words signify? Do they mean that the precipitation from the atmosphere and the invasion of the land by floods, caused by the upheaval of the ocean's bed, were sufficient to cover the highest mountains over the whole earth? When we remember that many of the peaks of the Andes and Himalayas are over twenty thousand feet high, and that the height of Mount Everest is nearly thirty thousand feet, and then call to mind the mean depth of the ocean—according to Murray,[1] twelve thousand four hundred feet—we shall see that the supply of water would be totally inadequate for such a submergence as is supposed.[2]

Some have imagined that God specially created a sufficient quantity of water to inundate the entire earth and cover the highest mountains, and that after all flesh outside of the ark had been destroyed He annihilated the water thus specially created. This, however, is an assumption for which there is no warrant in Scripture, and one which is so at variance with the known harmony of the laws of nature, and so contrary to our ideas of God's providence and wisdom in

---

[1] Mr. John Murray, of the *Challenger* expedition, is one of the highest living authorities on oceanography.

[2] Cf. *Le Déluge Biblique et les Races antediluviennes*, par Jean d'Estienne, *Revue des Questions scientifiques*, Oct., 1885.

the government of the world, that it has never been received with favor by exegetists of any weight. No one denies that God could have worked such a miracle had He so willed, but we are dealing with a question of fact, and not discussing what Omnipotence could or could not accomplish.

In the light of science, therefore, especially in the light of geology, zoölogy, and physical geography, the theory of a universal Deluge is untenable. On any ground it is untenable without assuming the existence of such a number of miracles that the theory perforce falls by its own weight.[1]

Explanation of Terms.

But it will be asked, What explanation is to be given of the universal terms employed in the biblical account of the Deluge? It is "*all* men" and "*every* living creature" that are to be destroyed; it is the "*whole* earth" that is to be submerged. The words "all," "every"—*totus, cunctus, omnis, universus*—are absolute and exclude nothing. And it is these words, we are told, that must be satisfactorily explained before we are at liberty to accept any other theory than that which proclaims that the Deluge was universal.

Nothing is of more frequent occurrence in the Old Testament than the employment of universal for particular terms. The same peculiarity is observed in

[1] Among the most distinguished of recent Catholic writers who teach that the Deluge affected only a portion of the earth's surface are Sorignet, Marcel de Serres, Geofroy, Lambert, Michelis, Schouppe, Pianciani, Zschokke, Reusch, Schoebel, Duihle de Saint-Projet, Vigouroux, Delsauz, Hettinger, Güttler, Bosizio, Brucker, and Lord Arundell of Wardour.

the New Testament, but not to such an extent as in the Old. It is a characteristic of all Oriental tongues to use hyperbole, and at times in a way that we should pronounce extravagant. St. Augustine in a letter to St. Paulinus of Nola states that it is the custom of Scripture to speak of the part as of the whole.[1] He likewise observes that it is frequently necessary to explain the word "all"—*omnis*—in a restricted sense. He tells his correspondent that there are many passages in the Sacred Text which at first sight present numerous difficulties, which, however, forthwith disappear on applying to the terms used a particular instead of a general or absolute signification.

A few examples will illustrate the principle of the great Doctor, and show how universal is its application in explaining even the simplest narratives.

In speaking of the famine which prevailed at the time of Jacob, Moses declares that "the famine prevailed in the whole world," that "the famine increased daily in all the land," and that "all the provinces came into Egypt to buy food and to seek some relief of their want."[2]

None of these passages, however, are to be taken literally, notwithstanding the use of the absolute terms "all" and "whole"—*omnis* and *universus*. Moses refers only to the countries and the peoples known to the Hebrews.

In a similar manner is to be explained the analogous passage in the book of Kings, where we read, "And

---

[1] Scripturæ mos est ita loqui de parte tamquam de toto, *Epist. ad Paulin.*, cxlix. See also Pianciani's *Cosmogonia Naturale Comparata col Genesi*, pp. 243-245.

[2] Genesis xii. 54, 56, 57.

all the earth desired to see Solomon's face and to hear his wisdom, which God had given in his heart." [1] Our Lord Himself uses similar language when He declares that the queen of Saba "came from the ends of the earth to hear the wisdom of Solomon." St. Luke in like manner speaks in the same general terms when he tells us in the Acts of the Apostles that at the time of the descent of the Holy Ghost on the apostles there were assembled in Jerusalem "devout men out of every nation under heaven."

In the case of the famine in the time of Jacob the people referred to did not live more than a few hundred miles, at the most, from the home of the patriarch. The queen of Saba dwelt, most likely, in Southern Arabia, distant, possibly, some ten or twelve hundred miles. The representatives of every nation under heaven in Jerusalem at the feast of Pentecost came from the countries that were then known to the Jewish people, and, to judge from those named, none who were present at the time came from points distant more than a few thousand miles at the farthest. No exegetist has ever thought of taking the words literally, or of imagining that there were then present in the Holy City, Chinese and Japanese, Indians from Peru and Mexico, and strangers from the Isles of the South Pacific. And yet if the words were to be taken literally one would be perfectly justified in making such a supposition.

A still more striking illustration of hyperbole, so characteristic of Hebrew thought and language is found in Sophonias: "Gathering, I will gather together all things from off the face of the land, saith the Lord. I will gather man and beast, I will gather

[1] III Kings, 24.

the birds of the air and the fishes of the sea: and the ungodly shall meet with ruin: and I will destroy men from off the face of the land, saith the Lord."[1]

Here, to take the words literally, we have a menace of universal destruction. Not only all men and all animals are to be destroyed, but all birds of the air and all fishes of the sea. The words threatening the destruction of animate nature by the Deluge do not imply more, are not more precise and far-reaching. But what are the object and extent of divine wrath as expressed in these sweeping words of the prophet? Some interpreters tell us that reference is made to the land and people of Juda; others say that the menace is directed against Babylon, while others still maintain that the prophecy refers to the Phœnicians and other peoples on the borders of Palestine. But, whatever be the exact meaning of the text, it is generally agreed among commentators that the universal terms employed have a meaning that is, if anything, more restricted than that of similar words in any of the passages yet quoted.

And so is it in many other instances that might be adduced. The whole earth—*omnis terra*—sometimes applies only to the Promised Land; sometimes it embraces only Egypt. At other times the same words are made to refer to the kingdom of David or of Solomon, and at others, again, to a stretch of country bounded by the visible horizon.[2]

It is a mistake to suppose that the words of Scripture are self-explanatory, or that we can arrive at the

[1] Sophonias, I, 2 and 3.
[2] *Le Déluge Biblique devant la Foi, l'Écriture et la Science*, par Al. Motais, p. 52.

signification of the words by considering them in themselves and apart from what precedes or follows them. In some cases we can determine the precise meaning of the terms used from the context. In others we must have recourse to parallel texts, and study the meaning of the passage in question in the light of the genius of the language and of the temperament of the people who spoke it. Many readers of the Scriptures fall into egregious errors by imagining that they are obliged to apply the same rules of interpretation and criticism to the florid, picturesque, and hyperbolical languages of the Orient as they would in studying the meaning of an author who had written in English, French, or German. Sound, logical exegesis, however, as Reithmayer has so clearly expressed it, requires us to interpret Scripture according to the mind of the writer and according to the mind of those for whom the author speaks.

Teaching of Fathers and Doctors.

But, conceding the gravity of the objections offered by science against the acceptance of the theory of a universal Deluge, and granting that the words of the Bible may, in certain cases, be interpreted in a restricted sense, are we justified in concluding from these facts that such a restricted use of language is applicable to the account that Moses gives of the Flood of Noah? Comparing the language employed in the description of the Deluge with that used in other passages of the inspired writings, it may be admitted that, *in se*, a restricted meaning *may* be attributed to the universal terms that occur in the narrative, but it will be asked, Will the traditional interpretation that has been assigned to the great catastrophe permit us any liberty of opinion on the subject under discussion?

What have the Fathers and Doctors of the Church thought and taught? What have the Schoolmen and commentators of a subsequent age believed and professed? And are we not obliged to accept the traditional teaching—the teaching of the early Fathers and that of the mediæval schools—as the teaching of the Church? And if it be found that these venerated and venerable authorities have, with almost unbroken unanimity, held that the Deluge was universal, can we as faithful children of the Church—*citra jacturam pietatis*, as Melchior Cano expresses it—reject their teaching and regard the contrary view as tenable?

We may for the nonce admit that the Fathers and Doctors, theologians and commentators, for the first sixteen centuries of the Church's history almost unanimously believed and taught that the Flood was universal. But, granting this to be true, are we obliged to regard their beliefs and teachings as anything more than the expressions of personal opinions concerning matters that any one is free to discuss? Or are we to consider their consensus of opinion regarding the Flood as a part of that body of doctrine which cannot be impugned without scandal and danger to faith?

Let us examine. It may at once be premised that very few of the texts of the Holy Scripture have been explicitly defined by the Church. And it may at the same time be further observed that an equally small number of passages are regarded as authoritatively and infallibly interpreted by the unanimous exegesis of the Fathers. Hence of the thousands of paragraphs of which the Holy Scripture is composed, the number on which the Church and her Doctors have pronounced authentic and solemn judgment is very small indeed.

The question now arises: Is the narrative of the Deluge to be classed among those parts of Scripture to which have been given an authoritative interpretation? We can say, unhesitatingly, that in so far as the Church is concerned, as represented by her supreme ruler, nothing whatever has been decided. There is no papal judgment or interpretation bearing on the subject. In this respect, therefore, we are at full liberty to elect any theory regarding the Deluge that may commend itself to our judgment.

But is not the consensus of opinion of the Fathers and Doctors of the Church of that kind which we are compelled to accept as a part of the dogmatic teaching of the Church? Let us see what are our privileges and what are our obligations in the face of patristic and scholastic teaching and opinion.

A decree of the Council of Trent, renewed by the Council of the Vatican, declares that in "matters of faith and morals pertaining to the building up of Christian doctrine . . . it is forbidden to interpret Scripture contrary to the unanimous consent of the Fathers."[1]

Now, according to Pallavicini, the great historian of the Council of Trent, "the Council had no intention to prescribe a new rule or to restrain by new laws the manner of interpreting the Word of God, but simply declared as illicit and heretical what was so by its

[1] Conc. Trid. Sess. iv.; Conc. Vatic. Constit. de Fide Catholica, 2.

nature, and what had always been held and proclaimed as such by Fathers, Pontiffs, and Councils."

The decree had no reference to certain questions of minor importance—*quæstiunculæ*, as St. Vincent of Lerins calls them—connected with biblical interpretation. It referred rather to fundamental questions of faith and morals—or, as the same St. Vincent puts it, to *his dumtaxat præcipue quæstionibus quibus totius Catholici dogmatis fundamenta nituntur*.

"When," says Cardinal Franzelin, "we inquire what is the measure of the authority which the unanimous consent of the Fathers possesses in a question of theology, it is necessary to distinguish the different ways in which a given doctrine may be proposed by them, and to consider whether their opinion regarding such a doctrine is or is not tantamount to a declaration that it belongs to the common faith of the Church, or whether, on the contrary, their consensus of opinion may not rather refer to a doctrine or an explanation of a doctrine, connected indeed with religion and truth, but not so clearly proposed as to entitle it to be regarded as a dogma of faith."[1]

When there is question of Councils or Popes giving decisions, it is necessary, the same theologian declares, that they speak "in the plenitude of their authority, and that they deliver authentically a dogma proposed for universal acceptance."

If, then, explicit and authentic definition is required when Popes and Councils speak, for a much stronger reason equal certainty of definition is demanded when there is question of the authority of the Fathers. It is important in this connection to remember the state-

[1] Franzelin, *De Divina Traditione et Scriptura*, sect. ii. cap. i.

ment of Bossuet, that " the Fathers in the interpretation of the Scriptures do not urge the literal sense except when confirming dogmas and refuting heretics."

Hence, Pallavicini teaches, it is necessary that there be question not only of doctrinal matters, but also of dogmas to be believed, and that the sense of the Sacred Text be *declared certain* by the unanimous teaching of the Fathers. It is necessary that the signification of the text be approved as a dogma of faith—*tanquam dogma fidei a cunctis Ecclesiæ Doctoribus comprobari*—and that the Fathers condemn, or show that they are disposed to condemn, as a heretic any one who rejects the truth which they enunciate or the article of faith which they proclaim. If, however, the Fathers regard a doctrine simply as religious and true, if they declare themselves only as if expressing an opinion—"*opinantium modo*"—they teach us by their example that we also may have the same liberty of opinion. Wherefore, in order that the *consensus patrum* may bear on the face of it the formula of Catholic truth, it must carry with it the evidences of undoubted and explicit dogmatic decisions.[1]

St. Thomas Aquinas makes a beautiful distinction between things which are necessarily of faith and things which pertain to faith only accidentally, which will serve to elucidate the question under discussion. The Trinity and Unity of God, for instance, belong necessarily—*per se*—to the substance of faith. Many things of an historical nature—*historialia*—appertain to faith only accidentally—*per accidens*—about which even the saints have entertained different views, and

---

[1] See Motais, *Le Déluge Biblique*, pp. 132 et seq., whose argument I have here followed.

regarding which they have given different interpretations. Thus, that the world was created belongs to the substance of faith, and such is the unanimous teaching of the Fathers. But the manner and order of creation pertain to faith only accidentally. Hence many different explanations have been given regarding these questions without in the least affecting the truth of Scripture.[1]

The distinction the Angelic Doctor lays down regarding the creation of the world applies, it seems, with equal force to the Noachian Deluge. The fact of the Deluge no one can deny. Neither may we call in question the prophecy announcing the Flood nor the purpose which it subserved. These are of faith, and explicitly declared so even by our Lord and His Apostles. The prophecy, we must admit, was miraculous, and therefore supernatural. The Deluge, although providential was, we may believe, but natural. The Almighty by His foreknowledge simply availed Himself of natural agents in carrying out the execution of His decrees. We are at liberty, therefore, to maintain that the occurrence of the Deluge was natural, as we may believe that the destruction of Jerusalem was natural. The latter event was foretold with even greater detail than the former, but in both instances it was natural causes—in one the forces of nature, in the other human agency—that were executors of the divine Will.

LIBERTY OF INTERPRETATION.

And if we are free to explain the Deluge by the

[1] In Lib. ii. Sent., Distinct xii. Art. 2.

action of causes purely physical, we may likewise, *a fortiori*, avail ourselves of the same liberty of interpretation regarding the extent to which the catastrophe prevailed. Father de Smet, the celebrated president of the Bollandists, expresses this idea forcibly when he declares that "the Catholic *savant*, when in presence of a prodigy whose miraculous character is not clearly attested by a divine witness, has full liberty to examine it with all the severity which characterizes the discussion of miracles by the members of the Sacred Congregation of Rites in cases of beatification and canonization." Even granting that the Scriptures declared not only the fact of the Deluge, but also informed us in detail as to its extent and the causes which operated in its production, such a recital would be an object of Catholic faith only accidentally, inasmuch as it constitutes a part of the Sacred Text, but it would not of itself, as St. Thomas and Franzelin teach, enter into the things of faith and morals that pertain to the building up of Christian doctrine as based on the infallible interpretation of the Fathers.

What St. Thomas says of matters which are purely historical—*historialia*—Patrizzi declares of matters of science and philosophy. "You will not find," this eminent theologian declares, "questions which are purely philosophical treated by the Fathers as pertaining to religion and Christian piety."[1] St. Augustine

---

[1] *Institut. de Interpretatione Bibliorum*, cap. v. Fessler, in commenting on the decree of the Council of Trent respecting the authority and scope of patristic teaching, declares: "Non itaque S. Synodus statuit piaculum esse a patribus discedere in quæstionibus historicis, philosophicis, mathematecis, physicis, astronomicis, geographicis aliisque hujus modi rebus,

expresses the same sentiment with equal force and clearness. "In the obscurities of natural things," the great Doctor observes, "in which we recognize the omnipotence of God, we must proceed, not by affirming, but by inquiring, especially when there is a question of treating books commended to us by divine authority."[1] In such matters, therefore—in questions, namely, that are purely historical, philosophical, or scientific, as prescinded from any clear and certain connection with matters of faith and morals—we have all the liberty of examination and discussion that even the most exacting investigator could reasonably desire. For this reason it is that Melchior Cano, when speaking of the nature and force of traditional interpretation, does not hesitate to declare, anent such subjects as the one under examination, that "if all the Fathers had erred in their opinions, they would have been wrong in matters of slight moment."

I have assumed, for the sake of argument, that the Fathers and Doctors of the Church were at one as to their views of the universality of the Deluge. This assumption, although in the main true, requires qualification. Their teaching, although apparently unanimous, admits of some exceptions which in the discussion of questions like the present have especial significance.

Thus, notwithstanding the absolute expression, "all the earth"—*omnis terra*—some of the Fathers and older writers exclude Olympus and Atlas from the effects of the inundation, contending that these moun-

---

quibus Sacræ Litteræ materiam vastam suppeditant."—*Institutiones Patrologiæ*, tom. i. p. 55.

[1] *De Genesi ad Litteram*, cap. i.

tains were too high for the waters of the Deluge to reach their summits. Others make the same exception for the Garden of Eden. Others, again, go much farther, and say that the waters of the Deluge did not reach the summits of any of the mountains, but remained only on the plains below.

More than this. They made exception, without any apparent hesitation, not only for different parts of the earth's surface, but also for different kinds of animal life. They found justification for such exceptions in various reasons—some of them very fanciful indeed—of science and history and exegesis.[1] But the important fact disclosed by these exceptions made by the Fathers and contemporary authors, who were faithful children of the Church, is that they throw light on the bearing of Scripture exegesis at the time in question on the meaning to be attached to the words "all the earth" and "all flesh." If one exception could be made—the Fathers made many—what is to prevent us from freely interpreting the narrative of the Deluge in the restricted sense which we have been advocating? Even aside from the principles of interpretation which we have been considering, we should be justified by the example of the Fathers themselves in upholding the theory of the non-universality of the Flood.

What has been said of the Fathers may with equal truth be affirmed of the Schoolmen and the exegetists who succeeded them. The Fathers in their capacity of witnesses and doctors of Tradition are, as Franzelin teaches, one of the essential parts of the magisterium and ministry divine-human instituted by God for the

---

[1] See Motais, *Le Déluge Biblique.*

propagation of Christian doctrine in the world. But if the opinions of these preordained witnesses to the truth of Tradition are not binding on our reason except when they possess all the characters demanded by theology and the Church, for a stronger reason the unanimous consent of the School cannot be said to have such authority over our reason and conscience. This is what Pius IX. means when he declares that the constant and unanimous consent of theologians must refer not only to *matters of faith*, but that the doctrine taught must be held as *true* and as of *Catholic faith*.[1]

And yet more. The common opinion of the Scholastics, even when deduced from sources of revelation, is not of faith, as Franzelin teaches, except when the truths it teaches are declared to be such. Suarez assigns several reasons why such an unanimous opinion may not be of faith: "First, the text of Scripture in question may be so worded as to admit of several interpretations. Second, because the Church has given no decision in the matter. Third, because Tradition is not decisive on the question."[2]

These declarations refer especially to opinions which are subject to change—to opinions which even the Schoolmen themselves did not hesitate to abandon when sufficient reasons for so doing were forthcoming. Opinions regarding certain matters of science, history, and philosophy would come under this head. They would naturally change with the advance of knowledge and the progress of research. The various opinions entertained regarding the six days of creation is a case in point. And scarcely less noteworthy in this

[1] Encyclical of Dec. 21, 1863.
[2] Quoted by Motais in *Le Déluge Biblique*, p. 174.

respect is the question of the universality of the Deluge. It is a question rather of science and archæology than of pure theology. Hence the changes of opinion that have been occasioned by modern scientific investigations and the new views that are now entertained by apologists and exegetists.

The Fathers, as we have seen, interpret the text regarding the total destruction of mankind according to its most obvious meaning. They had no reason to hold a different opinion from that which they professed. The state of knowledge in their time did not admit of any other view, and even if one could have been formulated there would have been no means of verifying it.

Like the Fathers, the Schoolmen gave an opinion on an equivocal passage of Scripture without any profound investigation, for the simple reason that the necessary data for such investigation were almost entirely wanting. As a matter of habit, as it were, without reasoning and without reflection, they accepted as true the opinions of the Fathers, but made no attempt to establish the truth of these opinions.

But while they took it for granted that the opinions taught were true, they did not propose them as necessary articles of belief. The very manner in which they express themselves evinces the contrary. Indeed, a brief examination of the way in which the Schoolmen treated the question of the universality of the Deluge will convince one that the common opinion that was held regarding the catastrophe was one of those which, as De Lugo says, might be universally defended in one age, and in consequence of the progress of research be as universally rejected in the next.

And no less an authority than Cardinal Franzelin tells us that an opinion that has obtained general acceptance among theologians may sometimes, by reason of the discovery of new data or because of more profound investigations, lose much of its pristine authority or even be abandoned entirely.

It may then be accepted as a fact, which no one can gainsay, that not a single Scholastic, nor indeed any Catholic theologian of repute, has ever taught, from any point of view whatever, that the universality of the Deluge is of faith. The consent of Doctors may have been universal, but it was regarding a matter that was always open for examination and discussion. The consent, therefore, was at best a matter of opinion, and not one of positive judgment or dogmatic definition. It was an opinion that obtained for centuries, not because it was not open to controversy, but because the materials supplied by modern criticism, and indispensable for successfully grappling with the question, were not then available. It was an opinion that had not been tried in the crucible of modern exegesis, and one, consequently, that never had any of the notes of truth and certitude possessed by a dogma of faith. The unanimity in question was, at best, something purely negative, and cannot be construed as authoritatively opposing a theory that, in the very nature of the case, was, at the time of which we speak, incapable of being formulated.

True it is, the opinion is one that prevailed for over a thousand years—one that was discussed in many bulky volumes from the times of St. Augustine and Tostatus to those of Mersenne and Pereira. But time alone in the discussion of such a question is not an important factor. If it were a question of principles or one of pure theology, where all the elements and documents necessary for the elucidation of the case were at hand, the application of the ordinary rules of logic would be all that was necessary to draw certain and infallible conclusions. In such a case the solution of the question would involve nothing more than simple reflection and ratiocination, and a genius like that of a St. Augustine or of a St. Thomas Aquinas would not demand time as an indispensable prerequisite for arriving at a conclusion.

But with questions of physical and natural science, of history and philosophy, of archæology and linguistics, it is quite otherwise. Hence St. Augustine, Origen, and other Doctors felt constrained to leave to time the clearing up of many difficulties which in the state of limited information in their day were insoluble. If the illustrious bishop of Hippo could, toward the end of his life, find in his writings materials for a volume of retractions, how much more, if he were now living, would he not discover, in those obscure natural questions that in his time were so puzzling, to amend or reject! And if now, in the light of modern research and with the aid of sciences that were unknown to the Fathers and the Schoolmen, we still encounter insuperable difficulties, even in connection with the question now under examination, how lenient should we not be in passing judgment on opinions that were then formed and generally received—opinions which their authors would be the first to modify or abandon if they were now living or if they had had the data and information that modern natural and physical science has placed at our disposal!

CHAPTER II.

THE ANTHROPOLOGICAL UNIVERSALITY OF THE DELUGE.

NOVELTY OF THE QUESTION.

WE are now prepared to go a step farther. The Deluge was not, as we may believe, universal as to the earth's surface nor as to the destruction of all forms of animal life. Was it, excluding those who were in the ark, universal as to man? Until the last few years scarcely any one would have thought of giving to this question other than an affirmative answer.

Whatever views may have been entertained as to the geographical universality of the Deluge, it was almost, if not quite, unanimously believed that no exception could be made to the total destruction of our race except that stated in the seventh chapter of Genesis, where only Noah and his family are explicitly excluded from the all-destroying cataclysm. To question and, much more, to deny, the universality of the Deluge was, and is still, with the majority of the people, considered tantamount to impugning the authority of the Bible or rejecting an article of faith. Nevertheless, if the question be examined without any preconceived notions, in the light of modern research and true exegesis, and with the seriousness and thoroughness to which it is entitled, it will, I think, be found that one may be justified in holding different views from those which have been so long current. This may, doubtless, surprise some of my readers, and yet I make the statement deliberately and with a full knowledge of all the objections urged against such an interpretation. I know that I am mooting a question that was not seriously discussed until a few years ago, and calling attention to a theory that has as yet but few defenders. But is it not a privilege and a right of ours to examine the latest phases of modern thought, to consider the theories that are now agitating the thinking world, as well as inform ourselves regarding facts and principles about which there can be no controversy? And if so, is it not our right, as well as our privilege, to scrutinize what we may believe as well as what we must believe—to discuss hypotheses and theories as well as doctrines and dogmas? And are we not justified, therefore, in pushing our investigations to the farthest limits permitted by reason and sound criticism? I think there can be but one answer to these queries— that we should fail to keep abreast with the advance of modern discovery and modern thought if we should not avail ourselves of all the sources of information that are placed at our disposal, and examine, as far as may be, even the tentative efforts that have in view the solution of problems in which all students have been more or less interested from time immemorial.

Universality of the Deluge an Open Question.

It will clear the way somewhat to premise that neither the Church nor Tradition nor the School has ever defined or taught that the universal destruction of mankind by the Flood, excepting, of course, those in the ark, is of faith. In this respect there is the same liberty of belief as there is regarding the geographical universality of the Deluge. And the principles laid down and the quotations from the Fathers and theologians which have been given as bearing on the latter case apply with equal force and truth to the former. There has been, it may be admitted, a common consent, which there was not until recently any reason for disputing, that all men except Noah and his family were destroyed; but it may, I think, be safely asserted that this common consent never amounted to anything more than an opinion, to stand or fall according to the evidence with which it might be supported. We have seen that the absolute expressions "all the earth," *omnis terra*, and "all flesh," *omnis caro*, may be used in a restricted sense—that science demands it, that exegesis allows it. The question now presents itself naturally and logically: Cannot the universal terms "all men," *universi homines*, be likewise interpreted in a similar sense? There is certainly nothing in the narrative of the Deluge nor in any collateral text bearing upon the subject that precludes such an interpretation. Besides, the laws of logic and hermeneutics oblige us, if we are to be consistent, to deal with all the universal expressions of the text in question in the same manner, unless there be some special and positive reason for doing otherwise. But such positive reasons, it seems, are wanting, whilst, on the contrary, both Scripture and science afford many motives for believing that the expression "all men" is to be taken in a restricted sense, as well as "all flesh" and "all the earth."

It has been said that the traditional teaching requires us to believe that the Deluge was universal, at least so far as man is concerned, whatever we may be permitted to hold regarding its extent in other respects. This, however, is scarcely an exact statement of the facts in the case. The general consensus of the Fathers and Doctors does indeed suppose the destruction of all men except Noah and his family. Some exceptions, however, are made, and these logically open the door to as many more as the advance of science and the demands of exegesis may render necessary.

According to the Septuagint, for instance, Methusalem lived fourteen years after the Deluge. But as he was not one of those in the Ark, some of the Fathers and commentators assume that he must have been saved by other means. Again, Henoch is numbered by some commentators among those who escaped from the waters of the Deluge, and we are told that he was saved because the water did not reach the summit of the mountain where he was sojourning. But if we can allow two exceptions, why not as many more as the circumstances of the case may require? This, if not a logical necessity, is at least exegetical consistency. To give a restricted meaning to some of the universal terms of the narrative of the Deluge—"all the earth" and "all animals," for instance—and an absolute meaning to others—"all men"—would, as Abbé Motais well observes, be tantamount to employing two systems of weights and measures, and without any scriptural warrant.

And what are the reasons, it may be asked, that make for a change in the opinion that has so long obtained regarding the universal destruction of mankind? They are twofold—some are biblical, others are scientific.

It would take far more space than I have at my disposal for a complete discussion of the subject, but I may at least indicate the nature of the argument on which the theory is based.

Objections on the Part of Science.

The first serious objections to a universal destruction of our race came from science. The relics of man found in various parts of Europe and Great Britain—skeletons in caves, flint and stone implements in gravel-pits, kitchen utensils in lake dwellings and round about shell-deposits—seemed to give man a much greater antiquity than was allowed by the generally-received interpretation of the Mosaic Deluge. These remains seem to evince that men had found their way to very distant parts of the earth at a much earlier period than is usually supposed—at a period certainly long anterior to the Deluge, if we are to rely on the dates ordinarily assigned to the occurrence of this catastrophe. Unless, then, we suppose the Deluge to have occurred much earlier than the majority of chronologists are disposed to concede, we must infer that some of the relics of man found in Europe and Asia, and possibly also in America, are antediluvian instead of postdiluvian. And if, further, the Deluge affected only a limited portion of territory at most—probably only a small part of Western Asia, as there is now reason to believe—then we are forced irresistibly to the conclusion that there were human beings in various other parts of the world who escaped the inundation described in Genesis.

The conclusions of geology are corroborated by the

teachings of archæology, ethnology, physiology, and linguistics. Egyptologists and Assyriologists, especially, tell us of races and peoples inhabiting Egypt and parts of Asia who could scarcely have descended from Noah, unless it be assumed that chronologists have been entirely wrong regarding the dates which they have fixed for the Deluge. Full three thousand years B. C. the Egyptians found in the valley of the Nile tribes belonging to the negro race—a race, there is reason to believe, that must have forestalled the Egyptians in the occupation of the country by at least several centuries.[1]

And then it is difficult, if not impossible, on any of the known principles of ethnology and physiology, to account for the great difference in color, in anatomical and social characteristics, that distinguish the negro from the Egyptian. It is scarcely reasonable to suppose that such a radical divergence could have occurred in a few years, as we are forced to conclude if we derive both races from Noah. The only alternative, therefore, is to admit that the negroes in Egypt and in other parts of Africa were of antediluvian origin, and that they escaped destruction because the waters of the Flood did not extend to the countries which they inhabited.

History and ethnology likewise tell us of antediluvians found by the descendants of Noah—the Hamites, Semites, and Japhetites—along the valleys of the Tigris and the Euphrates, and of an ancient yellow race that

---

[1] See Lenormant's *Histoire ancienne de l'Orient*, neuvième édition, tome ii. p. 47, and Maspero's *Histoire ancienne des Peuples de l'Orient*, quatrième édition, p. 17.

the sons of Japhet discovered when they reached the lands watered by the Ganges and the Indus. And this ancient yellow race was preceded by an earlier black, which had been driven to the forests and the mountains when the country was taken possession of by the former.

But, even granting it possible to explain away the difficulties urged by the sciences just mentioned, we are confronted with almost, if not quite, as insuperable objections presented in the name of linguistics. There are, as is known, three great families of languages— the monosyllabic and the agglutinate, spoken by the yellow, black, and red races, and the flexional languages, spoken by the white race or all those who can be traced with certainty to Noah or his sons. The monosyllabic and agglutinate languages are so entirely unlike the flexional that it is simply impossible to account for their difference, unless we put back the Deluge much farther than any system of biblical chronology will warrant, or admit that those who speak monosyllabic and agglutinate tongues belong to pre-Noachic races, and that they all, by reason of their being far away from the land of the Deluge, escaped unharmed.

If we admit what seem to be the logical and incontrovertible deductions of geology, archæology, ethnology, physiology, and linguistics, we remove at once all the difficulties that are urged in the name of these sciences, and find ourselves in a position to reconcile the many discrepancies which have so long puzzled the brains of exegetist and apologist.

The Deluge in the Light of Exegesis.

Singularly enough, when the results of scientific discovery proclaimed the necessity of revising the interpretations that had been in vogue regarding the total destruction of the race by the Deluge, it was found that there was nothing in the Sacred Text that forbade such a revision. On the contrary, it was found that the narrative of the Deluge might be reconciled with the opinion which excepts a part of the human race from the cataclysm. God, it was said, inspired Moses to write an account of the Deluge. Moses makes use of a written document or avails himself of an oral tradition which was faithfully preserved among the descendants of the patriarchs. Noah and the members of his family had seen the waters invade all the country which was visible to them, and had witnessed the destruction of all animals and men round about them. They were naturally persuaded, therefore, that all the earth and that every living thing on its surface had been submerged. Hence the universal expressions made use of by them in reporting the event: "All flesh," "all things wherein there is the breath of life," "all the high mountains under the heaven." Moses had appropriated the documents at hand, and, persuaded of the universality of the Deluge, made no change in the expressions used. The Holy Ghost, having in view only the narrative of a prodigious inundation destined to punish the crimes of mankind, did not prevent the inspired writer from using these general expressions, inasmuch as these, when compared with similar expressions in other parts of the Bible, were susceptible of a more restricted sense. This restricted sense, applied to the expressions used, would at a later date correct the inexact or false idea that had been entertained regarding the extent of the Deluge. "For this reason, then, if the whole question of the non-universality of the Deluge were to be limited to the discussion of the simple text of Moses, there would be in this reasoning a fruitful element of solution."[1]

Again, it had all along been assumed, at least by the majority of commentators, that the Deluge was primarily, if not entirely, an act of divine vengeance occasioned by the sins of the world. But the mercy of God, as displayed in the purification of the race; His providence, as manifested in the conservation in all its integrity of the patriarchal line, and in a still more ineffable manner in the great work of Redemption, from which the Deluge may not be disassociated, —are factors that are lost sight of in such a circumscribed view of the great catastrophe. "They forget," as Abbé Motais well observes, "the divine idea that embraces both Eden and Golgotha—the promise made in the garden of Paradise and its fulfilment on the summit of Calvary."

No, the Deluge was not simply an act of divine vengeance: it was rather a means which God, in His wisdom and goodness, employed for preserving intact the patriarchal line from which was to descend the Redeemer of the world; it was a necessity in order that "the sons of God" might be preserved from contamination by associating with "the daughters of men."

And just here we come upon one of the chief dif-

[1] P. Corluy, in *La Controverse*, pp. 74, 75, May, 1885.

ficulties in the way of a true insight into the providential reasons for the Deluge. What are meant by the expressions "sons of God" and "daughters of men"? Numerous and different interpretations have been given. Many have imagined that by the sons of God are understood the Sethites, and by the daughters of men are designated the Cainites. But a closer examination of the Sacred Text seems to evince that Moses intentionally ignored the Cainites, as he did the descendants of the other children of Adam. He was not concerned with them. They did not enter into the scope of his narrative. His object was to show the genealogy of the patriarchs from Noah through Seth to Adam. After the Deluge he deals only with Noah and the unbroken patriarchal line as descended from him. That there were among the mountains of Central Asia or along the valley of the Nile descendants of Cain and of other children of Adam he may or may not have known. But whether he knew of their existence or not—and we can scarcely believe that he was in ignorance of their existence—it matters not. He was not writing a history of the world. He was tracing out a synopsis of the history of the Hebrew people, the chosen people of the Lord, the sons of God. To him all who were not Hebrews were "Goim," as in the estimation of Athenian writers all who were not Greeks were barbarians. No others entered into the plan of his narrative.

The Cainites had long before emigrated to distant parts of the world. The other descendants of the children of Adam not mentioned in the ethnographic chart are absent from the record of the Deluge, because they too had long previously sought a home in other far-off lands, and did not, consequently, enter into the purview of the world spoken of by the inspired writer. To Moses, according to Abbé Motais, the patriarchs were the sons of God; the daughters of men were the women of the people who lived in their immediate vicinity. To Moses the sons of God and the daughters of men were "all men"—the *universi homines*—whose destruction was decreed and carried into execution by the Almighty. All the world was corrupt if the world of the patriarch became tainted. What matters it, from the Messianic point of view, that at the moment of the Incarnation virginity no longer existed in the world, provided it was still conserved in the heart of Mary? What matters it, from the same point of view, that at the time of the Deluge corruption infected the entire earth, provided that Noah, remaining true patriarch, is able to carry forward the world to Jacob and through Jacob to Jesus Christ? To effect the object in view it was not necessary to drown the entire race. Moses sees this, and does not, therefore, feel constrained to say it was necessary for God to do that which it was not necessary for Him to do. Viewing the Deluge, then, as affecting only a part of the human race, there is not a single word in the narrative that does not admit of a ready explanation.[1]

And yet more. Such an interpretation throws a flood of light on a number of other passages in Scripture that have always been involved in the greatest obscurity. It will suffice for our present purpose to adduce a couple of paragraphs from the celebrated prophecy of Balaam, as recorded in the book of Numbers.

[1] Motais, op. cit., p. 298.

"And when he (the prophet Balaam) saw Amalek, he took up his parable and said: Amalek, *the beginning of nations*, whose latter ends shall be destroyed."

"He saw also the *Cainite;* and took up his parable and said: Thy habitation indeed is strong: but though thou built thy nest in a rock, lo! he also, Cain, shall be exterminated."[1]

What are we to understand by the words "Cainite" and "the beginning of the nations"? Leaving aside the various interpretations that have been given by different commentators, is it not clear that, if we accept the theory of the Deluge as just explained, we have here meant the descendants of Cain who had escaped the great catastrophe—that the prophet refers to an antediluvian race, and that, as compared with the descendants of Noah, who were post-diluvian, they were in very truth *the beginning of nations?*

I might cite other passages from the Old Testament which corroborate this view in the most striking and unexpected manner. I might adduce numerous facts of archæology that seem to put such an interpretation beyond doubt, but to develop the argument in full would require more space than I am here granted.

From what has been said, it appears probable, if not certain, that the Deluge was universal neither geographically nor zoologically nor ethnographically. What the extent of the Flood was cannot be determined, but it seems to be almost certain that it was comparatively limited, both as to the amount of territory submerged and to the number of the human race destroyed.[2]

---

[1] Numbers xxiv. 20, 21.

[2] One of the first to advance the theory of the non-universal-

SUMMARY AND CONCLUSION.

The learned Oratorian, Abbé Motais, as the result of a critical and exhaustive examination of the latest

ity of the Deluge as to man was Oleaster, a Dominican inquisitor in Portugal, in the sixteenth century. He based his theory on the celebrated prophecy of Balaam. He was followed in 1656 by La Peyrère in his famous work on *Preadamites*. During the two following centuries the same theory was defended by several other writers of note, especially Cuvier and Quatrefages. In 1853 and 1856 attention was called to it by the works of Klee and Schoebel. In 1866, D'Omalius d'Halloy advocated it in an address delivered before the class of science of the Belgian Academy. In 1869 and subsequently the theory was developed and strengthened in a remarkable manner by the learned historian and Orientalist, François Lenormant. In 1877, Dr. Scholz taught it in the Catholic University of Wurzburg, whilst in 1881, 1882, and 1885, Jean d'Estienne supported it in a series of learned articles in the *Revue des Questions scientifiques*. In 1883 it was defended in *La Controverse* by Mgr. Harlez, a professor in the University of Louvain, whilst in the year following it was advocated by M. G. Dubor in the *Museon* and by Mgr. Clifford in the *Tablet*. But, by all odds, the most able and exhaustive work that has yet appeared on the subject is the one which I have so frequently quoted in these pages—*Le Déluge biblique devant la Foi, l'Ecriture et la Science*, by the late lamented Abbé Motais of the Oratory at Rennes. I may also refer to *La Non-universalité du Déluge* and *Encore La Non-universalité du Déluge* by the Abbé Robert, likewise of the Oratory of Rennes, who strongly champions the theory of his confrère, Abbé Motais, as well as to the masterly *Apologie des Christenthums* by Dr. Schanz, and to the admirable "Scriptural Questions"—Second Series, No. 4—contributed to the *Catholic World* by the erudite Father A. F. Hewit. More recent studies on the subject which will well repay perusal are the works of Howorth already referred to, and *Le Déluge devant la Critique historique*, par M. Raymond de Girard.

conclusions of science and biblical criticism anent the Noachian Deluge, summarizes his investigations as follows:

"The logic of exegesis, the laws of hermeneutics, the study of parallel passages and of the personages therein referred to, all keep us within the circle in which the author (Moses) confines himself. Not a word, not an idea, not a reflection obliges us to go outside of it. He is, then, in perfect accord with the plan and scope of his narrative and of his entire book when, after more than two thousand years of history consecrated solely to the patriarchs, we perceive in the event that is to reform the lineage of the sons of God an inundation which sweeps away the world of the patriarchs and not the world of humanity.

"And is this saying enough? Is not this conclusion more than permitted by logic? Does not Moses demand it? Do not sound criticism and prudent exegesis require it? All other systems leave the mind uneasy and in suspense. Many objections remain without even a plausible solution. It is necessary to multiply miracles and to have recourse to diverse expedients. But with the exegesis we have indicated every difficulty disappears, not as the result of multiplied and distinct efforts, but by a single stroke—by the simple admission of the non-universality of the Deluge. This is not a pure hypothesis. It is implicitly revealed in the plan of Genesis; it is explicitly proclaimed in the Pentateuch. The Rationalist is forced to admit it; the believer can accept it without denying any article of dogma. The imperfection and the insufficiency of the older traditional exegesis urge it; its tendencies and principles invite it. What is there, then, to preclude such a view? Only a single word—all—*Omnis;* that *Omnis* which neither the Fathers nor the Scholastics nor modern interpreters found to offer any special embarrassment; that *Omnis* which a hundred scriptural passages show is so often hyperbolic, which even the narrative of the Flood impels us to restrict, and which the design of the author explains always so naturally and so necessarily. No, in truth, we do not find any motives for rejecting a solution at once so simple and so comprehensive and so rational.

"Such is the thesis, or, if we wish, such is the hypothesis. Let it be taken up and studied, and contradicted even, but let it not be misrepresented. It is not the product of doubt, but of faith. It is the offspring not of indifference, but of a passionate love of the Scriptures—of a desire to defend and honor them, and of a firm conviction of the truth of their teachings. It has been written with the greatest respect for all the verities of religion as revealed in the Bible, and comes from the heart rather than from the pen. It is not born of the spirit of sect or party; its object is not to give support to the yet doubtful conclusions of profane science. The affirmations and attacks of science have been for us only an incentive to labor, and our study is one which is, before all and above all, one of pure exegesis. That which to our mind is most forcible and most convincing are arguments which are purely and simply biblical. He who adheres to the plan of Genesis as formulated by Moses is on solid ground. This is the true citadel. Unless driven from this no one can ever, unless the Church speaks, justly refuse to a Catholic the liberty to reject, in the name of Moses himself, the total destruction of humanity by the

Deluge. It is this right to liberty, we repeat in conclusion, that we have above all things wished to establish. In defending this hypothesis we have carefully measured our words and weighed our motives, and have all along had before our eyes the difficulties of other systems before which so many minds recoil. Let others judge of the value of these two motives, but let us be allowed to think that they are such as are justified by the severest and most exact exegesis.

"If criticism ratifies this thesis, it will have—and this is something in its favor—the honor of being established, not under the guarantee of profane science nor in consequence of some hostile discovery, but as the result of a free and respectful effort of Catholic exegesis. It cannot, then, be said that it is reason that dispossesses faith. Rather must it be affirmed that it is faith that perfects belief, since it is Moses who explains himself by what he has written.

"Those who may reject the thesis, if such there should be, cannot at least refuse it the merit of being produced under the domination of great and holy preoccupations, since its aim and purport are to remove objections urged against Catholic faith, to tranquillize souls, and to reassure consciences. Neither can any one deny that it is calculated to yield happy results. It makes God equally great in showing Him more benign, and the lesson it inculcates, being, as it is, less marked with the impress of vengeance, is also salutary. It exhibits, better than any other theory and in a brighter light, the lofty destiny of Israel; the genealogical union—by some perfidiously denied—of the Synagogue and the Church; the continued and merciful action of God toward the world in order to bring it to the Messiah. It places beyond all attack the grand dogma of Adamic descent. It reveals the majestic unity of the plan of Genesis, and affords a solid support to the authenticity of the Divine Book. Finally, it gives Catholic exegesis the advantage of acting on the offensive against the prejudices of a Rationalism which perversely avails itself of the imperfect information of its opponents and of the exaggerated opinions which they maintain, rather through apathetic confidence than from enlightened respect for the Book of books."[1]

[1] *La Déluge biblique*, p. 339, et seq. It affords me great pleasure to reproduce here the opinion of the learned Cardinal Gonzalez on the Deluge as summarized in his masterly work, *La Biblia y la Ciencia*. His Eminence is not only a profound theologian and philosopher, and one fully abreast with the latest advances in the natural and physical sciences, but he at the same time stands in the forefront of contemporary apologists on all questions bearing on science and religion. A man of pre-eminently liberal and comprehensive ideas, his views on all subjects which he has discussed deserve careful pondering. Referring to the question of the ethnographical universality of the Deluge, this illustrious author declares: "La lucha real está hoy entablada entre la teoria de la universalidad restringida que pudiera denominarse antropológica, la teoria que admite el exterminio de todos los hombres, fuera de la familia de Noé, y la teoria de la non-universalidad antropológica, la teoria que admite que, además de la familia de Noé, se libraron otros hombres del Diluvio. Considerado el problema con relación al testo biblico y á la tradición ecclesiastica, la primera teoria se presenta como más probable; considerado con relación á la ciencia, parece más probable la segunda: hoy por hoy, ninguna de las dos puede considerarse como cierta y demostrada, y una y otra pueden ser defendidas, como más ó menos probables, lo mismo en el terreno exegético que en el terreno cientifico.

"En todo caso, y cualquiera que sea la solucion cierta y de-

No better illustration than the subject we have been discussing could be instanced of the perfect liberty of opinion in matters not of faith which the Church permits her children. More than this. Not only does she grant us the greatest liberty of thought, but she also encourages us to add to her riches by appropriating the treasures of the Egyptians. Has not Leo XIII. in his admirable Encyclical of February 15, 1882, exhorted us to make use of the discoveries of modern science? and does he not declare in a few words, in his letter throwing open the treasures of the Vatican to the scholars of the world, what is the spirit which should animate every honest investigator and champion of science? The Church does not fear the truth. She cannot abet what is false.[1]

And let no one imagine that such liberty of opinion, such freedom of discussion, are calculated to foster rationalism and skepticism. The very opposite is the case. Has not Renan, in his *Souvenirs d'Enfance et de Jeunesse*,[2] told us that what he took as the Catholic teaching regarding the Deluge was one of the

---

finitiva del problema, si alguna vez llega á obtenerse, en nada affectará ni á la verdad de la Biblia ni á la verdad de la ciencia. Cualquiera que sea la solución, para el hombre de la fe y de la ciencia, para el escritor cristiano, la Biblia seguirá siendo depositaria de la palabra divina, la Iglesia seguirá siendo—*columna et firmamentum veritatis*, y la ciencia seguirá siendo hija predilecta del Dios de las ciencias—*Deus scientiarum Dominus est*."—*La Biblia y la Ciencia*, tomo ii. p. 683.

[1] The memorable words of the illustrious Pontiff are: "Illud in primis scribentium observetur animo; primam esse historiæ legem ne quid falsi dicere audeat: deinde ne quid veri non audeat; ne qua suspicio gratiæ sit in scribendo, ne qua simultatis."

[2] P. 293.

prime causes of his infidelity? And have not many others in a similar manner suffered the pangs of doubt, if not the loss of faith, in consequence of mistaking the opinions of the Fathers and Doctors in matters of science and philosophy for the dogmatic definitions of the Church? And have not others, again, forged intellectual fetters for themselves in consequence of the erroneous notions they entertained regarding the sense of the Church—the *Intellectus Catholicus*—which, far from impeding their researches in the domain of science, is as broad and as liberal as Truth itself?

There is such a thing as misguided zeal for the integrity of the Scriptures—a misleading reverence for the authority of traditional and scholastic teaching. It will not do to interpret the Sacred Text under the influence of preconceived notions, especially when such notions have no positive scriptural warrant. Neither will it do to attribute greater weight to the teachings of the Fathers and the Schoolmen than these eminent Doctors of the Church intended they should have. If St. Augustine, St. Gregory of Nyssa, St. Jerome, St. Thomas Aquinas, or Albertus Magnus had before them all the facts disclosed by modern science, would they have expressed themselves on many questions as they did? We do them a great wrong to suppose for a moment that they would. If they were living now, can we have any doubt about the character of their teaching? Surely not. It would be absurd to suppose that the keenest and the most comprehensive and the most liberal minds the world has ever known would feel that they were committed to views that had been expressed when most of the data necessary for a proper understanding of the subjects discussed were entirely wanting. Such an assumption, aside from being an injustice to them, would be an exhibition of egotism on our part that would be simply intolerable.

To find fault with them for having one or two thousand years ago a less extensive knowledge of the natural and physical sciences than we ourselves possess would be simply preposterous.[1] As well might it be affirmed that we should now know as much about the inductive sciences as will our successors ten or twenty centuries hence. Such an admission would be tantamount to asserting that the sum-total of natural knowledge is independent of research; that the natural and physical sciences are not of a progressive character; that, contrary to the very nature of these sciences—based, as they are, on the observation of facts and phenomena—they are incapable of development. It is obvious that no sane mind can hold, much less defend, such a view. We must judge the Fathers and Doctors of the Church as we ourselves, under similar circumstances, would wish to be judged. We must view their opinions on the "obscure things

---

[1] A fair sample of this irrational way of considering the opinions of the earlier commentators is afforded by Andrew D. White in his "Warfare of Science" and in his "New Chapters on the Warfare of Science," published in the *Popular Science Monthly*. A striking instance of *ignoratio elenchi* or of *suppressio veri* regarding the subject here discussed is seen in two articles—"Lights of the Church and Light of Science" and "Hasisadra's Adventure"—by Prof. Huxley in the *Nineteenth Century*, reprinted in his latest work, *Some Controverted Questions*. Prof. Huxley is a great biologist, but in these two articles he has conspicuously demonstrated his ability to outdo Don Quixote in his onslaught on windmills.

of nature" as they themselves, in the light of our present knowledge, would view them.

"It often happens," says St. Augustine, "that one who is not a Christian hath some knowledge derived from the clearest arguments or from the evidence of his senses about the earth, about the heavens, about the other elements of this world, about the movements and revolutions or about the size and distances of the stars, about certain eclipses of the sun and moon, about the course of the years and the seasons, about the nature of animals, plants, and minerals, and about other things of a like kind. Now, it is an unseemly and mischievous thing, and greatly to be avoided, that a Christian man, speaking on such matters as if according to the authority of Christian Scripture, should talk so foolishly that the unbeliever, on hearing him and observing the extravagance of his error, should hardly be able to refrain from laughing. And the great mischief is, not so much that the man himself is laughed at for his errors, but that our authors are believed by people without the Church to have taught such things, and so are condemned as unlearned and cast aside, to the great loss of those for whose salvation we are so much concerned. For when they find one belonging to the Christian body falling into error on a subject with which they themselves are thoroughly conversant, and when they see him, moreover, enforcing his groundless opinion by the authority of our sacred books, how are they likely to put trust in those books about the resurrection of the dead and the hope of eternal life and the kingdom of heaven, having already come to regard them as fallacious about those things they had themselves learned from observation or from unquestionable evidence? And, indeed, it were not easy to tell what trouble and sorrow some rash and presumptuous men bring upon their prudent brethren, who, when they are charged with a perverse and false opinion by those who do not accept the authority of our books, attempt to put forward these same holy books in defence of that which they have lightly and falsely asserted, sometimes even quoting from memory what they think will suit their purpose, and putting forth many words, without well understanding either what they say or what they are talking about."[1]

The Angelic Doctor, who quotes with approval these words of St. Augustine, is not less explicit in the statement of similar views. "As for myself," he declares, "I find that the safest way regarding those opinions held by the generality of philosophers and reconcilable with our faith is not to affirm them as dogmas, . . . and not to reject them as contrary to faith, for fear of affording the wise ones of the world an occasion to contemn the teachings of religion."[2]

Elsewhere he observes: "In questions of this sort there are two things to be observed: First, that the truth of Scripture be inviolably maintained; secondly, since Scripture doth admit of diverse interpretations, that we must not cling to any particular exposition with such pertinacity that if what we supposed to be the teaching of Scripture should afterward turn out to be clearly false, we should nevertheless still presume to put it forward, lest thereby we should expose the Inspired Word of God to the derision of unbelievers and shut them out from the way of salvation."[3]

[1] *De Genesi ad Litteram*, lib. i. cap. xix.   [2] *Opusc.*, ix.
[3] *Summa Theologica*, Pars Prima, Quæst. lxvii., art. 1.

In weighing the opinions of the Fathers and Doctors of the Church we must always carefully distinguish the object of faith from the motives on which it is based. Errors in physics, zoology, history, criticism, exegesis do not impair the authority or the magisterium of the Fathers and Doctors when speaking in their capacity of witnesses to Tradition and of the common faith of the Church. We may not, indeed, without new and weighty reasons—*novæ rationis pondere*, as Pallavicini expresses it—reject the teaching of such venerable authorities in questions like the one now under discussion, but when sufficiently grave reasons are forthcoming we may safely, and without incurring the note of rashness—*temeritatis nota*—modify our opinions so as to make them harmonize with the certain data and conclusions of science.

PART III.

The Age of the Human Race according to Modern Science and Biblical Chronology.

PART III

PART III.

The Age of the Human Race according to Modern Science and Biblical Chronology.

CHAPTER I.

THE ANTIQUITY OF MAN ACCORDING TO ASTRONOMY AND HISTORY.

INTRODUCTION.

"THE pivotal centre," says the learned Father Hewit, "around which a whole system of topics turns, is the topic of the antiquity of the human race."[1] With the exception of evolution, which has a literature of its own and counts its volumes by thousands and tens of thousands, no other scientific subject, it may be safely asserted, has provoked so much discussion as has the antiquity of our race. For a full hundred years the question of the age of the human species has engaged the attention of scientists and biblical scholars, and yet, notwithstanding all that has been done in the various departments of knowledge, we are still very far from having definite information on many of the points in dispute.

Many causes might be assigned for the interest that has been manifested in the question—an interest which, far from subsiding, seems to enhance as time

[1] "Scriptural Questions," the *Catholic World*, p. 645, 1885.

rolls on—but not the least potent has been, no doubt, the antagonism that by many was imagined to exist between the teachings of scriptural chronology and the findings of modern science. For this reason, therefore, the question of the age of the human race is one that must interest the biblical as well as the scientific student, and in consequence our modern scriptural exegetists have given to the subject almost as much thought and study as have the most zealous votaries of science. The topic is certainly a fascinating one, and we need not be surprised that so many investigators have spent so much time in attempts at its elucidation.

Like all scientific subjects which are tinged with a human and a religious interest, it has a charm that no subject of pure science can ever possess. And until all difficulties bearing on the question are cleared up, until all doubts arising from the supposed conflict of science with scriptural chronology are dissipated, and until it shall be demonstrated that there is and can be no difference of teaching by science on the one hand and Scripture on the other regarding the time man has existed on earth, so long will the question of the antiquity of our race continue to have, for many investigators at least, the paramount attraction that is now so notable.

Fully to appreciate the reason of the great interest which attaches to the study of questions like the one under discussion, and to understand the cause of the wide divergence of views of a certain class of scientists on the one hand, and of orthodox scriptural interpreters on the other, regarding many passages in the Bible, especially in the Pentateuch, it is necessary to take cognizance of the influences which have contributed to the development of that pronounced form of Rationalism which is such a striking and dominant characteristic of our age.

RATIONALISM AND DEISM.

In every age of the Church, Rationalism has been more or less prevalent. In the first centuries of its existence it was championed by Celsus, Porphyry, Hierocles, and Julian the Apostate. In mediæval times Averroes and his followers were its chief coryphei. At the present time—and during the past hundred years, for that matter—the great stronghold of Rationalism is in Germany. But it would be scarcely true to say that the Rationalism now so rampant is an indigenous growth among the Germans. Luther did, indeed, sow the germs of free thought when he proclaimed his principle of private interpretation of the Bible, but neither he nor his countrymen seemed to realize the consequences to which this principle would logically and inevitably lead. It is more consonant with the facts of history to regard German Rationalism as an exotic, greatly developed and transformed, it is true, by reason of congenial soil and favorable environment, but nevertheless an exotic, transplanted from lands where the genius and temperament of the people, although in some respects similar to, are yet in others entirely different from, those of the Teutonic race.

The first to perceive the full significance of the principles laid down by the heresiarchs of the sixteenth century, and the first to draw conclusions in accordance with the premises involved, were the Deists of England. Lord Herbert of Cherbury is usually regarded as the father of English Deism. In his work on truth and revelation,[1] published in 1624, he rejects revelation as useless and reduces Deism to a system. He soon had a large number of followers, and among them some of the keenest intellects and most famous wits of the time.

The noted Materialist, Hobbes, although differing from Herbert in philosophy, shared many of his views on religion and morals. Among later Deists who contributed much toward sowing the seeds of doubt and free thought and sapping the foundations of religion in Great Britain were Shaftesbury, Blount, Toland, Collins, Tindal, Morgan, Woolston, Chubb, Whiston, Somers, Shrewsbury, Buckingham, and Bolingbroke.

Toland regarded Christianity as a superstition, and had no respect either for revealed truth or the principles of natural morality. Tindal followed in the wake of Lord Herbert, and with Morgan united in considering the religion of Christ but a forerunner of natural religion. To Woolston the miracles of the Gospel were mere allegories. He, accordingly, with Chubb, Whiston, Shaftesbury, and, above all, with Hume, made his onslaughts on these evidences of revealed truth. Collins and Craig directed their shafts against the prophecies of the Old Testament. All combined to assail the authority of the Sacred Scriptures, and the consequence was that many whose faith was wavering soon found themselves deprived of the little they still possessed.

[1] *De Veritate prout Distinguitur a Revelatione, a Verisimili, a Possibili, et a Falso.*

Natural Religion and Rationalism were the first fruits of these persistent attacks on the Bible. But the work of religious disintegration was not to be confined to England. It was soon to affect France, and then Germany and other parts of Europe. During his enforced sojourn in England, Voltaire had found congenial associates among the leading Deists and free-thinkers of the day, and was not slow to imbibe their principles. As may easily be imagined, he was an apt pupil.

Of all the English Deists, Bolingbroke seems to have exerted the greatest influence on the "Sage of Ferney," and to have supplied him with much of the material with which he afterward so violently assailed both the Old and the New Testament. But it was not argument that Voltaire employed in his assaults on Christianity, which at one time he egotistically fancied he could destroy, but refined derision and irony. A peerless master of epigram and endowed with a keen, penetrating understanding, he made the Bible and the Church the butt of his brilliant, flashing wit and of his caustic and withering ridicule. Understanding thoroughly, as he did, the temperament of his countrymen, Voltaire was fully aware of the power of the weapons he employed. Nothing, he knew, would affect a Frenchman sooner than sarcasm or a well-turned epigram, and accordingly, during his long and eventful warfare against Christianity, he never deviated from the plan of campaign which he first adopted. To say that he was not in a measure successful in his nefarious purposes would be to controvert history. The evil that he accomplished can never be estimated.

As Herbert was the father of Deism in England, so

was Voltaire the father of infidelity in France. But he was not alone in his attack on the Church and all that the French people until his time had revered as sacred. He was aided and abetted by a number of kindred spirits, like Diderot, Rousseau, Helvetius, Condillac, and others, who by their writings generally, but above all by that monument of falsehood and impiety, the French *Encyclopédie*, made infidelity fashionable and paved the way for the Reign of Terror.

From France the tidal-wave of free thought soon passed on to Germany, where it issued in forms of Rationalism and Materialism, Atheism and Nihilism, before which the world stood appalled.

The work of destruction was inaugurated by Samuel Reimarus, a professor of philosophy in Hamburg. He died in 1768, leaving a collection of manuscripts from which Lessing subsequently published numerous extracts under the title of *Wolfenbüttelsche Fragmente eines Ungenannten*. Reimarus's production was a direct attack on the historical basis of Christianity, and opened the flood-gates for the deluge of Rationalism which has since extended its ravages from the mouth of the Elbe to the Mediterranean and from the Ural Mountains to the Irish Sea.

Prior to the time of Reimarus there had been exhibited in certain quarters a disposition to question the inspiration of the Scriptures, but the public was not yet prepared for the revolutionary teachings of Reimarus and Lessing. The illustrious Dutch jurist, Hugo Grotius, and the pantheistic Jew, Spinoza, had called in doubt some of the fundamental principles of theologians respecting biblical interpretation and criticism; but their doctrines lay practically dormant until the eighteenth century, when their influence began to be felt throughout the length and breadth of Europe—an influence which has continued unabated in power and extent until the present day.

Luther repudiated tradition; Lessing, who has been called the Luther of the eighteenth century, repudiated the Bible as a divinely-inspired work. Thenceforward, scriptural commentators seemed to vie with one another as to who could carry farthest the work of disintegration and demolition. Every book, every chapter, every verse, every word of the Old and New Testaments, was submitted to the microscope of the "Higher Criticism." Every statement of Scripture was compared with the teachings of profane science, and declared true or false according as it agreed or disagreed with the latest pronunciamentos of scientific thought.

The progress of Rationalism in Germany much resembled the advance of Deism in England. Good and pious men, in their frantic endeavors to save something of supernatural religion from utter shipwreck, threw everything overboard until they found they had left nothing but Natural Religion, which is but little more than Rationalism pure and simple. Such was the fate of Locke in his attempted answer to Lord Herbert, and such, too, was the fate of Semler, Henke, and Ernesti in their futile attempts to stay the torrent let loose by Lessing and Reimarus. They dissociated religion from theology, and fancied they could save Christianity by rendering it independent of Scripture.

The denial of the inspiration of the Bible was the first step toward the denial of Christianity. The second step was the denial of miracles, and this was made by Eichhorn and Paulus.[1] The latter was deeply imbued with the ideas of Kant, who, according to Lecky, was, with Lessing, the chief leader in Germany in the war against the Bible.[2] The third and last step consisted in denying the authenticity of the Sacred Books, and this radical movement was made by the notorious David Friedrich Strauss. Under the pompous name of biblical criticism or critical theology he brushed aside all that his predecessors had left of the Sacred Text, and made the negation of the supernatural one of his fundamental tenets. What for so many ages had been regarded as undoubted facts and truthful narratives were pronounced by the author of the *Leben Jesu* myths and mythical legends.[3]

I have briefly traced Rationalism through its full course and found it to issue in Atheism and Nihilism. The doubts of Lessing and the skepticism of Kant led to the negations of Strauss, and the Pantheism of Hegel to the Atheism of Feuerbach and Schopenhauer.

According to these representatives of the most advanced German thought, the value and truth of dogma are to be estimated by its conformity with the latest results of scientific research. The principal dogmas of the Christian faith are belief in a personal God, the creation of the universe out of nothing, and the immortality of the soul. But these beliefs are not in

---

[1] "Mélanges bibliques," *Les Inventeurs de l'Explication naturelle des Miracles*, par F. Vigouroux.

[2] *History of the Rise and Influence of Rationalism in Europe*, vol. i. p. 189, et seq.

[3] Cf. Einleitung of *Leben Jesu;* also, Introduction of *Vie de Jesus*, by Ernest Renan. See likewise Rawlinson's *Historical Evidences of the Truth of the Scriptures*.

accordance with the teachings of science, and are therefore false. Astronomy has driven God from heaven; reason has deprived Him of His court and taken from Him His angels and His saints. Geology and palæontology have demonstrated the falsity of the Mosaic cosmogony; linguistic and prehistoric archæology have shown the futility of biblical chronology; and historical criticism has proved that the Old and New Testaments are nothing more than a tissue of myths and fables. Religion is a bugbear invented by a wily priestcraft; morality is a name for something that does not exist; law and order, restrictions on personal liberty which should not be tolerated.

Such is the last word of modern Rationalism, such the latest utterances of that science that has arrayed itself against the Bible and against all forms of supernatural religion.

Certain Modern Tendencies.

We are now in a position to understand—what would otherwise appear difficult if not unintelligible—the attitude assumed by so many scientific men in the discussion of all questions that have even a remote bearing on the inspiration and the authenticity of the Scriptures and on the evidences of revealed religion. They affect to have persuaded themselves, and they try to convince others, that the Bible is false, that Christianity is a concatenation of falsehoods, and that it is the mission of science and of men of science to proclaim to the world the irreconcilable antagonism between revelation and science, between the teachings of religion and the latest conclusions of modern thought.

It must not, however, be inferred from the foregoing that there is any real antagonism between true science and religious dogma. Not only is this far from being the case, whatever modern Rationalists may declare to the contrary, but, what is more, it is impossible. There are, indeed, discrepancies and antagonisms between the protean theories of science and the teachings of faith, but this, from the very nature of the case, is inevitable. The doctrines of the Church are the expression of Truth itself, and therefore immutable. The hypotheses and the speculations which certain scientists set such store by are as changeable as the colors of the chameleon and as short-lived as the Mayfly. Such theories, so often foisted on a credulous world in the name of science, are truly characterized in the words of the poet who speaks of

> "Ephemeral monsters, to be seen but once—
> Things that could only show themselves and die."

What I wish specially to direct attention to is the *tendency* of modern science to inculcate Utilitarianism in morals, Materialism in philosophy, and Rationalism and skepticism in religion. True science and true scientists keep aloof from this tendency, but there are many students of nature who are unconsciously affected by it, even when they are absolutely free from any preconceived notions in their special lines of research. They live in an atmosphere of doubt, and are imbued with the spirit of criticism and Agnosticism which is everywhere rampant. Contrary to their own principles, and in spite of themselves, they are forced into the current of Rationalism, and ere they realize it they are engulfed in the maelstrom of Materialism or Pantheism.

For, strange as it may appear, and inconsistent as it really is, men of science, who are so restive under authority, spiritual or religious, and who are wont to boast of perfect intellectual freedom, are often the greatest slaves to those who for the nonce are saluted as the hierophants of "advanced thought." The influence which Häckel, Karl Vogt, Büchner, Oscar Schmidt, Paul Bert, Darwin, Huxley, Romanes, Spencer, and others of their ilk have over their followers, even in matters disconnected with the sciences which they profess, is evidence, if any were required, of the truth of this statement.

Contrary to what they assert, modern scientists are often more guided in their investigations by the *magister dixit* of some wild theorist than they are by the facts of science and the indications of nature. This will explain the variations and contradictions which are so often palmed off on the public as veritable science, and account for the vagaries and absurdities that frequently constitute such a striking characteristic of some of our "advanced thinkers." What on one day obtains universal acquiescence sinks on the next to complete rejection. For men of science, at least the majority of them, have yet to learn that when they leave the domain of nature, where their researches should keep them, and enter into the region of speculation, they are, Icarus-like, courting certain failure if not utter destruction. Their experience is sure to be like that of the Rationalistic school in questions of Scripture and religion—the verification of the old saying, *quot homines tot sententiæ*.

After this rather long preamble, we are now prepared to discuss the historical and the physico-scriptural question of the antiquity of the human species, and to appreciate many of the aspects of the controversy which would otherwise be ill understood. It will be found that the variations in the history of heresies so graphically described by Bossuet are fully paralleled by the various phases assumed by the protracted and heated debate between biblical scholars and scientists regarding the character of scriptural chronology, especially in its bearing on the always fascinating question of the age of our race.

The first serious onslaught by men of science on the biblical chronology in its relation to the antiquity of man was inaugurated in the latter part of the last century. The atmosphere was then impregnated with the poison of free thought and irreligion, and the minds of many, even good men, were in a condition of doubt and anxiety bordering almost on despair. It was a period of intellectual as well as of political revolution and anarchy, when the worst elements of society were in the ascendency and were bent on destroying thrones and altars and removing the last vestiges of the ancient *régime*. Bayle, Voltaire, Rousseau, Condillac, Diderot, Helvetius, D'Alembert had done their work. The "Encyclopædists," so it seemed, had conquered. Rationalism and infidelity had triumphed. A new era was to be ushered in, and all traces of the past, in so far as the Church and religion were concerned, were to be consigned to oblivion.

ASTRONOMICAL DISCUSSIONS.

The attack was made in the name of astronomy, and was led by some of the ablest minds of the age. A careful examination of the astronomical tables of the Hindus, it was averred, proved conclusively that the Indian astronomers had made observations on the heavenly bodies full three thousand years before our era, and had cultivated the science of the stars twelve hundred years earlier than their first recorded observations. In other words, it was contended that the Hindus had studied astronomy at least four thousand two hundred years before the Christian era—that, consequently, these people had an antiquity far in excess of that assignable by the usually accepted scriptural chronology. Professor Playfair, the distinguished Scotch mathematician, in referring to these tables, discloses the animus which actuated himself and his confrères by the statement: "It is through the medium of astronomy *alone* that a few rays from those distant objects" (the primitive inhabitants of India) "can be conveyed in safety to the eye of the modern observer, so as to afford him a light which, though scanty, is pure and unbroken and free from the false coloring of vanity and superstition."

It was not long, however, before it was demonstrated by some of the more prominent members of the Asiatic Society, notably by Mr. Bently of Calcutta, and by the celebrated French astronomer, Delambre, that the calculations of Playfair, Bailly, and their associates were based on a myth. It was shown, beyond question, that the earliest reliable astronomical observations of the Hindus, as given in their sacred books, do not date back farther than 1421 B. C., and that their oldest extant treatise on astronomy belongs to a period not earlier than 570 A. D.

Shortly after the excitement consequent on the discussion of the Hindu astronomical tables had subsided a still greater sensation was produced by the finding, by some of the French savants who accompanied Napoleon to Egypt, of the now famous zodiacs of Denderah and Esneh. According to the calculations of certain astronomers and mathematicians, these zodiacs, as well as the temples in which they were found, had an antiquity utterly irreconcilable with any system of chronology that could be deduced from the facts and the genealogies of the Old Testament.

The zodiac of Esneh, M. Nouet calculated, dated as far back as 4600 B. C., whilst M. Burckhardt's computations assigned it to a period about seven thousand years before our era. According to a writer in the *Edinburgh Review*, the zodiacs of Denderah could not "be referred to a period much later than three thousand eight hundred years ago," whereas that of Esneh was given an antiquity of "more than five thousand three hundred years." M. Dupuis went much farther, and estimated that the temples in which the zodiacs were discovered must have a minimum age of fifteen thousand years. "I have," he exclaimed with self-complacency, "cast the anchor of truth into the ocean of time." But, as the sequel showed, he was mistaken; his ocean of time proved to be an ocean of error.

"It was then," remarks a sagacious writer, commenting on the zodiacs and the speculations to which they gave rise, "that science struck out into very bold systems, and the spirit of infidelity, seizing upon the discovery, flattered itself with the hope of drawing from it new support." The enemies of religion and the Bible again raised a cry of victory, and gravely announced that the Christian chronology was a thing of the past.

But the shout of triumph, as in the case of the Hindu tables, was premature, for just when the infidels of France and England were rapturously singing their pæans of congratulation a young man—a scholar and an explorer—arrived from Egypt, bringing with him incontestable evidence that the calculations which assigned such great antiquity to the temples and zodiacs of Denderah and Esneh were entirely illusory and were utterly without foundation in fact. The young man's name was Jean François Champollion, the father of Egyptology, whose genius had unravelled the mysteries of the hieroglyphics that before his time disclosed as little regarding the past history of Nile-land, its monuments and its inhabitants, as the Sphinx itself. He had studied the zodiacs *in situ*, and was able to demonstrate to the satisfaction of even the most critical that, far from having the hoary antiquity claimed for them, they did not antedate the first two centuries. They did not belong to the times of some of the earlier Pharaohs, as many stoutly maintained, but were put in place during the Roman domination in Egypt, and some time during or between the reigns of Tiberius and Antoninus Pius.

The warfare waged in the name of astronomy against the biblical chronology was a signal failure. But, nothing daunted, the enemies of the Church betook themselves to a new arsenal, from which they fondly hoped to draw more effective arms. These arsenals were the histories and literatures of certain of the Oriental nations, especially India, China, Egypt, and Assyria.

Hindu Chronology.

Hindu literature and history, whose vast treasures had just been opened up to European scholars, seemed to promise them all they could desire. Herein, it was claimed, existed incontestable evidence of a civilization older than that of Greece and richer than that of Egypt—the fountain-head, it was averred, of all other civilizations whatsoever. The poems, mythologies, and the genealogical lists of kings as given in the Vedas, Purânas, and Sutras were carefully scrutinized and compared; but the results arrived at, when above mere conjecture, were far from reliable, or satisfactory to those who were in quest of weapons which they could use against the Christian cause.

Sir William Jones, the great Orientalist, and certainly no friend of the Church, was the first to make a serious attempt to unravel the intricate web of Indian chronology. In his examination of Sanskrit records he met with absurdities and contradictions innumerable, but still, far from despairing, he pursued his inquiries with a persistence and an enthusiasm that must extort admiration even from his bitterest adversary.

And what was the result of his investigations? One that was a grievous disappointment to the anti-Christian theorizers of his time, but one that was quite in consonance with the chronology of the Bible. Accepting as legitimate the conclusions of a prejudiced investigator, but one who was remarkably well qualified to give an opinion on the question under discussion, "we have the establishment of a government in that country [India] no earlier than two thousand years before Christ, the age of Abraham, when the book of Genesis represents Egypt as possessing an established dynasty, and commerce and literature already flourishing in Phœnicia."[1]

Wilfort, Klaproth, Heeren, and others continued the work inaugurated by Sir William Jones, and with essentially the same results. Heeren, after making a thorough examination of the Hindu writings, gives it as his opinion that "we cannot expect to find in them any critical or chronological history; it is one by poets composed and by poets preserved." And so completely are the early annals of India involved in mythological fable that Klaproth does not hesitate to bring down the commencement of true chronological history to a period as late as the twelfth century of our era.

The erudite Lassen, as the fruit of most laborious and extended researches in Indian history and literature, arrives at conclusions which admirably harmonize with those of his predecessors whom we have just named. He places the date of the establishment of regular government in India somewhere between 2000 and 1500 B. C.—a date quite in keeping with even the most conservative system of scriptural chronology.

According to some of the most recent authorities on the subject—Kruse and Littré, for instance—none of the Hindu records deserve the name of history. They are enveloped in a poetical mantle of myth that utterly precludes any determination of time or the establish-

[1] Cardinal Wiseman's *Science and Revealed Religion*, vol. ii. p. 33.

ment of any date which could serve as a certain basis of a system of chronology that would be even approximately correct.

According to Max Müller, the oldest of the Vedas, which are the most ancient monuments of Sanskrit literature, belong to a period not anterior to twelve or fifteen hundred years before the Christian era. For a long time the Laws of Manu—the Manavadharmasastra—were, like the Vedic hymns, supposed to have a venerable antiquity. Sir William Jones fixed their date at 1280, and Elphinstone at 900, B. C. The learned Oxford philologist, in referring to them, says: "I doubt whether, in their present form, they can be older than the fourth century of our era; nay, I am prepared to see an even later date assigned to them. I know this will be heresy to many Sanskrit scholars, but we must try to be honest to ourselves." [1]

Elsewhere the same distinguished authority observes: "I ascribe the collection and systematic arrangement of the Vedic hymns and formulas, which we find in four books, or the *Samhitas*, for the *Rig-veda*, the *Yagur-veda*, the *Sama-veda*, and the *Athrarva-veda*, to the Mantra period, from the year 800 B. C. to the year 1000." [2] Referring to the antiquity of the *Rig-veda*, he affirms: "One thing is certain: there is nothing more ancient and primitive, not only in India, but in the whole Aryan world, than the hymns of the *Rig-veda*."

In a recent exhaustive and scholarly work, *Brahmanism and its Relations*,[3] Mgr. Laouënan, vicar-apos-

---

[1] *India : What it Can Teach Us*, lecture iii.
[2] *Lectures on the Origin and Growth of Religion*, p. 145.
[3] This remarkable work—*Du Brahmanisme et ses Rapports*

tolic of Pondicherry, India, reiterates what has been so often remarked by others. "The special characteristics," he observes in the introduction to his book, "of all Indian literature is that it has almost absolutely no chronology; so all who have written on ancient India up to the Mohammedan invasion in the eleventh century are reduced to conjectures more or less risky." "India," he continues, "has no history, or rather it possesses no chronology; historical facts abound, but they have no dates, so that it is by confronting them with events in the history of other peoples who had relations with it that it is possible to determine in an approximate manner the time when the persons existed or the events took place." [1]

The utter impossibility of constructing anything like the chronological history of India from the materials supplied has been fully acknowledged by one who was singularly well qualified to express an opinion on the question. I refer to the distinguished scholar and Orientalist, M. Barthélemy Saint-Hilaire. Writing in the *Journal des Savants*[2] in reference to the subject we are now considering, he declares that everywhere in the world of India, except in Ceylon, "history is

avec le Judaisme et le Christianisme—was the fruit of thirty-five years of research under exceptionally favorable circumstances. It was specially approved—*couronné*—by the French Academy, and may be regarded as the ablest and most reliable exposition of the subject which has yet appeared.

[1] For a thoughtful discussion of this topic, as well as for an interesting notice of Mgr. Laouënan's book, see an article in the *Catholic World*, vol. lviii. No. 347, by the accomplished bishop of Vincennes, the Right Rev. Francis Silas Chatard, D. D.

[2] March, 1866, pp. 164, 165.

entirely absent, or, if it tries to show itself, it is so disfigured that it is absolutely unrecognizable. Who in the legends of the epic poems, the Brahmanas, the Purânas is able to discover an historical tradition? Is it possible, even according to the most liberal system of interpretation, to extract therefrom anything precise, anything real? The most important events of Brahmanic society are obscured by an impenetrable darkness which time intensifies instead of diminishing. In spite of all our erudition, so powerful and so sure, we must despair of resuscitating that past which was annihilated by the very ones who were its chief actors. India has not willed to awake from her dreams; we cannot historically call her from her tomb."

A careful study, therefore, of the astronomy, the literature, and what there is of the history of the Hindus leads us to the same conclusion at which the learned Cardinal Wiseman arrived more than half a century ago. In his admirable lectures on *The Connection between Science and Revealed Religion* — which, notwithstanding the remarkable strides science has made since 1835, when the lectures were delivered, is still, in many respects, a standard work on the topics treated — this scholarly prince of the Church summarizes in one sentence all that may be said on the subject of the antiquity of the Hindus when he says: "Instead of the six thousand years before Alexander attributed by some writers on the credit of Arrian, or the millions deduced from the fables of the Brahmans, we have, as Jones and others have conjectured, the age of Abraham as the earliest historical epoch of an organized community in India."[1]

[1] Op. cit., vol. ii. p. 37.

THE AGE OF THE HUMAN RACE. 197

Antiquity of the Chinese.

The boasted antiquity of the Chinese fares no better in the hands of modern historical criticism. As in the case of the Hindus, national pride and ambition impelled the Chinese to claim an extravagant remoteness of time for their origin and for the beginnings of their history. It is the boast of the Chinese that theirs is the oldest nation on the globe, and, if we are to credit their annalists, the history of the Celestial Empire stretches back to the venerable antiquity of three million two hundred and seventy-six thousand years before the Christian era. Like the Hindus, the Chinese tell us that in the earliest times their country was governed by celestial rulers or demigods, and their historians gravely give us long lists of kings and dynasties whose reigns extend over tens of thousands and hundreds of thousands of years.

When, however, we come to sift truth from fable, and determine how much of historical fact there is in their fanciful mythological creations, we find that the epoch to be assigned to the commencement of sober history is very recent indeed.

We are indebted to the Jesuit missionaries for the first reliable data bearing on the history of China. The learned chronologist, Father Gaubil, as the result of calculations based on certain eclipses mentioned in Chinese annals, is disposed to regard the date when the emperor Yao ascended the throne as the first event that can be fixed with any degree of accuracy. According to the computations of this able Sinalogue, the date in question is to be assigned to the year 2357 B. C.

Father Gaubil's chronological views were endorsed by many competent critics, but a number of eminent scholars who have made a careful study of the many difficulties involved in determining any of the remote dates of Chinese records think that the earliest date of authentic history belongs to a period far more recent.

The oldest of the classical books of China is the Chou-King, by the celebrated philosopher Confucius, which is alleged to give the history of the country between 2357 and 627 B. C.; but even those who are favorable to the great antiquity of the Celestial Empire are forced to admit that the Chou-King does not afford us a means of establishing a system of chronology for the long period of time which it embraces.

If there is no satisfactory evidence for the great antiquity of China, so often claimed for it in the native records, there is still less in the annals of any of the ancient nations of the world with which China may reasonably be supposed, if so ancient as she pretends to be, to have been in communication. Thus, Chabas has shown that the monuments of ancient Egypt include no mention of the Celestial Empire, although there are references made to all other then known peoples.

Klaproth, who devoted special study to the subject of Chinese history, denies the existence of historical certainty in the annals of China prior to the year 782 B. C.—"pretty nearly the era of the foundation of Rome, when Hebrew literature was already on the decline." In this view he is followed by Lassen, who does not hesitate to declare that the Chinese have no authentic history before the beginning of the eighth century before the Christian era. As a matter of conjecture he fixes the first dynasty of the Celestial Empire, that of Hia, at a period not antedating the year 2205 B. C.

At all events, whatever may be the antiquity of the Chinese as a race—and it does not appear that we shall ever have more light on the subject than we possess at present—we can heartily subscribe to the opinion of the erudite Abbé Vigouroux, who confidently affirms that there is nothing in Chinese chronology which proves that China as a nation dates back to the time of Noah, and that we have in the chronology of the Septuagint all the time required for the development of its history.

Egypt and her Monuments.

A special interest has always centred in Egypt for the reason that generations before India and China were known the land of the Nile was regarded as the cradle of civilization. As far back as we can penetrate into her dim and distant history we find her in full possession of that religion and of those arts and monuments which, from the earliest times, have ever remained the enigma of travellers and scholars. We know nothing of the infancy of her strange people. From the most remote ages they appear to us in full maturity and in all the splendor of their marvellous powers.

Long anterior to the Hebrew Exodus, before Abraham visited the land of the Pharaohs, Egypt was old and the seat of a government that had endured through many and powerful dynasties. Centuries before "the Father of the Faithful" had left Ur of the Chaldees the pyramids of Gizeh, looking down upon the broad valley of the Nile to the east and the great Libyan desert to the west, stood as monuments that were then the evidence and the pride of a great nation, as they were the wonder and the inspiration of Napoleon and his warriors; and this at a period so long subsequent that nothing remained to attest the pristine glory of two of the nation's greatest capitals, both within sight of Cheops and his companions, but a mutilated sphinx where Memphis once stood, and a solitary obelisk on the site of Heliopolis.

Our knowledge of Egyptian chronology is derived from three different sources: from Greek travellers who visited the land of the Nile; from the historian Manetho, an Egyptian priest, born about 300 B. C., who wrote in Greek a history of his country under the reign of Ptolemy Philadelphus; and from various original monuments, papyri, and inscriptions, the most important of which have been brought to light during the present century.

Relying on information obtained from the priests of Heliopolis, Solon and Herodotus attributed to Egypt a very high antiquity. According to the former, the Egyptian monarchy stretched back full nine thousand years, while according to the latter the earliest annals of the Egyptian kings dated from an epoch more than two thousand years earlier. Historians, however, have given little credence to the opinions of the Greeks regarding the age of Egypt as a nation, and hence we may dismiss what they have to say on the subject without further comment.

Manetho's history, unfortunately, has been lost, and all of it that has come down to us are the lists of kings and dynasties as preserved in the works of Julius Africanus, Eusebius, and Syncellus. Like the Indian and Chinese authors, Manetho gives as the first rulers of his country long dynasties of gods and heroes. The reign of the gods, according to him, lasted no less than thirteen thousand nine hundred years—far from the hundreds of thousands and millions of years claimed for the reigns of their gods by the Chinese and Hindu writers, but a long period in comparison with the time allowed to the reign of the kings of whom we have authentic records.

Rejecting as mythical the reigns of gods and demigods, the majority of critics are disposed to regard as historic the thirty dynasties of Manetho, which begin with Menes, the first ruler of Egypt, and end with Nectanebo II. In his scheme of chronology the Egyptian historian purposes giving not only the number of dynasties, but also the greater part of the names of the kings belonging to them, together with the duration of their reigns and the order of their succession.

But an objection to Manetho's lists is that he enumerates all the dynasties as if they were successive, whereas it is well known by all students of Egyptian history that several of the dynasties were contemporaneous. Again, he never speaks of two rulers being associated on the throne, when we know, from incontestable evidence, that in several instances two kings occupied the throne at the same time. A notable case in point is that afforded by the joint reign of Seti I. and his famous son—often called the Napoleon of ancient Egypt—Rameses II. A third objection is that he frequently exaggerates the length of time during which his monarchs bore sway. For this reason critics generally are of the opinion that the lists of Manetho require the control and support of other and more authentic sources of information. These are supplied by various papyri, inscriptions, and monuments.

Undoubtedly the most important as well as the most authentic chronological record yet discovered is the celebrated Turin papyrus. It gives a list of those who ruled from the time of the gods and heroes to the epoch of the Hyksos, or shepherd kings. Of the greatest value so far as it goes, it unfortunately exists only in tattered fragments and lacks completeness. For this reason Brugsch, in his *History of Egypt under the Pharaohs*, says of it: "As the case stands at present, no mortal man possesses the means of removing the difficulties which are inseparable from the attempt to restore the original list of kings from the fragments of the Turin papyrus. Far too many of the most necessary elements are wanting to fill up the *lacunæ*."

Besides the Turin papyrus we have the tables of Abydos, Sakkarah, and Karnak, and others of less importance, all of which have been discovered in various parts of the Nile Valley within the past few decades. They exhibit the cartouches of a large number of the rulers of Egypt, as well as their order of succession, and, in spite of certain omissions and discrepancies, are invaluable to the student of Egyptian history and chronology.[1]

But, important as are the records just mentioned, they do not by any means enable us to construct a

---

[1] Cf. Lenormant's *Histoire ancienne de l'Orient*, tome ii. pp. 37 *et seq.*

system of chronology that can be considered even approximately correct. They tell us, indeed, how long each king reigned and how long each Apis lived, but they do not inform us as to the connection of the reign of any one sovereign with that of the ruler who preceded or followed him—of the time that elapsed between one Apis and the next in succession. Neither do they give us any direct information regarding the time during which a sovereign was alone on the throne and when he had a coadjutor. It is certain that there was a number of simultaneous dynasties, but just how many there were is still a matter of great diversity of opinion. According to Lenormant, there were but two; according to Brugsch, five; Leiblein and Bunsen admit seven; while Poole and Wilkinson extend the number to twelve.

"The greatest obstacle in the way of establishing a regular Egyptian chronology," says the accomplished Egyptologist, Mariette, "is the fact that the Egyptians themselves had no chronology." And they had no chronolgy because they had no era. Hence, as Mariette well observes: "Whatever be the apparent precision of our computations, modern science will always fail in any attempt to restore that which the Egyptians never possessed."[1]

According to M. de Rougé, the first event to which a certain date can be assigned is the expulsion, in the year 665 B. C., of the Ethiopians by Psammatik I. of the twenty-sixth dynasty.[2] In this opinion Mariette,

[1] *Aperçu de l'Histoire de l'Egypt*, p. 66.
[2] Cf. Felix Robiou, a disciple of De Rougé, in his scholarly article, "Chronologie de l'Egypt," in the *Dictionnaire apologétique de la Foi catholique*, par l'Abbé J. B. Jaugey.

Brugsch, and others fully concur. There are numerous documents belonging to this period which put the matter beyond doubt. Besides, Egypt was then in constant communication with Greece, so that we have information from the writers of the latter, as well as from the monuments of the former nation, of events that occurred during this period in the land of the Pharaohs.

Astronomical calculations based on the heliacal rising of Sothis—Sirius—enable us, with some degree of exactness, to carry back the chronology of Egypt to the year 1322 before the Christian era.[1] There are some historians who incline to the belief that we can go back still farther—to the eighteenth or nineteenth century B. C., about the time of the expulsion of the Hyksos.

Beyond this all is conjecture, and we enter into the region of what De Rougé has designated "uncertain chronology." Authorities and monuments are vague and conflicting. In numerous cases it is impossible to decide whether certain dynasties were successive or contemporary; whether they bore rule over the whole of the Nile Valley; or whether, as in certain undoubted instances, their authority was limited to only a small portion of the Delta.

It is these *lacunæ*, imperfections, and contradictions in all existing records that render so difficult the construction of a system of chronology, and that have given rise to so many and such diverse estimates regarding the age of Egypt as a nation.

Wilkinson assigns the date at which Menes, the first

---

[1] See *La Monde et l'Homme primitif selon la Bible*, par Mgr. Meignan, pp. 333 et seq.

monarch of the first dynasty, ascended the throne, to the year 2691 B. C., while Stewart Poole fixes on the year 2717 B. C. as the date of this event. Bunsen makes the figure 3051 or 3623; Lepsius, 3852; Lieblein, 3893; Pessl, 3917; Chabas, 4000; Lauth, 4157; Brugsch, 4455; Lenormant and Mariette, 5004; Unger, 5613; and Bockh, 5702. This, as Rawlinson well observes, "is as if the best authorities upon Roman history were to tell us, some of them, that the republic was founded in B. C. 508, and others in B. C. 3508."[1]

How long the Egyptians were in the valley of the Nile before Menes ascended the throne is, if anything, a still more vexed question. Prof. Owen claims seven thousand years as the time that has elapsed since the origin of primitive Egyptian civilization. Others demand ten thousand and fifteen thousand years, while Baron Bunsen puts the figure at twenty thousand years.

With such conflicting data before us, furnished by those who are most competent to pronounce judgment in the premises, it were unwise for us to attempt to untie the Gordian knot. One of the latest authorities on the subject, the learned Egyptologist, M. Felix Robiou, says in reference to the question: "We do not know, even approximately, the duration of the history of the Pharaohs; but the least improbable conjecture, one which cannot be far from the truth, is that it commenced in the fourth millennium before the Christian era, possibly in the first part of this millennium."[2] The Abbé Vigouroux is disposed to accept a still higher figure, and to admit that the

[1] See *History of Ancient Egypt*, chap. xii.
[2] *Dictionnaire apologétique de la Foi catholique*, loc. cit.

reign of Menes dates from a period 5000 years B. C. But even granting this figure to be correct, he insists that "Genesis, properly understood, allows Egyptologists full liberty to attribute to Egypt any antiquity that a just study of its monuments may demand."[1]

How long the descendants of Noah had been established in the valley of the Nile before the time of Menes is a question on which the monuments of Egypt throw no light whatever. It may have been but a few, and again it may have been several, centuries. But, whatever time may have elapsed between the advent of the Noachidæ and the accession of Menes to the throne, we can rest quite assured that when we shall have full information on the subject, Egyptian chronology on the one hand and biblical chronology on the other will be found to be in perfect harmony.

CUNEIFORM INSCRIPTIONS OF WESTERN ASIA.

During the past fifty years much valuable information regarding the antiquity and early history of our race has been gleaned from investigations which have been conducted and discoveries which have been made in various parts of Western Asia, and notably in the valleys of the Tigris and the Euphrates. Prior to this period our knowledge of the language and literature, as well as of the history, of Chaldea, Assyria, and Babylonia was as limited as was that which we had of Egypt before the famous discoveries of Champollion, Young, and Rosellini.

It is true that Berosus, a priest of Belus at Babylon, had about 250 B. C. written in Greek a history of Bab-

[1] *Revue des Questions scientifiques*, October, 1886, p. 400.

ylonia, but of it nothing is now extant except a few fragments preserved in the writings of Apollodorus, Polyhistor, Eusebius, Syncellus, and some of the early Greek Fathers. Enough, however, is known of his chronology to convince us that it is no more deserving of credence than that of Manetho. Both cater to the vanity of their countrymen by assigning a fabulous antiquity to their respective nations and by making their earliest rulers gods and heroes. But, whereas Manetho is satisfied with an antiquity of thirty thousand years for his country up to the time of Alexander the Great, Berosus carries the history of Babylonia back to a period antedating the Christian era by over four hundred and sixty-eight thousand years. According to this annalist, there were ten kings before the Flood, whose aggregate reigns had a duration of four hundred and thirty-two thousand years. It is no wonder, then, that even the old Greeks and Romans, addicted as they were to myths and fables, felt themselves called upon to reject such pretensions as absurd.[1]

But although the first part of the lists of Berosus, like the first part of Manetho's lists, is mythical, the latter portions of his chronological scheme, like that of the Egyptian historian, is substantially correct, at least so far as concerns the time demanded for the various dynasties and rulers mentioned. According to Rawlinson, the earliest historical date of Berosus is

---

[1] Cicero in his work *De Divinatione*, in referring to the Chaldeans, says of them: "Condemnemus hos aut stultitiæ aut vanitatis aut impudentiæ, qui CCCCLXX millia annorum ut ipsi dicunt monumentis comprehensa continent et mentiri judicemus."

about 2458 B. C., considerably more remote than the earliest authentic date of Egyptian history.

It is, however, from the inscriptions on tablets, cylinders, and other monuments that have been discovered where once stood the flourishing cities of Assur, Sippara, Erech, Accad, and those famous capitals of the ancient world, Nineveh and Babylon, not to speak of numerous other localities in Western Asia, that we derive our most accurate knowledge regarding the antiquity as well as the history of the peoples who in ages long past constituted the great kingdoms of Chaldea, Babylonia, and Assyria.

And here we meet with new triumphs of erudition and genius that remind us of the wonderful achievements that have rendered the name of Champollion immortal. For centuries past specimens of wedge-writing, or nail-like inscriptions, found among the ruins of various cities of the Orient, had attracted the attention of scholars and travellers, but until a few decades ago the meaning of these strange figures was involved in even greater mystery than that which enveloped the hieroglyphics of the temples and obelisks of the land of the Pharaohs. To the wandering Arab they were the work of the genii, while to the European they were often but the expression of the fantasy of some architect who wished to show in how many different ways he could combine these nail-like forms.[1]

In 1765, during his journeyings in the East, Karsten Niebuhr, the father of the illustrious historian, copied some of the inscriptions at Persepolis, and offered sev-

[1] Cf. Vigouroux's *La Bible et les Decouvertes modernes*, tome i. pp. 34 et seq.

eral theories regarding them which subsequent investigators have confirmed. Scholars in various parts of Europe now became interested in cuneiform writing, but all attempts to decipher it were fruitless. A Champollion was required for the task, but he appeared not. A genius like his is vouchsafed to the world only at rare intervals.

In 1802, Grotefend succeeded in making out the names of Darius and Xerxes, and thus supplied a key for the reading of the cuneiform characters, as Champollion at a later date discovered the key to the Egyptian hieroglyphics by deciphering the names of Ptolemy and Cleopatra on the now-famous Rosetta Stone. But Grotefend's work was far from being as thorough as Champollion's. While the former was able to read but a few names—he never accomplished more—the latter was fortunate enough, unaided and alone, to decipher not only the writing of ancient Egypt, but also to resuscitate its grammar and language as well.

A third of a century elapsed before anything further was done. At the end of this period Burnouf in France and Lassen in Germany, independently and almost simultaneously, announced the discovery of the alphabet of the trilingual inscriptions of Persepolis. This was a giant step forward, and contributed materially toward the solution of a problem on which, for a long time, some of the keenest intellects of Europe had been engaged.

The next great advance made was the publication, in 1857, in the *Journal of the Royal Asiatic Society*, by Sir Henry Rawlinson, of the Babylonian text of the trilingual inscription of Darius on the rock of Behistun. This rock often, and justly so, called the

Rosetta Stone of Assyriology, had on it inscriptions in three different languages, ancient Persian and Medic and Babylonian or Assyrian. As soon as the Babylonian text was deciphered by the brilliant English colonel a key was supplied for the interpretation of the thousands of unilingual inscriptions found everywhere along the valleys of the Tigris and the Euphrates.

These conquests of genius, added to Botta's discovery, a few years before, of the ruins of Nineveh, which for nearly twenty-five centuries was so effectually buried under the earth that even its site was unknown, spurred on antiquaries and explorers to new achievements, and a long succession of triumphs was the result. Botta had unearthed the palace of Sargon and discovered a large number of tablets and inscriptions of the utmost value. Layard, Loftus, Place, Oppert, George Smith, Hormuzd Rassam, and others followed him and exhumed monuments and palaces which were bewildering in their number, extent, and magnificence.[1]

THE OLDEST LIBRARY IN THE WORLD.

But by far the most important discovery, the one in which we are at present most interested, and the one which, more than all the others combined, contributed to put Assyriology on a firm and permanent basis, one which has proved of untold value to biblical students, was the discovery by Layard in 1850 of the celebrated library of Assurbanipal.

This library was one of many that formerly existed

---

[1] Cf. Rawlinson's *Seven Great Monarchies*, Assyria, chap. vi., and Lenormant's *Histoire ancienne de l'Orient*, tome iv. chap. iv.

in all the large cities of Chaldea and Assyria, but the only one that so far has been discovered, and, it may be, the only one that has been preserved.[1] The Assyrians had neither papyrus, like the Egyptians, nor parchment, like the Greeks and Romans, nor paper, such as we possess. Their books were composed of tablets of clay—*coctiles laterculi*, Pliny calls them—a fortunate circumstance, indeed, as they would doubtless have otherwise been destroyed long centuries ago. As it is, we have a great portion of them, and many of them in a good state of preservation.

Assurbanipal—the Sardanapalus of the Greeks, the *grand monarque* of Assyria, the patron of art, science, and literature—had in his library, besides works on history, astronomy, astrology, theology, politics, geography, and other branches of knowledge, a valuable collection of syllabaries, grammars, and dictionaries, which the Assyrians themselves had used in learning the significance of the symbols and in mastering the difficulties of their written language. By means of the contents of this library—undoubtedly the oldest in the world—which Providence at an opportune moment placed in the hands of the scholars of Europe, Assyriologists were able to lift all that was left of the veil that still obscured the secrets of the mysterious wedge-writing of Western Asia. In the words of Maspero:[2] "In less than thirty years a world of languages and of

---

[1] The noted German writer, Scholz, speaks of it as "eine Bibliothek aus dem 9 Jahrhunderte v. Chr., und zwar Alles im Original." Cf. *The Higher Criticism and the Monuments*, chap. ii., by A. H. Sayce.

[2] *Histoire ancienne des Peuples de l'Orient*, quatrième édition, 1886, Appendice, p. 712.

peoples, before unknown, was discovered; thirty centuries of history were brought from the tomb to the full light of day."

To realize fully the extent of this wonderful find, it is sufficient to state that the number of tablets estimated to have existed originally in the royal library of Nineveh was not less than ten thousand. According to Mr. Birch, there were in 1872 about twenty thousand fragments of these tablets in the British Museum, not to speak of the countless fragments in other museums and in the possession of private individuals in various parts of the world. It has been computed that before the destruction of the library these books of baked clay would have made full five hundred printed quarto volumes of five hundred pages each.

The books of this wonderful library, relating to the manners and customs, the religion, science, and governments, of the ancient peoples who inhabited the lands watered by the Tigris and the Euphrates, are interesting and valuable, but the tablets bearing astronomical records are, for our present purpose, far more important. Thanks to the computations and tabular statements of the old Chaldean astronomers, we are now able to fix the dates of many historical facts of Babylonian history as far back as the sixth century B. C. with almost mathematical precision.

Chaldean Astronomy and Assyrian Chronology.

It had long been known that the origin of astronomy could be traced to Mesopotamia, and that the Chaldeans were the first astronomers. But beyond this general fact all was fancy and conjecture. Few or no details were known or available. About all that could be said on the subject was included in the following poetical paragraph of Lalandé's *Astronomie*, which was published more than a hundred years ago:

"The inhabitants of the vast plains of Sennaar, where was built the city of Babylon, were, according to many savants, the oldest astronomers and the first of all observers; at least their observations are the oldest which have come down to us. Everything concurred to direct their attention toward the heavens. The care of their flocks was their principal occupation. But the heat of the day made them select the night for their labors and their journeyings, so that the spectacle of the heavenly bodies forced itself, as it were, on their attention in spite of themselves."

Within the last few years, however, a great advance has been made in our knowledge respecting the beginnings of the science of astronomy, and our information regarding the early work and methods of the first of the world's star-gazers is comparatively complete. The learned palæographists and mathematicians Fathers Strassmaier and Epping of the Society of Jesus, as the result of a careful decipherment of some of the cuneiform inscriptions found in the library of Assurbanipal, and of a series of long and complicated calculations that only astronomers can fully appreciate, have demonstrated conclusively that as far back as the sixth century before our era the astronomers of Babylonia had a very accurate knowledge of the science of the stars, and that they made observations of the eclipses of the sun and moon, of the oppositions and conjunctions of the planets and of some of the stars, with a degree of accuracy that is simply marvellous. More than this, they had a calendar remarkable for its exactness, and a collection of tables based on observations and calculations that approximated in many respects to our modern ephemeris.[1]

But remote as is the past to which the tablets of the Chaldean astronomers convey back the chronologist, there is reason to believe that new discoveries will supply still other dates of a much greater antiquity. The study of Chaldean astronomy from cuneiform inscriptions is but in its infancy, and yet it has already disclosed a number of facts of which not even the most sanguine Assyriologist ever dreamed. One of these facts—and it is of paramount importance—is that the Assyrians (and the same may be said of the Chaldeans and Babylonians) had a chronological sense —something which, as we have seen, was entirely wanting to the ancient Hindus, Chinese, and Egyptians. This fact, if no other, should inspire more confidence in the chronological records of Assyria, Chaldea, and Babylonia than we are warranted in feeling in those of any of the other ancient peoples of the Orient.

The Assyrians, unlike the Egyptians and Chinese, did not reckon time by the years during which their

[1] See "Astronomie à Babylone," by the Rev. J. D. Lucas, S. J., *Revue des Questions scientifiques*, October, 1890, and April, 1891. Also, by the same writer, "Ephemerides planetaires des Chaldéens," in the same *Revue* for January, 1892. Consult likewise "Astronomisches aus Babylon oder das Wissen der Chaldäer über den gestirnten Himmel," by Fathers Strassmaier and Epping, S. J., published in 1889 as a supplement to the *Stimmen aus Maria Laach*.

kings held the sceptre, but rather by the names of eponym officials, called *limmu*, who, like the archons at Athens and the consuls of Rome, gave their names to the years during which they held office. By means of eponym canons or lists, some of which have been preserved, we are able to assign with comparative certainty the dates of events that occurred at very remote periods of Assyrian history.

Thus, from inscriptions at hand we know that the institution of the *limmu* dates as far back as the fourteenth century B. C., and there are valid reasons for believing that it existed long prior to this epoch. Other inscriptions that Assyriologists seem disposed to credit carry us back to the year 2274 before our era, while the celebrated tablet of Nabonidos, about which so much has been written, gives us a date nearly fifteen centuries more remote. This remarkable monument, now preserved in the British Museum, seems to fix the date of the reign of Sargon I., the father of Narsam-Sin, at about thirty-eight centuries before the Christian era—a date much earlier than was formerly attributed to this sovereign.[1]

[1] Lenormant, *Histoire ancienne de l' Orient*, tome v. p. 79, in referring to this tablet, observes: "Si cette indication est exacte, comme rien ne s'y oppose, Narsam-Sin regnait vers 3750 et Sargon, son père, vers 3800 avant J. C.; c'est la plus ancienne date certaine de l'histoire." Mr. Sayce, the distinguished English Assyriologist, hesitates about accepting this date as reliable.

Certain statues found by M. de Sarzec at Tel-loh are, we are assured, to be referred to even an earlier date than the tablet of Nabonidos. According to the inscriptions which these statues bear, they have been supposed to date back as far as 4000 or 4500 years B. C. The eminent French Assyriologist, M. Heuzey, however, contends that they belong to a more recent period.

According to the testimony of other monuments, quite a number of kings occupied the throne during the time that intervened between the reign of Sargon I. and the Deluge of Noah. This, contrary to the generally received opinion, would place the Flood at a period 4000 years B. C. at least, and possibly at a date much earlier. Certain inscriptions from the library of Assurbanipal relating to the Deluge, and deciphered by Mr. George Smith,[1] led Sir Henry Rawlinson, than whom no one is more competent to express an opinion on the subject, to ascribe to the great cataclysm so graphically described in Genesis a date preceding our era by six or seven thousand years.

Whatever of truth there may be in Rawlinson's estimate, it seems certain that Assyriologists are able to carry back the history of our race to a more remote period than can possibly, with any show of reason, be claimed for it by the chronologies of India, China, or Egypt. And it appears quite reasonable that this should be so. Central Asia, if not Mesopotamia, according to tradition and science, was most likely the birthplace of the human species, and hence it seems probable that the people who inhabited the valleys of the Tigris and the Euphrates should have a greater antiquity than those who lived in the land of the Nile or in regions more distant from the first home of the race. If, therefore, it should be proven that Egypt had a civilization antedating the Christian era by five thousand years or more, as many suppose, we should be quite warranted in claiming for the ancient peoples of Mesopotamia a civilization several centuries older,

---

[1] Cf. *Les Premières Civilizations*, par François Lenormant, tome ii., "Le Déluge et l'Épopée babylonienne."

THE AGE OF THE HUMAN RACE. 217

and thus fixing the beginnings of its history somewhere near unto six millennia before the time of Christ.

Linguistics and ethnology tell the same story as history and astronomy. They demand a greater antiquity for mankind than biblical scholars have hitherto been disposed to concede.[1] Like history and astronomy, they seem to fix the dispersion of the sons of Noah at about five or six thousand years before Christ— a much longer period than is indicated by any of the versions of the Bible as usually interpreted. Adding this time to the two thousand years that are ordinarily supposed to have elapsed between the creation of Adam and the Deluge, and the nineteen centuries that date from the coming of Christ, we have for the age of the human race a period that covers nearly ten thousand years.

It cannot be urged that these figures are too liberal. On the contrary, the estimate is rather conservative. There are many, as we have seen—and I have mentioned but a few of those who have studied the question—who insist on it that history and astronomy, as well as linguistics and ethnology, teach us that man has been on the earth fifteen or twenty thousand years, if not more. But even these figures, high as they are, are small in comparison with those furnished us by geology and prehistoric archæology.

How reconcile these dates and figures with scriptural chronology? Are not the Bible and science hopelessly

---

[1] Cf. Mgr. de Harlez in *La Controverse*, 1881, pp. 577, 578; also the admirable criticism, by the learned Father Van den Gheyn, S. J., of the *Origines ariacæ* of Karl Penka, in the *Revue des Questions scientifiques*, p. 605, April, 1884.

at variance in regard to the antiquity of man, and have we not here at least an instance of that irreconcilable conflict we hear so much of between the certain results of modern scientific research and the inspired record? I do not think so. On the contrary, I am firmly convinced that a careful and unprejudiced study of the question of man's antiquity will issue in proving, as has been so often done heretofore in other matters, that the Bible and science are at one regarding the question now under discussion, and will eventually render the same testimony.

Before, however, attempting to demonstrate the truth of this proposition, I shall take up certain objections that are deemed more formidable than any which have yet been urged, and which, during the past third of a century especially, have attracted an attention and assumed an importance that render all other difficulties comparatively insignificant. The objections referred to are presented in the names of geology and that newer science, prehistoric archæology. The examination of these objections and the discussion of this, the most interesting portion of our thesis, I reserve for the following chapters.

CHAPTER II.

THE ANTIQUITY OF MAN ACCORDING TO GEOLOGY AND CLIMATOLOGY.

PRIMITIVE MAN.

THE ancient peoples of the Orient, as we saw in the last chapter, were one in asserting for themselves a venerable antiquity. Not content with tens of thousands, many of them demanded hundreds of thousands of years as the period of time covered by their annals. They were likewise a unit in claiming descent from gods and demigods and in attributing godhead to all of their earlier rulers. Many, if not all of them, were firm believers in a golden age, an age of justice and happiness, which distinguished the first era of the world's history from all subsequent periods, and placed the beginnings of humanity on a much higher plane than our race has since been able to attain. "Then," says Hesiod, in his *Works and Days*, "without chagrin or disquiet, exempt from labor and sorrow, men lived like gods. Infirmity, the companion of old age, was unknown. Enjoying, even in advanced years, the pleasures of youth, death to them was but as a sweet sleep. A fruitful earth furnished spontaneously the most delicious fruits, and the abundance thereof removed all occasion of envy. The peaceful and voluntary occupation which they found in providing for their daily needs removed the tedium of leisure and the weariness entailed by idleness."[1]

The golden age, in which we may see a faint recollection of the Garden of Eden, was followed, in the order given, by the ages of silver, brass, bronze, and iron. The last was the worst of all, and was marked by sorrow and suffering and misery—ills which in the earlier ages were unknown.

Modern science also, especially geology and prehistoric archæology, makes great demands on time, as well as on our faith, in its teachings regarding the age of the human species. But in marked contrast with the tenets of the ancients concerning the origin and primitive condition of mankind are the views entertained on the same subjects by the majority of our modern scientists and "advanced thinkers." Instead of ages of gold, silver, brass, bronze, and iron, which were supposed to characterize, in the order named, the beginnings of humanity, prehistoric archæology tells us we must substitute ages of stone, bronze, and iron. According to the sages of antiquity—and they gave but a dim reflection of the biblical teachings on the subject—the earliest inhabitants of the earth were a more perfect race of men than the world has since known. But they fell from their high estate and degenerated into degraded sons of once noble sires. Modern scientists hold an opposite view. The history of humanity, they tell us, is not one of degeneration, but one of development; not one of descent from a higher plane, but one of ascent from a lower; not one that makes mankind of noble lineage, as we have long been wont to believe, but one that declares the species

[1] Cf. Ovid's *Metamorphoses*, lib. i.

to have had a far humbler and a more ignoble beginning. We are not of

> "Adam, the goodliest man of men since born,
> His sons;"

but the descendants of some speechless pithecanthrope —*alalus*, Häckel calls it—or some tailless, narrow-nosed ape that lived and disappeared untold æons before the advent of the traditional ancestor of our race.

If we are to credit geologists and archæologists, the time which has elapsed since the appearance of the first man on earth is a very variable quantity, for no two persons have yet been able to agree upon the precise number of years to be assigned as the age of the species.

Le Conte, in concluding his discussion of the antiquity of the human race, says: "We have, as yet, no certain knowledge of man's time on earth. It may be one hundred thousand years or it may be only ten thousand years, but more probably the former than the latter."[1] M. Mortillet, one of the founders and chief representatives of the new science of prehistoric archæology, is more positive in his statements. "Man," he says, "appeared in Europe at the commencement of the Quaternary age, at least two hundred and thirty or two hundred and forty thousand years ago."[2] These figures are nearly the same as those given by Lyell and Lubbock, who estimated the age of the human race to be about a quarter of a million years.

Büchner, although less definite, is not less positive, about the great antiquity of man. He regards it as

[1] *Elements of Geology*, p. 570.   [2] *Le Préhistorique*, p. 628.

perfectly certain "that the known historical period is a mere nothing, in point of time, when compared with the periods during which our race has actually inhabited the earth."[1] According to A. Laugel, whom Büchner quotes with approval, modern science has thrown back "the origin of man to a period so distant that in comparison with it our written history appears like a passing moment in a series of centuries which the mind is unable to grasp."

HÄCKEL AND MONISM.

But it was reserved for the notorious professor of Jena, Ernst Häckel, to settle for once and for all any doubts that the Darwinian school of science might still entertain regarding the antiquity and origin of the human race. In his *History of Creation*, after referring to the researches of some of his compeers, he declares that "the numerous and interesting discoveries presented to us by these extensive investigators of late years on the primeval history of the human race place the important fact, long since probable for many other reasons, beyond a doubt, that the human race, as such, has existed for more than twenty thousand years. But it is also probable that more than a hundred thousand years, perhaps many hundred thousand years, have elapsed since its first appearance."[2]

The professor, however, is not satisfied with this simple but vague statement. As if guilty of some great blunder in underrating the antiquity of man,

[1] *Man in the Past, Present, and Future*, p. 43, English translation.
[2] Vol. ii. p. 298.

he hastens to correct himself. He remembers that he is the hierophant of Monism, and that, according to the theory of Evolution, of which he has always been an ardent champion, there never was, properly speaking, a first man. The countless transformations, extending through long geological eras, which resulted in giving to one or several animals whose environment was specially favorable the distinguishing characteristics of the human species were so insensible that it is impossible not only to fix the date of the apparition of man, but also equally impossible to predicate of any given individual that it was the first representative of humanity in its last stage of development. He therefore tells us, unambiguously, that the evolution of our race from the lower forms of animal life "took place so slowly that we can in no wise speak of the first man."

"Now," he continues, "whether we reckon the period during which the human race, as such, has existed and diffused itself over the earth as twenty thousand, a hundred thousand, or many hundred thousands of years, the lapse of time is in any case immensely small in comparison with the inconceivable length of time which was requisite for the gradual development of the long chain of human ancestors."

And the professor is good enough not to leave his readers in ignorance regarding the genealogy of man and the processes which obtained in his development from the lower forms of animal life. All is clear to him, and he is desirous of giving others the benefit of at least the reflected light of his brilliant intellect. He exhibits a genealogical tree of twenty-two parent-forms which, he assures us, "may be regarded, with more or less certainty, as the animal ancestors of the human race, and which must be looked upon as, in a sense, the most important stages of evolution in the long evolutionary series from the one-celled organisms up to man."[1] But he would not have us infer that the twenty-two types he gives us afford the complete pedigree of the human species. Far from it. He is very explicit in stating that "the number of species —or, more accurately, form-stages which are distinguished as 'species'—must, in the human ancestral line, in the course of many millions of years, have amounted to many thousands, the number of *genera* to many hundreds."

The original ancestor of our species, according to Häckel's teaching, was a simple moneron, a small particle of structureless protoplasm, a creature of primitive slime or plasson. This moneron, which actually stands "on the very boundary between organic and inorganic natural bodies," Häckel is frank enough to tell us, is like that "most remarkable of all monera," the *Bathybius Hæckelii*, discovered and described by Huxley in 1868, and named after his friend, the professor of Jena and the fantastical author of *Natürliche Schöpfungsgeschichte*. To this last statement we may give our cordial assent, especially in view of the fact of its ignominious fate at the hands of the eminent Catholic geologist, M. de Lapparent,[2] who showed that its reputed existence was a myth; and in view of the further fact that the inventor of this missing link between the inorganic and organic worlds was obliged,

---
[1] *The Evolution of Man*, vol. ii. p. 42.
[2] *Revue des Questions scientifiques*, January, 1878.

in the presence of the British Association for the Advancement of Science, assembled at Sheffield, to admit that what he had heralded forth to the world, with a great flourish of trumpets, as the long sought-for primal form of organized matter was, in reality, nothing more than a simple precipitate of sulphate of lime.

From Häckel's moneron "the infinitely long series of slowly and gradually differentiating animal forms" finally "attained to the amphioxus, from that to the primeval fish, from the primeval fish to the first mammal, and again from the latter to man." This development of our species from the original speck of protoplasm which, away back in the Laurentian period, spontaneously evolved itself from a few favorably collocated atoms of carbon, oxygen, hydrogen, and nitrogen, was, as might be expected, a slow process. Hence we are informed that "the organic history of the earth must not be calculated by thousands of years, but by palæontological and geological periods, each of which comprises many thousands of years, and perhaps millions or even milliards of thousands of years."[1]

It is true that the high priests of evolution or transformation are not at one as to some of the details of man's genealogy. Vogt traces our pedigree in its earlier stages through the annelids and earth-worms. Häckel demurs to this, and affirms that at this stage of development our ancestors were ascidians and amphioxi.

But, however much evolutionists may disagree as to details, they are unanimous in asserting the animal origin of man. To bridge over the chasm between brute and organic matter they invented the monera,

[1] *History of Creation*, vol. ii. p. 337.

which resulted from a fortuitous concourse of certain atoms of hydrogen, oxygen, carbon, and nitrogen. The nearest living analogue of this primitive form of protoplasm is, Häckel assures us, the ill-starred *bathybius* of Huxley. To bridge over the chasm between the irrational and the rational, between animals and man, they invented the anthropoid or the pithecanthrope, the speechless man-ape, of which, like so many other links in Häckel's genealogical chain, there is not the slightest trace in geology or palæontology,

Juvenal ridiculed the credulity of those who believed that Mount Athos was sailed through of yore:

> . . . creditur olim
> Velificatus Athos, . . .

but how much more deserving of the satirist's derision and invective are the fantastic teachings of those who declare that brute matter can of its own motion bridge the chasm that separates it from sentient and conscious beings! Truly, "beyond all credulity is the credulousness of atheists who believe that chance could make the world, when it cannot build a house."

But the theory of descent advocated by the evolution school of science requires the existence of these links, and we are told to look to the future for their discovery. This is about as satisfactory as Häckel's defence of spontaneous generation, which is one of the prerequisites of his hypothesis. Spontaneous generation, in spite of the crucial experiments of Pasteur, is, Häckel assures us, still going on, but at the bottom of the deepest oceans and in other places to which access is barred to the investigator. Similarly, man, as man, as well as the all-important missing link—*alalus*—had his origin in Lemuria, an imaginary continent now at the bottom of the Indian Ocean, far out of reach of the modern fossil-hunter; and thus we shall for ever be denied the privilege of looking upon any of the relics of our venerable ancestors or of their immediate progenitors, a race of catarrhine apes long since extinct.

Mark Twain, in his *Innocents Abroad*, laments the absence of a monument to the memory of our common ancestor, Adam—something that the world, for some unaccountable reason, seems to have lost sight of until its attention was directed to the matter by the great American humorist. Häckel seems even more solicitous about the memory of the primitive plasson—the *Bathybius Haeckelii*—from which, he will have it, humanity is descended. According to the professor of Jena, we are indeed an ignorant and ungrateful offspring.

And yet these advocates of the animal origin of man are proud of the favored mud-fish and of the ambitious sea-squirt to which they trace back their ancestry. This is not a libel on them, because they take pains to inform us of the fact. "It is better," says Claparède, "to be a perfectionated ape than a degenerate Adam." To this sapient utterance of the Swiss naturalist, Häckel, Vogt, Büchner, and their disciples say "Amen," and all further discussion is pronounced impertinent.

But a little reflection will teach us that the Monists or Transformists, whose views we have been considering, have "method in their madness." They assume evolution, in the sense in which they teach it, to be true and to rest on an impregnable basis of fact. They assume also that matter is eternal, because science, by which they mean physics, can tell us nothing, because it knows nothing, of creation. They pin their faith to spontaneous generation because their theory demands it. "If we do not," says Häckel, "accept the hypothesis of spontaneous generation, then at this one point in the history of development we must have recourse to the miracle of a *supernatural creation*."[1] But this is something that cannot for a moment be admitted. For the professor of Jena continues: "To me the idea that the Creator should have in this one point arbitrarily interfered with the regular process of development of matter, which in all other cases proceeds entirely without his interference, seems to be just as unsatisfactory to a believing mind as to a scientific intellect." Carl Vogt endorses these views when he declares: "There can be no doubt that Darwin's theory ignores a personal Creator and his direct interference in the transformation and creation of species, there being no sphere of action for such a being." The notorious French Darwiness, Madame Clemence Royer, proclaims the same doctrines with even greater crudeness and barbarity. With her, creation is impossible, contradictory, unimaginable, and the Creator—the "Absolute" is her word—has no ex-

[1] Op. cit., vol. i. p. 349.

istence, but is simply the last term of regression of an order purely logical, which does not correspond to any objective reality.[1] In lieu of a Creator, Virchow tells us "the process of life, both in its beginning and in its repetition, must be referred to a special kind of mechanics." For we must understand that "at a certain period of the earth's evolution unusual conditions supervened;" that "a thousand circumstances, which we are now unable to produce," existed; that under such conditions and under such circumstances certain "elements, entering into new combinations, *in statu nascente*, assumed the vital movement, and thus the ordinary *mechanical* conditions were formed into vital ones.[2]

But the truculent Büchner, impatient of such euphemistic phraseology, expresses himself more bluntly, if not more positively. "The belief in God," he tells us, "is a creation of the uneducated human mind," arising "from defective knowledge of the laws of nature"—a disposition on the part of man to refer what he cannot explain in a natural way to an invisible mysterious cause. "Science," he affirms, "is a continued struggle with this notion, and with every step she makes forward she drives back the belief in supernatural forces, or the need of such belief, into more remote and untenable positions. Hence every science, and especially every philosophy, that seeks reality instead of appearance, truth instead of pretence, *must necessarily be atheistic*, otherwise it blocks up against itself the path to its end, the truth. As soon, then, as in a *philosophic* book the word 'God'

---

[1] *Origine de l'Homme et des Sociétés*, p. 6.
[2] Büchner: *Force and Matter*, pp. 176 et seq.

occurs, except in criticism or reference, one may confidently lay it aside; in it will found nothing capable of promoting the real progress of knowledge. In properly scientific works the word will seldom be met with, for in scientific matters the word 'God' is only another expression for our ignorance."[1] Hence, says the blasphemous Carl Vogt, "we must dismiss the Creator without ceremony, and not leave any more the least place for the action of such a being."

Here, as in the preceding chapter, we see Rationalism run wild. With Strauss and his school it issued in Atheism and Nihilism; with the leading German Transformists it results in Monism and an explanation of the universe by a "special system of mechanics."

But whether the subject of study be philosophy, theology, science, or Sacred Scripture, the object of the Rationalist is ever the same—to minimize the supernatural, or to relegate it, as the outgrowth of ignorance and superstition, to the domain of myth and fable. Anything, therefore, that refers directly or indirectly to God or religion; anything that bears on the authenticity of the Bible or the integrity of Christian dogma; anything that will tend, even by implication, whether by distortion of fact or suppression of the truth, to cast discredit on the traditional teaching of the Church or shake the faith of her children, is eagerly seized on, as if the highest act of virtue and the sole end of science were to banish for ever from the minds of men the very idea of God.

That which M. Gustave Flourens wrote the scientists of the Monistic school imply, if they do not express it in words: "Our enemy is God! Hatred of

---

[1] *Man in the Past, Present, and Future*, p. 329.

God is the beginning of wisdom. If men would make progress, it must be on the basis of Atheism."[1]

From what we have already seen, and from what we shall learn in the sequel, the subject of the antiquity of man is one that has been particularly grateful to the skeptics and the scientific Atheists of our day. They fancy they see in the disproof of the scriptural chronology a condemnation of the traditional teachings regarding the Adamic origin of the various races of the human family, if not a demonstration of the falsity of the entire Bible as a divinely-inspired record. A certain class of geologists, and prehistoric archæologists especially, have taken this view of the question, and hence have bent their best energies to show that the teachings of their science are utterly irreconcilable with any of the accepted systems of biblical chronology, and would now have us believe that they have succeeded without peradventure in their purpose. They display the animus that actuates them in their investigations by their inability to refrain from giving frequent expression to their contempt for the Inspired Record and for those beliefs which have so long been the solace of countless millions of our race. This is particularly so in the case of the question under discussion. They affect to be surprised that any one endowed with ordinary reasoning power or the faculty of weighing the simplest kinds of evidence should any longer find anything in scriptural chronology to claim his assent or to stand in the way of his unreserved acceptance of the prevailing teachings of the evolutionary school of geology and anthropology regarding the age of human kind.

[1] Quoted by W. S. Lilly in *The Great Enigma*, p. 68.

I have been thus explicit in what precedes in exhibiting the character, views, and methods of the modern scientists, from whom I have quoted at some length, in order that what shall follow may appear in its true light, and in order, too, that the reader may appreciate the nature of the pressure that is brought to bear on many votaries of science who have no sympathy whatever with the principles of the Monistic and Atheistic school which we have been considering. Without these prefatory observations it would be impossible to understand the attitude of contemporary geologists and archæologists—of those, even, who make profession of Christianity and belief in the Book of books as a divinely inspired record—regarding the question of the antiquity of man in its connection with the reputed teaching of the Bible on the subject.

What, then, does modern science—and by this term we mean conservative, veritable science, and not wild hypothesis and fantastical speculation—teach concerning the age of mankind? What answer has geology, and that newer science, prehistoric archæology, to give to a question which has excited such interest and received such attention during the last third, we might say during the last half, of a century? What is the nature of the evidence offered in elucidation of this much-vexed subject, and what is the value of the testimony by which the case is to be adjudicated? What kind of chronometers do geologists and archæologists employ? Are they reliable, or are they utterly lacking in all the elements of certitude? What are the criteria by which we are asked by scientists to be guided in arriving at a conclusion respecting this all-important problem, and are they of such a character as to command the assent of one whose reason tells him that he must be governed in his researches by at least the ordinary laws of dialectics? Let us see.

Tertiary Man and Uniformitarianism.

The evidence usually adduced in support of the great antiquity of man is based on observed geological and geographical changes, on changes in climate, on changes in the fauna, and on changes in the objects and implements of human industry, which have taken place since man's appearance on earth.

One of the indisputable facts, it cannot be gainsaid, of geologic science is the fact of the very recent origin of our race. Man, according to the almost universal teaching of geologists and archæologists, did not appear before the opening of the Quaternary Age. But this age, whatever may have been its duration in years, is conceded on all hands to have been incomparably shorter than the various ages that preceded it.

Some decades ago, it was thought by many—among them by the learned French archæologists Abbé Bourgeois and Abbé Delaunay—that men existed during the Tertiary Age. Thence the long and heated discussions about Tertiary man, who, a few years ago, occupied such a prominent place in periodical literature. The question has lost the interest which it formerly possessed, although there are not wanting, even now, prominent men of science who believe, or affect to believe, in the existence of Tertiary man. The evidence, however, in support of the theory that man existed before the Quaternary Age is so slight and inconclusive that even those whose preconceived notions would incline them to favor the theory of Tertiary man are forced to declare that we must await further light on the subject before a final decision is warranted.

But truth is, the deathblow to Tertiary man, at least in France, was dealt by the Scientific Congress held at Blois in 1884. At the conclusion of a long and heated debate, and after a visit to Thenay, where Abbé Bourgeois had discovered in 1863 his alleged relics of Tertiary man, and a thorough examination of the flint-flakes that had been imagined to be of human handiwork, the section of anthropology, composed of forty members, declared, with only one dissenting voice, that the proofs in support of the learned abbé's theory were entirely inadequate. It is true that even after this M. Mortillet insisted that if the flints of Thenay were not the products of human industry, they were at least the work of some intelligent creature. So convinced is he of this that he does not hesitate to ascribe them to an imaginary being whom he burdens with the name of *Anthropopithecus*, who, he will have it, was man's immediate predecessor and the missing link for which geologists and archæologists have so long been seeking. But M. de Mortillet, if not alone with his *anthropopithecus*, has but a small following, for, as far as any evidence goes, his pretended precursor of man is fully as mythical as Tertiary man himself.[1]

[1] Cf. Appendix by H. W. Haynes, in Wright's *Man and the Glacial Period;* "La Question de l'Homme Tertiaire," by Abbé Bourgeois, in the *Revue des Questions scientifiques*, 1877.: "L'Homme Tertiaire," in the same *Revue*, January, 1889, by M. Arcelin. See also "L'Homme Tertiaire," in the *Dictionnaire apologetique de la Foi catholique*, per Abbé Jaugey, and chap.

But if man did not live during the Tertiary Age, it is quite certain that he was contemporary with many species of animals that are long since extinct. He therefore existed during one of the geological periods, properly so called—the Quaternary—because the Recent Period, as understood by geologists, was not ushered in until the disappearance of the animals now found in a fossil state. In this connection it may be observed that a fossil, in scientific terminology, is any organic body buried in the earth at a period preceding the so-called Recent Period, in which we now live. But the existence of men during the Quaternary Age does not, as has been so often stated, presuppose for him a greater antiquity than is consistent with a legitimate deduction from the chronological facts of Scripture. The truth of this statement will appear as we proceed.

Among the geological and geographical evidences advanced in support of man's great antiquity are those supposed to be afforded by alluvial deposits, peat-bogs, stalagmitic formations, and by oscillations of the earth's surface.

In various parts of Europe and America, not to speak of other portions of the globe, relics of man and of human industry have been found entombed at various depths in layers of clay, sand, and gravel

ii. of Abbé Hamard's admirable work, *L'Age de la Pierre et l'Homme primitif.* So late as August, 1892, in an address before the Congress of Anthropologists in Moscow, Professor Virchow boldly declared: "Jamais personne n'a trouvé, dans les conches vierges d'un terrain tertiaire, quelque morceau de silex qui ait été reconnu par le monde savant comme un vestige irrécusable de l'existence de l'homme."

which have been deposited by flowing water. In deposits made by rivers and streams it has been contended—and, at first sight, quite naturally—that all that was necessary to determine the age of human remains in fluviatile detritus was to find the average rate of deposition per annum. Thus if an arrowhead or a stone hatchet were to be found in an argillaceous stratum at the depth of five feet, and it were known from a number of observations that the mean annual rate of sedimentary accumulation was one inch per annum, the inference would at once be drawn that such implements were left in the place where they were found sixty years ago. Such reasoning would be perfectly just if we could be certain that the same conditions obtained throughout the entire sixty years as during the period of observation.[1]

If there were a question of only sixty years, as in the instance given, there might not be much room for doubt. When, however, there are thousands and tens of thousands of years to be considered, the case assumes a new phase. Then the Uniformitarianism, of which Sir Charles Lyell was such an ardent champion, makes greater demands for our acceptance than the known facts of geology and physical geography will justify. For we know as a fact that the rate of fluvial deposition

---

[1] So difficult, indeed, is it to make any calculations worthy of acceptance regarding the rule of fluviatile deposits that a distinguished scientist, in referring to the chronological supputations based on the monuments buried in the valley of the Nile, does not hesitate to assert that a "Fellah who makes a dam around the lower end of his field can in one year introduce a few thousand years into the cleverest calculations of a European savant."

is far from being the same in different times and places—that in France, for instance, it was far greater during the first centuries of the Christian era than it has been at subsequent periods. This is demonstrated so plainly, both by history and archæology, that it is incontestable.[1]

To give but a single case: the waters of the Somme, according to M. de Mercy, who made a special study

---

[1] Regarding "the dwarfing influence of Uniformitarianism," the regulating of everything " by a martinet measure of time and change," Professor Prestwich, the Nestor of English geologists, whose knowledge and judgment no one can suspect, writes as follows: "We trust we have now said enough to show upon how insecure a basis the Uniformitarian measures of time and change stand. They have probably done more to impede the exercise of free inquiry and discussion than any of the catastrophic theories which formerly prevailed. The latter found their own cure in the more accurate observation of geological phenomena and the progress of the collateral sciences; but the former hedge us in by dogmas which forbid any interpretation of the phenomena other than that of fixed rules which are more worthy of the sixteenth than of the nineteenth century. Instead of weighing the evidence and following up the consequences that ensue from the assumption, too many attempts have been made—not unnaturally by those who hold this faith—to adjust the evidence to the assumption. The result has been strained interpretations framed to meet one point, but without sufficient regard for the others. We repeat that we would not for a moment contend that the process of erosion, the modes of sedimentation, and the methods of motion are not the same in *kind* as they have ever been; but we can never admit that they have always been the same in *degree*. The physical laws are permanent, but the effects are conditional and changing in accordance with the conditions under which the laws are exhibited."
—*The Position of Geology*, in the *Nineteenth Century* for Oct., 1893. Cf. also Preface to Howorth's *Mammoth and the Flood*.

of this river, were during the Roman period fully fifty times as abundant as they are now. During the Quaternary Age the deposition of alluvium must have been far more rapid than at any time since. In consequence of the great humidity of the atmosphere, the precipitation was then ten or twenty times as abundant as it is at present.[1] Indeed, so exceptionally active during the Quaternary Period were the agents of erosion and transportation that nothing which we may now witness can give us an adequate idea of their power and violence unless it is an occasional torrential storm in the tropics or a destructive cloud-burst in the mountains. For this reason alone, not to speak of others, we can declare with certainty that none of the remains of man thus far discovered in the alluvium of either Europe or America can be produced as proof that the age of the human race is other than that which is indicated by the chronology of the Sacred Record.

The peat-beds of the Old and New Worlds have likewise been appealed to as chronometers for settling the question of the age of man, at least in the localities which have yielded undoubted human remains.

But here, as in the case of alluvial deposits, we are confronted with a fundamental difficulty—that of estimating the growth of peat-formations. The most divergent results have been arrived at by different investigators, varying greatly according to the localities studied.

According to Lyell, the rate of growth of peat is of extreme slowness. M. Boucher de Perthes, as the result of his investigations, came to the conclusion

[1] De Lapparent, *Traité de Géologie*, p. 1283.

that it was not more than four centimetres per century. Having found in the Somme Valley specimens of Roman pottery sixty centimetres below the surface of a peat-bed eight metres in depth, he calculated that the time required for the formation of the peat, assuming that the pottery was fifteen hundred years old, was no less than twenty thousand years. The error in the computation was in assuming that it required fifteen hundred years for the growth of the peat overlying the pottery. The time demanded may have been, and undoubtedly was, far less than this. From what we know regarding the rate of peat-formation in other places, there is no reason for believing that the time actually consumed in the growth of the peat above the pottery was more than two or three centuries at most. Boucher de Perthes assumes as known what in reality is a totally unknown quantity, and hence his supputations are vitiated and count for naught.

In America, according to Andrews, peat is formed at the rate of twenty to twenty-five inches per century —from twelve to fifteen times as rapidly as was imagined by Boucher de Perthes. In Ireland it has been known to grow at the rate of two inches per annum— more in one year than the French savant allowed for a hundred. In view of these and other facts of similar import, M. Rioult de Neuville, an acknowledged authority on the subject, does not hesitate to assert: "It seems proven that under favorable circumstances the thickest peat-bogs may have formed within a period of time not exceeding one or two centuries, and in those places even where in our day, for lack of the conditions essential to its development, it is no longer produced." For this reason, therefore, we are fully warranted in rejecting entirely the exaggerated statements of Lyell and others regarding the length of time required for the growth of peat, and substituting hundreds for the thousands of years their calculations demand. Even geologically speaking, peat is of very recent origin, and it is quite futile to attempt to deduce from any human relics found in it an argument for the great antiquity of man or against the biblical chronology.

In the stalagmitic deposits of certain caves, especially in Europe, have been found human remains associated with those of animals now extinct. These relics have long been thought to indicate a great antiquity for our race, but the reasoning by which this conclusion is arrived at is fallacious, for two reasons: First, because it assumes that the extinct animals, whose fossil remains are found alongside those of man, existed at a much earlier period than the facts of the case will allow. Secondly, it is taken for granted that the rate of deposit of stalagmites in the caves in question was much slower than is known to be the case elsewhere where the conditions are not dissimilar. The truth is, we encounter the same difficulty here as in our attempts to measure time by the deposition of alluvium or the growth of peat. Thus, according to one author, a million years was required for the deposition of the carbonate of lime on the floor of the celebrated Kent cavern in England, while according to another authority, equally competent to give an opinion on the subject, a period of a thousand years was all that was necessary.

As in the case of alluvial deposits, there is every

reason to believe that the rate of formation of stalagmites during the Quaternary Age was much more rapid than it is at present. There was then more moisture in the atmosphere, and consequently a greater abundance of water percolating through the limestone formations in which the caves are found. The natural result under such conditions would be that quite thick deposits of calcareous matter would be formed in a comparatively short time. Visitors to the Yellowstone National Park know how rapidly, at the Mammoth Hot Springs for instance, calcareous and siliceous deposits are made. Objects placed in these waters are heavily incrusted in a few days. The conditions here are, it is true, exceptionally favorable, but it would be rash to assert that they were not equally favorable in some of the caves in which human remains have been found, and which belong to the Quaternary or even to the Recent Period.

For this and other reasons we may declare with De Lapparent that there is no foundation whatever for "generously distributing among the different phases of the Quaternary Epoch the hundreds and thousands of centuries," as has so long been the vogue of a certain school of geologists. And, contrary to the findings of this same school of geologists, I am unable to see in any of the fossil cave-men or other human remains found in the caverns of Europe any evidence whatever for that fabulous antiquity of the human race that has so often been claimed for it. Nothing, to my mind, has yet been discovered in any of the caves that in the slightest degree tells against the teachings of scriptural chronology regarding the age of our race. We may concede to the remains of man found in the drift, in caves, and peat-bogs an antiquity of three or four thousand years, but, so far, we have no irrefragable evidence of such antiquity. We may admit even that cave-men—troglodytes they have been called—existed in Europe three or four thousand years before Christ, and still they would have been posterior, according to a chronology that we may accept, by a thousand years to colonies established by the descendants of the patriarchs along the valleys of the Nile, the Tigris, and the Euphrates, and probably also along those of the Ganges, the Indus, and the Brahmapootra.

For the sake of argument we may go yet farther. If the evidence from science were forthcoming, I should have no hesitation in believing that parts of Europe were inhabited in antediluvian times. Indeed, the science of linguistics and the existence of the Basques and Finns, who have no connection with the great Japhetite or Aryan branch of the human family, seem to point to prediluvial migrations that may have antedated the Christian era six or seven thousand years. But until geologists and archæologists shall have produced much stronger evidence than anything that has yet been offered regarding the age of man in Europe, we may feel that there is little difficulty in reconciling the age of human remains found in the peat-beds, caverns, and gravel-pits with the chronology of the Bible as it is usually given for post-diluvial, not to speak of antediluvian, times.

Cataclysmic Action.

Certain oscillations of the earth's crust, which have notably affected the contour of the surface of the globe, which are assumed—or, it may be, which are known—to have occurred since the advent of man, have frequently been signalized as arguments in favor of a greater than biblical antiquity of man. But here, as in the other instances which we have considered, the flaw in the argument consists in taking for granted the validity of Lyell's Uniformitarian theory, and in considering as a known that which is positively an unknown, and in the most cases an indeterminable, quantity. All cataclysmic action is denied, and this in spite of the fact that we have numerous striking evidences of its reality within historic times, not to consider those that obviously pertain to the domain of prehistory.

The coast-line of various parts of the world, as the reader is aware, is continually changing by reason of the elevations and subsidences of the earth's crust which are always in progress. In consequence of these oscillations the sea at some places encroaches on the land, while at others the land rises from the sea. For this reason the coast-line of France is quite different from what it was in the time of Cæsar, and for this reason too the topography of certain parts of Southern England is quite changed from what it is known to have been a few centuries before the Christian era. According to Diodorus Siculus, the Phœnicians who voyaged to Cornwall for tin were able at low tide to transport the metal to the Isle of Wight dry-shod. Such a thing, as every one knows, would now be very far from possible. There is no doubt, moreover, that the British Isles were formerly connected with the continent of Europe, and probably, too, only a few centuries before the intrepid navigators of Tyre and Sidon betook themselves to the far-off Cassiterides in quest of tin—that all-important constituent of bronze—which in their time was known to exist in large quantities only in this *Ultima Thule* of the then known world.[1]

Lyell, basing his conclusions on observations made along the coast of Sweden, thinks that the rate of elevation of land does not amount to more than two or three feet in a century.[2] Here again, true to his Uniformitarian theory, he assumes that the rate of upheaval is regular and, in the long run, practically the same in all parts of the earth's surface. But such an assumption is demonstrably false. Not only is there a variation in time, but also a variation in places quite contiguous.

To cite but one instance from among many similar ones that might be adduced illustrating the nature of the argument based on oscillations of the earth's crust which are assumed to have taken place since the appearance of man, shall give a typical case, often

---

[1] Wilkinson suggests that the Egyptians may have obtained tin from India or Spain long previously to this period. There does not, however, seem to be any evidence that the Phœnicians had any knowledge of the mines of India, while those of Spain, even if worked, would have supplied only a small fraction of the metal they actually used. Speaking of the bronze used by the Chaldeans and Egyptians in the earliest periods of their history, the Marquis de Nadaillac thinks that we must admit either "l'exploitation des mines dont toute trace est perdue," or the importation of tin from England or Malacca. Owing to the imperfect knowledge of navigation at the time, he regards its importation from England as impossible. Even its transport from India he considers "une hypothèse bien osée."

[2] *Antiquity of Man*, p. 58, and *Principles of Geology*, chap. xxxi.

referred to, which was brought to light in Sardinia. Here, at an elevation of about ninety metres above the sea-level, products of human industry were found in deposits of undoubted marine origin. Assuming that the rate of upheaval was one metre a century, the conclusion was that man lived in Sardinia full nine thousand years ago. The calculation, however, was nullified, not only by the assumption of a regular rate of elevation of the land, but by the assumption of regularity of movement in a part of the world where earthquakes and other cataclysmic actions are of frequent occurrence. But this is not the most serious objection urged against the computations based on the remains here found. It was discovered on a more careful examination that the accumulations of marine shells, pottery, etc. at the height stated were not necessarily any evidence whatever of upheaval. On the contrary, there are now the strongest reasons for supposing that these deposits are similar to the shell-mounds or kitchen-middings of Denmark, and that they may originally have been at the same altitudes above sea-level as they are at present.

The cataclysmic causes of upheaval and subsidence are indeed of much more frequent occurrence and affect much greater areas of the earth's surface than the Uniformitarian school of geology would have us believe. As cases in point it will be sufficient to recall instances with which every one is familiar, and which do not date back more than a few years—of islands suddenly rising from the bed of the ocean, and as quickly disappearing; of earthquakes whose effects embraced areas of hundreds, and often of thousands, of square miles; of volcanoes whose eruptions occasioned untold losses of life and property. As special instances of an earlier date may signalize the elevation of a considerable part of New Zealand during the night of the 23d of January, 1855, and the uplifting in Chili in 1822 of fully two hundred thousand square miles of territory between the Andes and the coast to a height of from two to seven feet; of the memorable earthquake at Lisbon in 1775, whereby no fewer than sixty thousand persons perished in the space of six minutes, and whereby a large portion of the city was permanently engulfed six hundred feet beneath the waters of the bay, and of the still more destructive earthquake that visited Calabria in 1783, which occasioned the death of one hundred thousand persons and was felt throughout the greater portion of Europe.

If such sudden and extensive changes in the configuration of the earth's surface have taken place during the short period of time of which we have a record, how many other, and even greater, changes may not have occurred in times prehistoric? And if we have such evidence of catastrophic action during the Recent Period, which all authorities admit to be one of remarkable quiescence, geologically speaking, what may we not believe of the period immediately preceding—the Quaternary—which affords so many indications, especially toward its close, of having witnessed oscillations and disturbances by the side of which all subsequent changes were comparatively insignificant? The wonder, then, is not that the surface has undergone so many and so violent mutations since the advent of man, but rather that the revolutions experienced have been so few. Certain it is that far from being an argument for the great antiquity of the race, the changes referred to rather corroborate the view of those who think that five thousand or six thousand years are amply sufficient to explain all the vestiges of prehistoric man, not only in America, but also in Europe.

The Ice Age.

We come now to a more interesting phase of our subject—the argument for the antiquity of man that is based on the changes of climate that are supposed to have supervened since his appearance on our planet. To do justice to this part of the discussion would require a special chapter, or more truthfully a special treatise; hence we must be satisfied with merely indicating a few of the reasons that have connected the age of our species with climatic changes.

The whole argument hinges on the celebrated glacial theory, about which so much has been written, but regarding which so little has been definitely ascertained. Men of science are not yet agreed as to the cause of the Ice Age, still less are they able to tell us how long it prevailed. More than this, those who have studied the matter most carefully are yet undecided as to whether there was one or several glacial periods. The opinions held by individual investigators depend entirely on the point of view which is taken or on some preconceived notion which has been raised to the dignity of a legitimate working hypothesis.

The theories that have been brought to bear on the subject may be divided into two classes—cosmical and terrestrial or astronomical and geological; and of these there are nearly a dozen, all having able advocates and all claiming recognition.

It is an indisputable fact that there has been since the close of the Tertiary Period, and probably since the apparition of man, what has been called a Glacial Period or an Ice Age. If man did not witness the beginning of this period of low temperature and extensive glaciers and ice-sheets, it seems certain, as all geologists and archæologists acknowledge, that he lived during a portion, probably the greater portion, of the period. The interesting part of the problem, so far as it concerns our present subject, is to determine just when the Ice Age began and how long it endured.

According to the theory so ably advocated by Lyell in his *Principles of Geology*, the growth and distribution of glaciers are to be attributed to the changes in the distribution of land and water over the earth's surface. As these changes must have been very great to produce the glaciation we know to have existed, and as mutations of this character must, according to the distinguished English geologist, have taken place with extreme slowness, we are asked to believe that the inception of the Reign of Ice dated back several hundred thousand years at least. Glacialists like James and Archibald Geike tell us that great areas of Europe and North America were then "drowned in a widespread *mer de glace*," attaining in Norway a thickness of six or seven thousand feet,[1] and giving rise, when sent adrift into the waters of the Atlantic, to "whole argosies of icebergs," in comparison with which those now furnished by the ice-seas of Alaska and Greenland sink into insignificance.

[1] A. Geike, *Text-Book of Geology*, p. 890.

Croll, adopting the astronomical theory of Adhémar, attempts to fix exactly the number of years that have elapsed since the beginning and end of the last Ice Age. An estimate of this kind based on Lyell's theory is impossible, both by reason of the complexity of the problem from a geological standpoint, and because of the utter absence of any reliable chronometer.

According to the astronomical theory, of which Croll, James Geike, and Sir Robert Ball are the chief English exponents, the cause of the Ice Age—or rather of the ice ages, because the theory supposes a succession or "groups" of them, to use Ball's term[1]—is to be sought in the climatic changes due to the precession of the equinoxes and to the variations in the eccentricity of the earth's orbit. To this may also be added, as a less potent factor, the variations in the obliquity of the ecliptic. Thanks to the investigations of Leverrier, Poisson, Lagrange, and other eminent mathematicians, astronomers are able to compute with great accuracy the periods of these variations both for past and future time.

The precession of the equinoxes, which gradually alters the relative lengths of winter and summer, has a period of twenty-one thousand years. According to the theory which ascribes glaciation to the precession of the equinoxes alone, there should be alternately, in the northern and southern hemispheres, an ice age every ten thousand five hundred years. Geologists most competent to interpret the facts of their science deny the existence of such a series of glacial periods, for the simple reason that they are not warranted by any evidence so far produced.

[1] *The Cause of an Ice Age*, chap. viii.

Croll, with whom Lyell and Lubbock substantially agree, seeks the cause of the Ice Age in the greater secular change occasioned by the variation of the eccentricity of the earth's orbit. This change, like the precession of the equinoxes, causes a difference in the relative lengths of summer and winter, but the difference due to variations of eccentricity are much greater than is possible by any change in the position of the line of equinoxes. At present the difference is only seven days, the summer being that much longer than the winter, but a difference of full thirty-six days may be occasioned by variations in the eccentricity of the earth's orbit.

The period of this change is likewise much longer, and embraces not tens of thousands, but hundreds of thousands, of years.

The last period of a state of high eccentricity, according to Croll's calculations, began two hundred and forty thousand years ago, and persisted for one hundred and sixty thousand years, terminating, therefore, eighty thousand years ago. During the greater portion of this period the winters were more than twenty days longer than the summers, and the temperature, we are told, was many degrees lower than it is at the present time. Another high state of eccentricity, that next preceding the one just referred to, embraced a period extending from about nine hundred and eighty thousand to about seven hundred and twenty thousand years ago. Both Croll and Lyell at one time assigned the Glacial Epoch to this period, but subsequently they adopted the later period, which culminated about two hundred thousand years since. With this view Sir John Lubbock and other glacialists are in accord.

And as the Glacial Period was wholly or in great part subsequent to the Tertiary Period, and as man, according to the majority of the authorities, appeared immediately or shortly after the close of the Tertiary, we are called upon by the school of Lyell, Croll, and Geike to grant man an antiquity of at least two hundred thousand years, if not more.

The conclusions arrived at by Prestwich, one of the most eminent of English geologists, are quite different from those just enunciated. As the result of a careful examination of the subject, he declares that "the time required for the formation and duration of the great ice-sheets of Europe and America—the Glacial Period —need not, after making all allowances, have extended beyond fifteen to twenty-five thousand years, instead of the one hundred and sixty thousand years which have been claimed." He also limits the time of the so-called post-Glacial Period, or of the melting away of the ice-sheet, to from eight thousand to ten thousand years or less.[1]

Mr. G. Frederick Wright, in his exhaustive work on *The Ice Age in North America*, states in one sentence the difficulty that confronts those who would attempt to fix even approximately the date of the Ice Age. He declares that "the sum of the whole matter, so far as theory is concerned, seems to be that, as yet, we do not know what was the ultimate cause of the Glacial Period."[2] "Everything here," as he truly observes, "depends upon the forces which distribute the heat and moisture over the land surfaces." Owing "to the general state of uncertainty as to the laws regulating

[1] *Geology*, vol. ii. pp. 553, 554.
[2] P. 440.

the absorption, retention, and distribution of the sun's heat upon the earth, it is by no means certain that when the winters of the northern hemisphere occur in aphelion they will be colder than now. Whether they would be so or not depends upon the action of forces whose laws cannot now be accurately calculated."[1]

The same writer deprecates the idea of geologists abandoning their own field to accept the glittering results of celestial mathematics, and favors the leaving the discussion of the theories of ultimate causation of the Glacial Epoch "to where it belongs," not to astronomers, or geologists even, but "to the more enlightened meteorologists of the future."

Referring to the theory of a succession of glacial periods, he maintains that local glaciers are amply sufficient to account for all the facts observed. Le Conte concludes a discussion of the subject with the statement: "The evidence at present, therefore, is overwhelmingly in favor of the *uniqueness* of the Glacial Epoch."[2] These conclusions "with reference to Croll's theory are those pretty generally adopted at the present time by the American geologists best qualified to interpret the facts."[3]

From the foregoing we learn that neither geology nor astronomy can give any answer to the questions regarding the cause, time, or duration of the Ice Age. The opinions entertained on the subject by even the ablest exponents of these sciences are most diverse, and

[1] Op. cit., p. 427.   [2] *Elements of Geology*, p. 557.
[3] Wright, op. cit., p. 439; cf. also Upham's paper on "Accumulation of Drumlins," in *American Naturalist* for December, 1893.

often as contradictory as they are extravagant.[1] Are we then to remain in complete ignorance of these mat-

[1] To realize how utterly at variance are the foremost representatives of science on the subject of the Glacial Theory, compare the views of Agassiz, Croll, and James Geike, on the one hand, with those of Prestwich, the Duke of Argyll, and Sir Henry Howorth, on the other. According to Agassiz, during the Glacial Age "the polar ice, which at the present day covers the miserable regions of Spitzbergen, Greenland, and Siberia, extended far into the temperate zones of both hemispheres, leaving probably but a broader or narrower belt around the equator ; nay, . . . the whole surface of the earth was, according to all probability, for a time one uninterrupted surface of ice, from which projected only the highest mountain-ridges covered with eternal snow." And not only was all this land enveloped in a huge winding-sheet of ice and snow during the Glacial Age, but also "all the northern seas," Croll declares, "must at that period have been blocked up with solid ice," and "the entire Atlantic, from Scandinavia to Greenland, was filled with land ice." These massive ice-sheets we are assured, flowed like water, or at least like pitch or treacle, and pushed their way over plain and mountain hundreds and thousands of miles, and, like a gigantic machine, "scooped out all our glens, rounded all our hills, and dug out all our lakes."

This theory of the Ice Age, as understood by glacialists generally, Howorth pronounces "the wildest dream which a fertile imagination ever imported into science." In the most positive manner he asserts that he does not "believe in interglacial periods, in a great overwhelming ice-cap, in the physical possibility of land ice moving for hundreds of miles over level plains like that of Poland, or in the possibility of tropical America being so glaciated that the valley of the Amazon was filled with ice."

For a clear exposition of the views of extreme glacialists and of those of their opponents see the *Great Ice Age*, by James Geike ; *Climate and Time*, by James Croll ; *The Mammoth and the Flood* and *The Glacial Nightmare and the Flood*, by Sir Henry Howorth. For interesting and thorough discussions of the

ters? or may we not expect information from other sources? I think this latter question may be answered in the affirmative. The light, however, will not come from astronomy or geology, but rather from a more neglected but nevertheless a more reliable witness—history. This, after all, notwithstanding what scientists may say to the contrary, is the witness that we are ultimately forced to appeal to in nearly all the difficulties that arise in discussing the much-vexed question of the age of our species.

REIGN OF ICE DURING HISTORIC TIMES.

Leaving aside the question as to the cause of the Ice Age as not relevant to our present purpose, may not history afford us at least a portion of the information we are seeking concerning the time of occurrence and the duration of that reign of ice of which we have, both in America and Europe, so many and so striking traces? As for myself, I am satisfied that it can, and I shall briefly indicate a few of the reasons for the faith that is in me.

Many, if not the majority, of those who have treated

same topic see the *Scottish and Edinburgh Reviews* for Oct., 1893; the *London Quarterly Review* for Jan., 1894; the *Nineteenth Century*, for Feb., 1894, in which there is a forceful article on "The Glacial Theory" by the Duke of Argyll; and recent numbers of the *Geological Magazine*, in which the subject has been treated by some of the most eminent of contemporary geologists. It has now been demonstrated that current notions respecting the Ice Age must be abandoned, and that the Glacial Theory, as held by extreme glacialists, must be materially altered in order adequately to account for the facts which it purports to interpret.

of the Ice Age have taken it for granted that the temperature which characterized this period was much lower than it is at present or has been during recent times. Such an assumption, however, is unwarranted. M. Charles Martin has shown that a lowering of the temperature by four degrees would be sufficient to explain all the phenomena of glaciation of the Ice Period. And this diminution of temperature may be regarded as a maximum, for it is a well-known fact, which no glacialist will deny, that moisture is even a more important factor in the production of glaciers than extreme cold. The river-beds and the alluvial deposits of the Ice Age attest the fact that this period was one of great humidity, as well as one of reduced temperature—that if it was characterized by an extraordinary extension of ice-fields in both the Old and New Worlds, it was no less marked for the great precipitation which then prevailed, and for the immense volumes of water which then coursed along channels that now convey but little water or are at times almost dry.

It is, too, a mistaken notion to imagine that we must go way back to the dim prehistoric past to find in Europe such a condition of humidity and reduced temperature. We have history to assure us that it obtained long after the advent of man in this part of the world—that we need not go back more than fifteen hundred or two thousand years to find climatic conditions quite different from those which are now prevalent, and winters whose rigors were far greater than anything that has ever been known in more modern times.

According to Herodotus, the climate of Scythia in

his day was about like that of Alaska or Labrador in our own. It as well as the country along the Danube was completely frost-bound during eight months of the year. The summer was characterized by torrential rains, a reminder of which we occasionally have—but at rare intervals—in those inundations that carry death and destruction before them, and which, when they do occur, are looked upon as national disasters.

Cæsar's account of the climate of Gaul, of the rigor of its winters, and of the excess of its rainfalls is the same as that given by the Father of History regarding the region of the Danube. The testimony of Varro, Cicero, Strabo, and Diodorus Siculus concerning the severity of the winters of Gaul are but confirmatory of that of Cæsar. So great, says Diodorus Siculus, is the cold of Gaul in winter "that almost all the rivers are frozen over, and natural bridges are formed over which large armies with their chariots and baggage pass in safety." Virgil and Ovid say the same thing of the glaciation of the Danube and the Euxine. Ovid tells us that not only has he seen the Danube frozen over, but that he has witnessed the whole of the Euxine covered with ice, and that he has walked on it when in this condition. More than this: he declares that so intense was the cold that even wine congealed and was broken into lumps when drunk. Virgil and Horace testify to the low temperature which prevailed in Italy, and picture to us climatic conditions existing in their day, as far south as the Campania of Rome and the ramparts of Tarentum, such as now characterize the winters of Northern Europe.

So intense was the cold of Scythia, declares Herodotus, that the ass, one of the hardiest of animals, was unable to live there. Aristotle makes the same statement about Gaul. For a similar reason, we are assured by Theophrastus, the olive could not be raised in Greece more than four hundred stadia from the sea. And according to the testimony of both Greek and Roman writers the arctic rigor of the climate of Gaul made it impossible to cultivate either the vine or the olive.

During the first centuries of the Christian era the climatic conditions of the portions of Europe we have named were, according to all contemporary writers who refer to the subject, essentially the same as they were in the times of Herodotus, Horace, and Ovid. It is unnecessary to indicate how much the climate has since changed, how entirely different it now is from what it was when Aristotle taught and Virgil sang. In reading the accounts left us of the former intense cold of countries where the climate is at present so mild we can almost imagine ourselves perusing the fanciful descriptions of some of our modern geologists and archæologists descanting on the rigors of the climate of the Glacial Period, when our troglodytic ancestors, clothed in the skins of wild beasts, shivering and suffering, huddled together in damp and gloomy caverns which afforded them their only available shelter from the biting blasts of winters that lasted for the greater portion of the year.

M. Fuster, who has made a profound investigation of the subject, declares emphatically that "if there is a settled fact of history, it is that of the extreme rigor of the climate of ancient Gaul. All testimonies, all opinions, all circumstances forcibly and unanimously proclaim the intensity of its cold, the superabundance of its rains, and the violence of its tempests. It is futile to contend against such a fact by invoking the aid of false notions or prejudices that are wholly without foundation. Like truth itself, it is sure, sooner or later, to be triumphant."[1] What M. Fuster here says of Gaul can with equal truth be predicated of the other countries of Europe just mentioned, for, from what we have already learned, they belong to the same category.

The change, then, from extreme cold to genial warmth has occurred within historic times. Might we not, if we had the light of history to guide us back a few more centuries or a few more thousands of years—for even the traditional chronology allows us this time—find all the rigor of climate, all the abundance of snow and ice, and all the excess of precipitation which geologists tell us were among the distinguishing features of that portion of the Quaternary Period known as the Ice Age? My opinion is that we should. A mean annual temperature a few degrees lower than it is at present, and a more humid condition of the atmosphere, are, as we have seen, all that is necessary enormously to augment the volume of our water-courses and to produce those mighty glaciers that at one time in the indefinable past wrapped extensive areas of both the Old World and the New in a deadly mantle of ice. Given a slight variation in our present thermometric and hygrometric conditions, and we should in a short time, as meteorology teaches us, witness all the phenomena of the Glacial Epoch. And such a variation would

[1] Quoted in the *Dictionnaire apologétique*, p. 215.

THE AGE OF THE HUMAN RACE.

effect in a few centuries—in a few thousand years at most—all the grand mutations for which geologists and archæologists demand tens of thousands and hundreds of thousands—yea, millions—of years.

In view, therefore, of these facts, and of a growing conviction which I entertain that many of the phenomena which modern scientists are wont to refer to the early Quaternary Period, or at least to the remote and unknown prehistoric past, really occurred within historic times, I decline to accede to the extravagant demands made by geologists and archæologists. Many, it is known, fall into error because, forsooth, they have some pet theory to support, or because, by reason of their environment, they are the victims, unconscious it may be, of delusions and of prejudices that color all their observations and vitiate all their conclusions. The antiquity of man may be much greater than has hitherto been supposed, but the evidence evoked from climatic changes which are presumed to have taken place since the advent of man is not conclusive. Hence of all inferences drawn from such premises we may simply and unhesitatingly say, *Non sequitur*.

The Age of the Mammoth and the Reindeer.

Another specious argument often advanced in favor of the remote antiquity of our race is the occurrence of undoubted human remains with those of animals long since extinct. Among the animals whose remains have most frequently been found with those of man are those of the elephant, the cave-lion, the cave-bear, the Irish elk, the cave-hyena, and the reindeer. But these animals, it was contended, all belonged to the geologic past—to the Quaternary Age at latest—and hence the universally received opinion that the appearance of man on the earth antedates by far the epoch assigned for his advent by the traditional chronology.

It has long been accepted as a fact that could not be gainsaid that man was contemporary with the mammoth. Remains of this species of elephant and human relics have been discovered in many places in Europe and America—especially in Europe—in the same deposits, and so commingled that it was regarded as certain that they belonged to the same epoch. And many were the ingenious theories that were evolved to account for the disappearance of this monster of "the forest primeval" to which not the slightest allusion has been made by any record that can be regarded as authentic. In America, in Great Britain, and in various parts of Europe bones of this giant pachyderm have been found in countless numbers. In Siberia the tusks are of such frequent occurrence as to give rise to a considerable traffic. All are familiar with the finding, in 1799, of one of these huge beasts encased in a large block of ice near the river Lena on the border of the Arctic Ocean, and remember that the flesh was in such a perfect state of preservation that dogs and other carnivorous animals ate it with avidity.[1]

---

[1] This singularly well-preserved specimen of the mammoth —or hairy elephant, as it is sometimes called—is now, as my readers are aware, in the great Museum of Natural History of St. Petersburg. It is by far the best specimen of the kind yet discovered. Some years ago, during a visit to the Czar's dominions, had an opportunity of examining it, and whilst pondering over some of the thoughts suggested by this

The mammoth, according to the majority of geologists, was regarded as the oldest of the animals coeval with man which are now found in a fossil state. Hence, as it was supposed to have disappeared some scores of thousands of years ago, man, if its contemporary, would have a very hoary antiquity indeed. Passing over the divers explanations that have been offered at various times of the difficulty raised, it will be quite sufficient for our present purpose to state that some of the ablest living archæologists deny *in toto* the coexistence of man and the mammoth. Among these may be signalized the distinguished and venerable archæologist of Copenhagen, J. Steenstrup, and Prof. Virchow of Berlin. The former, as the result of a critical examination of "the discoveries in Europe which are supposed to prove the contemporaneity of man with the mammoth, reached the conclusion that not only is the evidence inadequate, but for climatic and geologic reasons no such coexistence is possible." [1] This opinion is cordially endorsed by Virchow, who, with many of the members of the German Anthropological Association,

creature of another age and clime, addressed myself to the curator of the Museum, a learned German savant, well known in the world of science as one of the ablest of European naturalists, and asked him how long, in his estimation, it was since the mammoth became extinct. "How long?" quoth he, "how long? Forty thousand years, fifty thousand years, a hundred thousand years." He was not very positive about the exact number of years, as his answer indicates, but, like all the members of the school to which he belonged, he was an evolutionist of the most pronounced type; he affected to be certain that the lapse of time was to be measured by nothing less than multiples of tens of thousands of years.

[1] *Science*, February, 1893.

at their meeting in August, 1892, went even further, and declared that "the Reindeer Period was the remotest to which they were willing to assign the appearance of man in Europe on existing evidence."

According to the division of geologic time here referred to, the Mammoth Period was the first subdivision of the Quaternary Age. The Reindeer Period immediately followed. But the reindeer is still among existing animals. It did not become extinct, as did so many others that are alleged to have been contemporary with early man, but simply migrated to a colder climate. As all are aware, it is still found in large numbers in Northern Europe, especially in Lapland. In Cæsar's time it lived in much more southerly latitudes. In his *Commentaries* the Roman commander describes it as one of the strange animals in the Hercynian Forest.[1] The occurrence, therefore, of human remains in France and Germany together with those of the reindeer would not be evidence of the great antiquity of man, for it would not necessarily carry back the age of our race more than a few thousand years at most. And as there is reason to believe that the reindeer kept to the forests of Central Europe long after Cæsar's time, we are evidently dealing with a species of mammal that belongs to the historic as well as to a geologic period.

What has been said of the reindeer may, in a measure, be asserted of the urus, cave-bear, cave-lion, cave-hyena, and Irish elk. The urus is described by Cæsar, and at the time of the Roman invasion it ran wild in Gaul. It has, however, long since become extinct. As to the cave-bear, there is reason to believe that it

[1] *De Bell. Gall.*, vi. 26.

did not disappear until comparatively recent times. Certain it is that its remains have been found associated with those of some of our domestic animals. For this reason there are not wanting those who maintain, and not without show of reason, that the great bears referred to in the chronicles of the Middle Ages were none other than the cave-bears, also remarkable for their size, of the geologist and archæologist. The documents referring to the cave-lion and the cave-hyena as belonging to the fauna of Western Europe have not the same authenticity possessed by those that make mention of the cave-bear, the urus, and the reindeer. But the absence of all reliable historical data regarding them is, after all, no more than negative evidence. Considering to what an extent the whole of this part of the world was, even long after the time of the Romans, an immense *terra incognita*, it is not surprising that these animals, like many others that are known to have existed during this period, should have eluded observation or been passed over *in silence*. In view of the fact that immense numbers of lions are known formerly to have frequented parts of Northern Africa where they are now rarely if ever met with, and in view of the further fact that they existed in parts of Europe from which they have long since disappeared, it is far from unlikely—it seems, on the contrary, quite probable—that the king of animals was one of the denizens of the forests of Southern Gaul not only during the Roman period, but also during times long subsequent. We learn from the Greek writers that he formerly inhabited the forests of Thrace, Thessaly, and Macedonia, and from this and other facts of like import we may feel fully warranted in considering him as being, in Europe, the contemporary of the known fauna of the historical period. Regarding the great Irish elk—*Cervus megaceros*—whose remains are found in so many portions of the Old World, especially in France, Great Britain, and Ireland, it suffices to say that everything known about him seems to point to his extinction within historic times. Certain ancient records referring to him inform us that he was much sought after by the Romans, who had him brought from regions so remote as England.

There is, then, no valid reason for attributing to the animals named the great antiquity so frequently claimed for them. And there is, consequently, no reason for insisting on the great age of mankind because human relics have been found associated with the remains of animals that have been extinct for a long time, it is true, but not certainly during those untold ages of which geologists and a certain school of archæologists speak. There is surely nothing surprising in the fact that a half dozen or a dozen animals —the contemporaries of primitive man—should have disappeared in prehistoric times, when a much larger number of mammals and birds—forty or fifty species, at least—are known to have become extinct within historic times.[1] The wonder is rather that the number of species that died out in prehistoric times was not far greater—that there was not a hundred or more of them—considering the long lapse of time that intervened between the advent of man in Europe and the beginning of the historical period.

[1] See an interesting discussion on this subject in *Knowledge* for January, 1893. Cf. also *The Epoch of the Mammoth*, chap. xi., and *The Recent Origin of Man*, by James Southall.

In the early part of the last century the island of Rodriguez, in the Indian Ocean, was, according to the French writer Leguat, remarkable for the number and variety and uniqueness of its fauna.[1] Before the close of the century it had so completely disappeared that Leguat's testimony regarding it was called in question. Long subsequently, however, certain fossil remains were found in the soil which the eminent naturalist Milne-Edwards showed to be the relics of the identical species described by his fellow-countryman a century and a half before. The extinction of the bison in this country, where a few decades ago it roamed over our Western prairies in herds of thousands, if not tens of thousands, is an example before our own eyes of the short space of time required for the utter destruction of a numerous and a powerful species. For this and similar reasons that it is unnecessary here to multiply we should hesitate long before attempting to base an argument in favor of the great antiquity of man on the disparition of a few species of animals that are known to have been coetaneous with primitive man, but which, for all we know to the contrary, may have lived in historic as well as in prehistoric times.

[1] See "Adventures of François Leguat," in the *Edinburgh Review* for April, 1892.

CHAPTER III.

THE ANTIQUITY OF MAN ACCORDING TO PREHISTORIC ARCHÆOLOGY.—GEOLOGICAL CHRONOMETERS.

THE ARCHÆOLOGICAL ARGUMENT.

THE argument of all others in favor of man's great antiquity is that founded on the gradual and peculiar evolution of the industrial arts, the conclusiveness of which argument most archæologists consider as now beyond dispute. During the last few decades especially this argument has had a special interest attached to it, and a new force given it, on account of the numerous and important finds made not only in Europe, but also in America. Various objects of human industry, of ancient but uncertain date, tools, weapons, and implements of divers kinds employed by primitive man, have been unearthed and compared, and the result arrived at, we are informed, has been that the teachings of history and the Bible anent the age of our species have to be either greatly modified or altogether abandoned.

We have seen, in a previous chapter, that Hesiod, together with the majority of the earlier Greek and Oriental writers, regarded mankind as having descended from a higher to a lower plane—that the men of the later periods of the world's history were degraded—or decivilized, to use a more expressive word—in comparison with those who lived happy and god-

THE AGE OF THE HUMAN RACE. 267

like lives in the Golden Age of humanity's first beginnings.

Archæologists divide the first period of human history into three ages, called, in the order of succession, the Stone Age, the Bronze Age, and the Iron Age. These ages have, by certain writers, been divided into a greater or less number of sub-ages, but shall here retain the division just given, which was the one adopted by Danish archæologists when the foundations of the science of prehistoric archæology were first laid.[1]

If the evolution theory of the origin of man and of the development of civilization be true, we should expect to find the archæological division universally true and apply equally to all peoples in all parts of the world. But is this a fact? An answer to this question necessarily precedes a reply to the query regarding the antiquity of the human species.

THE STONE AGE.

There does not seem to be any doubt that in certain parts of Europe, perhaps throughout the greater por-

---

[1] The division of primitive time into periods of stone, bronze, and iron, although brought into general use by the Danish archæologists, notably E. C. Thomsen, is not of modern origin. It occurs in a book written by one Gognet nearly a century and a half ago. More than this: the same division is found in the *De Rerum Natura* (Lib. V. v. 1282 et seq.) of the Roman poet Lucretius. His words are:

> "Arma antiqua manus, ungues dentesque fuerunt
> Et lapides. . . .
> Posterius ferri vis est ærisque recepta,
> Et prior æris erat quam ferri cognitus usus,
> Quo facilis magis est natura et copia major."

tion of it, the Stone Age preceded the ages of Bronze and Iron. The reason for this belief is that the earliest implements met with are invariably of stone, at first rough and rude, but at a later date often beautifully polished and of delicate workmanship. With these are also found implements of horn and bone, which, in lieu of metal, constituted for primitive man the chief if not the sole materials available for the manufacture of the simple tools and weapons necessary for purposes of defence or for hunting beasts of the chase. In localities marked by several successive civilizations we frequently, but not always, find a series of deposits, the lowest of which contain only stone implements, those immediately above bronze, while the last in the order of time are characterized by the occurrence, in greater or less numbers, of implements of iron.

It would be a mistake, however, to imagine that the Stone Age marks a fixed period in human history, and that it prevailed at the same time in all lands and among all peoples. Nothing could be farther from the truth. While one nation or one tribe was living in the Age of Stone, its next neighbor may have been enjoying the advantages of the Age of Bronze or of Iron. Even now, in all the effulgence of the much-vaunted civilization of the nineteenth century, the Stone Age still continues in some parts of the world. To give only a few instances, it still persists in some of the islands of the South Pacific, among the Fuegians, the Esquimaux, and certain other tribes of the Pacific coast of North America. In Europe the use of stone for implements was not abandoned until a comparatively recent period, if, indeed, it can even now be said to be entirely discarded. According to two archæologists of recognized authority, Lartet and Christy, weapons and tools of stone were employed by the inhabitants of Western Europe until the Roman invasion, and probably until a later period. Records of undoubted authenticity tell us that flint hatchets and stone battle-axes were used from the fifth to the seventh century. At a much later epoch—about the year 920—according to Irish chronicles, stone projectiles were employed in a battle against the Danes near Limerick. Similar projectiles, we are informed, were used at the battle of Hastings in 1066. Nor is this all. There is every reason to believe that over a century later, in 1298, stone weapons were employed by the Scottish soldiery under Wallace. In Japan the Age of Stone and Bronze lasted until the present century, and in parts of China it still endures.

The Ages of Bronze and Iron.

If there is no fixed period of time for the Stone Age, neither is there a hard and fast line of demarcation between the Age of Stone and that of Bronze, or between the Age of Bronze and that of Iron. They frequently overlap one another, and are in many instances even quite synchronous. This is especially so in the case of the Age of Polished Stone and the Age of Bronze. Indeed, to so great an extent is this true that many eminent archæologists have not hesitated to declare that implements of polished stone and bronze must be referred to one and the same age. Thus the distinguished Dutch archæologist, M. Leemans, denies the distinction between the Age of Bronze and the Age of Stone in Holland. And M. Alexandre Bertrand, one of the most eminent of French archæologists, at the Congress of Archæologists held a few years ago at Stockholm declared that "there was in reality no Age of Bronze in Italy and Gaul."

Again: it would be equally wide of the truth to assert, as is so often done, that all peoples passed through the three phases of civilization indicated by the Ages of Stone, Bronze, and Iron. This is so far from being the case that numerous instances are citable where there are but two ages, and sometimes even not more than one. M. Bertrand in referring to this subject does not hesitate to assert that "this absolute doctrine of the succession of three ages, which has been proclaimed a law without exception, is, in our opinion, the opposite of the truth."[1]

Thus some of the more barbarous tribes of the earth are still in the Stone Age, and have never known any other. Again, there are others, even in Europe, that have never known a Bronze Age, properly so called, but who passed directly from the Stone to the Iron Age. In some parts of the world the Ages of Stone and Bronze have been synchronous; in others, those of Bronze and Iron. In still others, notably in parts of Western Asia, we have evidence of the contemporaneous use of stone, bronze, and iron from time immemorial. From the fact that stone, bronze, and iron implements are found together in Chaldean tombs and Assyrian ruins, and that, too, from the earliest dawn of the human period, archæologists of note have inferred that neither Chaldea nor Assyria ever knew the Ages of Bronze and Iron as distinct from that of Stone. M. Oppert declares that Babylonia and Assyria had

[1] *Revue archeologique*, p. 334, for the year 1875.

neither a Bronze nor an Iron Age, while M. Chabas rejects altogether the distinction of the three ages for Egypt.[1] But, more remarkable still, we find that in the case of the majority of the tribes of Africa, excluding the Egyptians, the only age that has ever existed is the Age of Iron. Stone has been used, and is still employed, but from the most remote period that archæology has been able to reach iron has been in common use, while bronze has been entirely unknown. Dr. Livingston, in his interesting *Narrative of an Expedition to the Zambesi and its Tributaries*, informs us that no flints are found in this part of the "Dark Continent," and that there are no indications whatever of a Stone Age. So universally is iron used for tools and weapons that rude furnaces for smelting it are met with in every third or fourth village, and the metal here produced is preferred by the natives to that imported from England.[2]

Yet more. Not only are the distinctions based on the existence of the three ages vague and misleading —not only do the ages vary in time and place, being earlier in some countries and later in others, lasting for long and indefinite periods among some peoples, and being among others of short duration—but there is also a more important fact to be noted, one indeed,

---

[1] Mr. Flinders Petrie, in his *Ten Years' Diggings in Egypt*, has demonstrated conclusively that implements of stone, copper, and bronze were long concurrent in the valley of the Nile, and that stone implements of the twelfth dynasty are identical in form and workmanship with those found in tombs belonging to the fourth dynasty. Indeed, instruments of stone were in general use in Egypt until shortly before the Christian era.

[2] P. 561 et seq.

that is entirely subversive of the evolution theory of primitive man.

According to the brilliant researches of Dr. Schliemann at Hissarlik, the site of ancient Troy, and at Mycenæ, there was neither a Stone Age nor a Metal Age in Greece and Asia Minor. More than this: the arguments that the evolution school of archæology has based on the development of civilization, as attested by the alleged gradual transition from the use of stone to that of bronze and from bronze to iron, is here decidedly negatived. In the finds at Troy especially there is the most striking evidence of devolution, or degeneration of the inhabitants who successively occupied this historic spot. Here, as well as at Mycenæ, the ornaments and implements discovered even in the lowest strata, far from indicating a state of savagery and utter degradation, betoken one of high civilization, and of as thorough an acquaintance with the working of metals and the fictile arts as was displayed at subsequent periods. In the light of Schliemann's discoveries, not to speak of others pointing in the same direction made in Egypt and among the ruins of Assyria and Babylonia, bearing on the condition of primitive man in the Orient, the conclusion seems to be inevitable that Hesiod was right, and that the modern evolution school is wrong—that the history of our race is not one of development, but one of degeneration. Thus the story of the Fall as recorded in Holy Writ is corroborated by the declarations of the newest of the sciences, which is but of yesterday—prehistoric archæology.[1]

[1] It is well to state here, once for all, that the word *prehistoric* does not have the absolute signification so often attributed to it

The chronological system of the Scandinavian archæologists has been prolific of other errors besides those just enumerated. It has, for instance, assumed that primeval man understood the manufacture and use of bronze before he had learned the art of smelting iron. In the opinion, however, of the most expert metallurgists this view is so improbable that it borders on the absurd. Thus, Mr. John Percy, one of the ablest metallurgists of the age, declares that from the point of view of metallurgy the Age of Iron should precede that of Bronze. "When archæologists," he tells us, "maintain the contrary, they should remember that iron by its very nature cannot be preserved in the earth so long as bronze." Col. Tschering, a Dane, as the result of long experience in the manufacture of ordnance, stated emphatically at a recent archæological congress at Copenhagen that a knowledge of iron should date back much farther than that of bronze, for the reason that the latter is much more difficult to prepare than the former, and requires the employment of iron and steel tools. "So undoubted is this fact," declares Horstmann in his criticism of the "three-age theory," "that it would involve a contradiction of all our technical knowledge to admit that objects of bronze have been fabricated by means of bronze tools.

by certain archæologists. It refers to that which is anterior only to *local* history, and not that which is prior to all history. Everything in America is prehistoric that antedates the discovery of the country by Europeans. It is evident, therefore, that certain objects found in one part of the world may be classed as prehistoric, while similar objects in other countries would be regarded as historic.

Such teaching is the disgrace of contemporary archæology."[1]

PHŒNICIAN BRONZE.

The bronze used in Europe in prehistoric times, and even much of that which was used in historic times, was an imported product. It was undoubtedly brought by the Phœnicians, the great manufacturing and trading nation of the ancient world, and given in exchange for other articles of commerce. So well attested is this fact that it cannot, I think, be disputed. The use of bronze, therefore, in parts of Northern and Western Europe prior to the use of iron in these same portions of the world, does not, then, as many have erroneously imagined, prove that man acquired the art of working bronze sooner than he did that of producing iron, but simply that with the Phœnicians bronze wares were more common articles of merchandise than those of iron.

As to the time that has elapsed since the beginning and the close of the Stone, Bronze, and Iron Ages, it may readily be surmised that the most diverse and extravagant views have obtained. Of these I shall have nothing to say, but shall confine myself to a brief consideration of facts that are known to be authentic and to conclusions that may be accepted as most probable.

The Age of Iron, even according to those who claim a great antiquity for our race, was posterior to the alleged Age of Bronze. But when in European countries was the Age of Bronze ushered in, and when did

[1] Quoted in the *Revue des Questions scientifiques*, p. 256, July, 1880.

it close? A satisfactory answer to this question is of paramount importance, because it is the pivot on which turns much of the controversy regarding the antiquity of man.

What has just been stated regarding the bronze traffic of Phœnician traders, together with what history tells us concerning the mining for tin by the Phœnicians in the Cassiterides, and possibly also in Spain, supplies us with a key for the solution of all apparent difficulties.

The period of commercial prosperity for Phœnicia, when her ships—those famous "ships of Tarshish"—sailed all known seas, and her merchants carried on traffic with the inhabitants of the most distant lands, and even with those of far-off Scandinavia, it is thought extended approximately from the twelfth to the fifth century before the Christian era. And this is the epoch, according to the latest and most reliable researches, during which the many objects of bronze, mostly of Phœnician design and manufacture, there is reason to believe, were distributed over Western, Central, and Northern Europe. This would place the so-called Bronze Age in the neighborhood of 1000 years B. C. But this probably is assigning it a maximum antiquity. From observations made on alluvial deposits at the mouth of the Loire, M. Kerviler fixes the beginning of the Bronze Age at 500 B. C. The stratification of the alluvium at this point indicates in the most remarkable way the annual rate of accretion, and furnishes the nearest approach to a reliable geologic chronometer of anything yet discovered. For this reason, and because they agree so well with the teachings of history, we may regard M. Kerviler's conclusions as approximately correct.[1] According to the Danish archæologist Worsaae it did not terminate in Denmark until A. D. 200. Bertrand tells us that it prevailed in Germany until the fourth century after Christ, and in Ireland it is known to have lasted until the eighth or ninth century.[2]

IMPOSSIBILITY OF FIXING DATES OF THE THREE AGES.

As to the Iron Age in Scandinavia, it belonged, if we are to credit two of the ablest authorities on the subject, Desor and Worsaae, to the fourth and sixth centuries after Christ. The Age of Iron in Gaul dates back to a much earlier period, probably to the fourth century before our era. This is about the time when the Gauls, properly so called, crossed the Rhine and the Alps and made themselves masters of Eastern France, then occupied by the Celts. Judging from the finds in the celebrated necropolis of Hallstatt, the Iron Age began in Austria one or two centuries earlier.

The Stone Age terminated in Denmark, according to Worsaae, about 500 or 600 B. C. This, however, may be questioned, because stone, as is well known, continued in use in Asia Minor until 700 B. C., and in many parts of Western Europe, as we have already learned, until a much later period. As the result of an extended series of observations made on the alluvial deposits of the valley of the Saone, M. de Ferry attrib-

---

[1] Southall's *Epoch of the Mammoth*, chap. xxiv.
[2] According to Siegfried Mittler, in his *Merkbuch Alterthümer Aufzugraben*, the introduction of metals into Europe does not antedate the fifth century B. C.

utes to the Stone Age an antiquity of nine or ten thousand years. From similar observations the distinguished French archæologist, M. Arcelin, obtains for the Stone Age an antiquity of from six thousand seven hundred to eight thousand years. These figures closely agree with those which historians assign for the beginning of the civilizations of Egypt and Mesopotamia. They are, however, in opposition to those derived from the generally accepted chronology of the Bible, unless, indeed, we admit, as it seems we may, the existence of antediluvian man in Europe, and allow further that he escaped the great cataclysm known as the Noachian Deluge.[1] It seems impossible otherwise to account for the existence in Europe of the Basques and Finns, whose peculiar ethnological position separates them entirely from the Aryan or Japhetic branch of the human family. Regarding them of Adamic instead of Noachic descent, and admitting that they, as the precursors in Europe of the Celts and Gauls, escaped the devastating waters of the Flood, we have no difficulty, as we shall see in the sequel, in reconciling even the high figures of prehistoric archæology with those of scriptural chronology.

But the fact is, it is utterly impossible to arrive at anything even approximating exact dates for any of the three ages. They are, as we have seen, different for different peoples. In some parts of the world we have only one age represented, in others two, in others still all three. Sometimes they occur in succession, more frequently they overlap one another, very often

---

[1] See the author's article on this subject in the *American Ecclesiastical Review* for February, 1893.

they are synchronous. For this reason, therefore, to construct a system of chronology based on the implements of stone, bronze, and iron that have been used by man in the prehistoric past is, at least in the present state of science, clearly impracticable.

Relics of Primitive Man.

What has been said of the futility of all attempts to arrive at a system of chronology based on the various objects of human industry to which we have referred obviously applies with equal force to the skulls and other bones of primitive man that have attracted so much attention during the past few decades. They can no more than the implements of stone and bronze and iron so far discovered be accepted as evidence of the great antiquity of the human race. Referring to the Canstatt and Neanderthal skulls, about which so much has been written, and the numerous theories based on them, Dr. Brinton, one of the most competent of American archæologists, well observes that "it should be recognized, once for all, that there is no sort of foundation for these dreams. In neither instance did the locality in which these skulls were found guarantee them any high antiquity." The same views were expressed at the meeting, August, 1892, of the German Anthropological Association "by such speakers as Von Holder, Virchow, Kollman, and Fraas. Their arguments leave no room to doubt the importance of these remains." [1]

Of the tumuli and megalithic monuments of Europe,

[1] "Current Notes on Anthropology," in *Science* for February 10, 1893.

which have been thought to argue so great an antiquity for man, it will suffice to state here that, on closer examination, objects of bronze and relics of the Roman period have been found in many of them. Even in the oldest of them, in those that archæologists were wont to consider as belonging to the Stone Age, iron is of frequent occurrence. Hence it is safe to affirm that most of these structures, far from having the great age so often attributed to them, postdate the Christian era, and in some instances by several centuries.

The shell-mounds or kitchen-middings that are found in various parts of America and Europe, especially on the eastern coast of Denmark, are likewise often appealed to as evidence of the great age of our species. Since, however, objects of bronze and iron and articles of undoubted Roman workmanship have been found in many of them, most archæologists have been forced to admit for them a much more recent date, and to allow them "to be taken out of the category of the evidences for the antiquity of man."

About forty years ago special attention was directed by Dr. Keller to the *palafittes* or lake-dwellings of Switzerland. They were at once seized upon as proof positive of the venerable antiquity of man. Prof. L. Agassiz, in referring to them some years after their discovery, did not hesitate to assert that "humanity is now connected with geological phenomena." Further investigation, however, disclosed, even in the oldest of the lake-dwellings, traces of copper and bronze, thus showing that they belonged to a recent epoch. Then, too, it was pointed out that the Roman soldiers under Trajan must have encountered pile-dwellers on the lakes of Austria or on the Danube, as they are represented on the celebrated triumphal column of Trajan in Rome. It was remembered also that both Herodotus and Hippocrates expressly mention lacustrine villages as existing in their day. The former tells of pile-dwellers who lived on Lake Prasias in Macedonia; the latter describes a similar settlement on the Phasis in Asia Minor. Still later and more careful researches showed conclusively that lake-dwellings in various parts of Europe were inhabited during the Middle Ages. In Switzerland there is incontestable evidence of their being occupied as late as the sixth century of our era. M. Chantre has proved that in France "there existed lacustrine habitations down to the Carlovingian epoch." In the north of Europe, we are told by Prof. Virchow, they were in existence as late as the tenth or the eleventh century, whilst in Ireland, under the name of *crannoges*, they are known to have been occupied as late as the sixteenth century. More than this, they are still found in various parts of the world—in equatorial Africa, in the islands of the Pacific, in Venezuela, in New Guinea, in Borneo, and elsewhere. But yet more remarkable is the fact that "the fishermen of Lake Prasias still inhabit wooden cottages over water, as in the days of Herodotus."[1]

In view of all these facts we may heartily endorse the words of Mr. W. H. Holmes of the Smithsonian Institution when he says that "the whole discussion of early man has been so surcharged with misconceptions of fact and errors of interpretation that all is vitiated as a stream with impurities about its source.

[1] *The Epoch of the Mammoth*, p. 60.

Until an exhaustive scientific study of the origin, form, genesis, and meaning of all the handiwork of man made use of in the discussion is completed the discussion of man and culture is worse than useless, and speculation can lead but to embarrassment and disaster." [1]

Geological Chronometers.

The great difficulty, as already intimated, experienced by scientists in arriving at accordant conclusions respecting the antiquity of our species arises from the total lack of anything approaching a reliable natural chronometer. The most satisfactory one so far known is, as has been said, that discovered at St. Nazaire by the French engineer, M. Kerviler. But this has been either ignored or rejected as unavailable by the new school of prehistorians, "because," as Canon Hamard shrewdly observes, "it labors under the grave inconvenience of harmonizing too closely with the traditional chronology." [2] The futile attempts to estimate time by the rate of growth of peat or the deposition of alluvium or the formation of stalagmites we have already considered. Arguments based on certain lava deposits, on the rate of growth of coral-reefs or erosion of rocks, or on the former extension of glaciers over portions of Europe and America, are equally worthless. As an illustration of the utter insufficiency of any of the various methods employed by men of science in evaluating

[1] "Gravel Man and Palæolithic Culture," etc., in *Science* for January 20, 1893.
[2] *Dictionnaire apologétique*, art. "Chronomètres naturels."

geologic time, and of the widely-different results to which such methods may give rise, I shall instance the chronometer to which geologists most frequently appeal, and which is regarded by the majority of them as the most reliable time-measurer which they, thus far, have at their disposal.

The chronometer in question is the well-known gorge between Niagara Falls and Queenstown. Assuming that the entire gorge from Lake Ontario to Niagara has been eroded by the gradually-receding cataract, and assuming further, as all glacialists do, that the birth of the falls dates from the retrogression of the great ice-sheet that enveloped this portion of territory during the Glacial Period, the problem is to determine the amount of time that has been required for the formation of this gorge, and to estimate the number of years that have elapsed since the close of the Ice Age at this point.

It is perfectly manifest that if we could ascertain the rate of recession of the falls the problem would become a very simple one indeed. All that would then be necessary would be to divide the length of the gorge—about seven miles—by the rate of recession per annum.

But two grave difficulties present themselves. It is not, in the first place, certain that the entire gorge is the result of post-glacial action. On the contrary, there are many able glacialists who contend that a portion of the ravine was eroded before the Glacial Period, and that we have, as yet, no means of knowing just how much of the work has been done since the torrent of Niagara began to pour over its escarpment at Queenstown. In the second place, in spite of the

THE AGE OF THE HUMAN RACE. 283

numerous attempts to determine the rate of recession of the falls, the most conflicting results have been reached, and that, too, by those who, we should think, were most competent to grapple with the problem.

According to the distinguished Swiss geologist, Desor, the rate of recession of the falls is not more than one foot in a century. This would carry back the date when this grand chronometer was first set going full three million five hundred thousand years. Sir Charles Lyell estimated the maximum rate of erosion to be one foot per annum, and fixed the beginning of the cataract at thirty-five thousand years ago. The English geologist, Bakewell, together with other careful observers, calculated the rate of retrogression to be two or three feet a year. Mr. C. K. Gilbert, of the United States Geological Survey, and Mr. R. S. Woodward of Washington, as the result of very careful measurements determined the average rate of recession to be five feet per annum. Hence, Mr. Gilbert, who is universally recognized as one of the most careful and reliable of observers and one of the most eminent authorities in such matters, does not hesitate to declare that the "maximum length of time since the birth of the falls by the separation of the lakes is only seven thousand years, and that even this small measure may need significant reduction."

An evidence of the truth of the conclusions arrived at by Gilbert and Woodward is the remarkable manner in which they agree with the results obtained by other observers by the employment sometimes of similar, and sometimes of different, methods of computation.

If the beginning of Niagara Falls marks, as has been

assumed, the disappearance of the great ice-sheet at this point, it is but natural to infer that observations made at other cataracts in the same or nearly the same latitude would indicate, at least approximately, the same date for the close of the Glacial Period. Thus, according to Professor Winchell, the average rate of recession of the Falls of St. Anthony since they first started at Fort Snelling, a little over eight miles below the present cataract, has been a trifle more than five and a half feet per year. This would fix the date of the birth of the falls at Fort Snelling at 7803 years. A detailed study of divers minor waterfalls and gorges in Ohio by Professor Wright fully sustains the calculations regarding the falls of St. Anthony and Niagara. After carefully examining Lake Lahontan in Nevada and Lake Bonneville in Utah—two bodies of water which M. de Lapparent aptly designates as *fossil pluviometers*—Gilbert and Russell regard ten thousand years as the maximum of duration for the Post-Glacial Epoch. By a study of the modified drift in the Connecticut Valley a like estimate is obtained. From observations which he made concerning the average rate at which the waters of Lake Michigan are eroding its banks and washing the sediment into deeper water, Dr. E. Andrews of Chicago concludes that the lakes which date from the Glacial Period cannot have been in existence more than seventy-five hundred years. M. Arcelin arrives at precisely the same result by the study of the alluvial deposits of the Saone. Calculations based on lakes and kettle-holes in New England and the North-west all lead to identical conclusions.

It seems, therefore, demonstrably certain that the age of the chronometers just referred to is much less than certain even eminent geologists have imagined. We hence infer that the Ice Age, far from having the antiquity so often attributed to it, is of quite recent date. The same must then be said of man, whose advent was probably synchronous with the latter portion of the reign of ice. It is consequently impossible for the gorges, lake-basins, and kettle-holes which we have been considering to " have existed for the indefinite periods sometimes said to have elapsed since the Glacial Era, while eternity itself is scarcely long enough for the development of species if the rate of change is no greater than is implied if man and his companions, both of the animal and vegetable kingdoms, were substantially what they now are as long ago as the date often assigned to the great Ice Age."[1]

AGE OF THE EARTH.

It is because it has fancied that it has unlimited time at its disposal, that it has almost "eternity itself" to draw on, that the evolutionary school, "under the influence of Darwinian prejudices," has handled time with such a strange laxity, and has talked of the millions of years that must be attributed to even the shortest of the geologic periods.

According to the Uniformitarian school of geologists, the origin of life upon the earth must be referred back full five hundred million years. As the result of certain calculations regarding the rate of erosion of the earth's surface and of the deposition of sedimentary rocks, the Rev. H. N. Hutchinson thinks that no less

[1] Wright's *Great Ice Age in North America*, chap. xx.

than six hundred million years have been required for the formation of the known stratified rocks of the earth's crust.[1] To accomplish this same work Sir Archibald Geike requires a period lasting somewhere between seventy-three million and six hundred and eighty millions of years.[2] Professor Samuel Haughton requires "for the whole duration of geological time a minimum of two hundred million years." T. Mellard Reade's estimate is ninety-five millions. Dana places the earth's age since the formation of the first fossiliferous rock sat forty-eight million years. Alfred Russell Wallace reduces the figure to twenty-eight millions. Mr. C. D. Walcott, as the result of a study of the sedimentary rocks of a restricted area of the Western portion of the United States, opines that the time which has elapsed since the Archæan Era has been about forty-five million years. Professor Warren Upham thinks that "the time needed for the deposition of the earth's stratified rocks and the unfolding of its plant and animal life must be about a hundred million years." Mr. W. J. McGee, reasoning from the same premises, demands seven billions of years for this portion of the earth's duration, and twice this amount of time for the period that has elapsed since it began its existence as a planet.[3] In the first edition of his *Origin of Species*, Darwin claimed three hundred and six million six hundred and sixty-two thousand four hundred years for "the denudation of the Weald," which he informed us was "a mere trifle" in comparison with that which was requisite for the establishing

---

[1] *Knowledge*, September, 1893.
[2] *Nature*, August 4, 1892.
[3] *American Anthropologist*, October, 1892.

of his theory. These are large figures, it is true, but they are still small beside the "milliards of thousands of years" which Häckel assures us have elapsed since man's original ancestor—the primal, self-created moneron—appeared on this globe of ours.

Unfortunately, however, for geologists and biologists who worship at the altar of Chronos, mathematicians and physicists and astronomers have interposed a strong demurrer against the assumption of such countless æons, and have shown cause why their demurrer should stand.

According to computations made long ago by Sir William Thomson—now Lord Kelvin—and based on a study of the earth's internal heat and its rate of radiation into space, the whole of geologic time must be limited within a period of one hundred million years. Proceeding from similar data, Professor Tait affirms that if the earth existed at all one hundred million years ago, it was in a fluid condition and at a white heat, and concludes that it is impossible to allow geologists "more scope for their speculation than about ten million, or say, at most, fifteen, millions of years."[1]

The distinguished French astronomer, Faye, in his profound work *Sur l'Origine du Monde*,[2] and Prof. S. Newcomb, hold substantially the same views. The latter says in reference to this subject: "If we reflect that a

[1] *Recent Advances in Physical Science.* The distinguished French geologist, M. de Lapparent, in referring to the computations of geologists and physicists, remarks : "Contentons-nous de ces résultats et admettons qu'il ne soit pas déraisonable de renfermer entre 20 et 100 million d'années le temps nécessaires au dépôt de tous les terrains de sediment."—*Traité de Géologie*, p. 1468.

[2] Chap. xiv.

diminution of the solar heat by less than one-fourth its amount would probably make our earth so cold that all the water on its surface would freeze, while an increase by much more than one-half would probably boil the water all away, it must be admitted that the balance of causes which would result in the sun radiating heat just fast enough to preserve the earth in its present state has probably not existed more than ten millions years."[1]

Mr. George H. Darwin, professor of Mathematics in Cambridge University, by computing the influence of tidal friction in retarding the rotation of the earth, arrives at the conclusion that fifty-seven millions years ago the length of the day was less than seven hours, that the moon was only one-seventh of its present distance from the earth, whilst the time of a lunar revolution was but a trifle more than a day and a half. Such a condition of things as Ball has pointed out would suppose, if there were then any water on the earth's surface, the existence of tides six hundred feet high, sweeping around the world every four hours and utterly destructive of every form of animal or vegetable life.

From a long series of careful experiments on the rock diabase in its relations to heat and pressure, Clarence King, of the United States Geological Survey, computes the entire age of the earth from the beginning of its planetary existence to be not more than twenty-four million years.[2] Accepting as true Lord Kelvin's conclusions regarding the age of the sun, as given in a lecture at the Royal Institution of Great Britain some years ago, Sir J. W. Dawson reduces "the

[1] *Popular Astronomy*, p. 511.
[2] *The American Journal of Science*, January, 1893.

whole of geological time since the formation of the oldest Laurentian rocks" to about six million years, or possibly less,[1] and concludes that the facts both of geology and astronomy beautifully "harmonize in point of time with those of the Bible history."

Fantastical Theories.

Another great source of error has been the disposition of geologists to build theories on trifles and to draw conclusions from facts but partially or imperfectly observed. Thus from a few flint flakes discovered in France and Portugal, M. de Mortillet does not hesitate to deduce an argument for the existence of Tertiary man, or for that of some intelligent being who was man's predecessor, to whom he assigns an antiquity of more than a quarter of a million of years. On more careful examination, however, these flints are proven by the most eminent authorities—Virchow and Evans among others—to have been produced by the operation of natural causes—by solar heat or accidental percussion, for instance—and to afford no evidence whatever of the action of man or other intelligent being. The flint flakes, bulbs, or conchoids of percussion, as they are sometimes called, on which M. de Mortillet bases his fanciful hypotheses are numbered by hundreds of thousands. If he could demonstrate that they were fashioned by human hands, and were not the product of natural forces, he would, considering the number of specimens at his disposal, have a very strong argument indeed. This he is unable to do. There are others, again, who are prepared to make

[1] *Modern Science in Bible Lands*, p. 175.

a profession of faith regarding the existence of Tertiary man on much slighter evidence. *Two* flint flakes, such as those just instanced, are offered by Boyd Dawkins as evidence of the existence of Tertiary man in England. *Credat Apelles Judæus!* A few years ago a bone was found in one of the English caves under glacial clay, and pronounced by some of the best-known scientists of the day to be a human fibula, and to be therefore a certain indication of the existence of man in Pre-Glacial times. The bone was subsequently submitted to a careful examination by experts, and pronounced to be that of a *bear*, or, in the learned phraseology of the committee, it was declared to be "ursine" rather than "human," while others equally competent to diagnose the case came to the conclusion that it might be almost any bone. In like manner certain notched or incised bones have been adduced as evidence of the existence of Miocene man. The incisions, it was argued, were such as could be made only by instruments of human manufacture. It is now known that similar cuts are made on bones that have been gnawed by the porcupine and other animals. Nor is this all. Sundry sharpened sticks found in certain Inter-Glacial deposits are appealed to as the handiwork of man and as conclusive evidence of the great antiquity of the human race. But scarcely is this ingenious theory advanced when it is shown that similar sharpened sticks can be and have been fashioned by beavers.[1] From a number of rudely-flaked stones found in the gravel-beds of Trenton, Dr. C. C. Abbott builds up an ingenious theory regarding the existence of a race of men of peculiar culture in the Delaware Val-

---

[1] *Epoch of the Mammoth*, pp. 407, 408.

ley in Glacial times, ten thousand or more years ago. Mr. Holmes makes a critical investigation of these deposits and flaked stones under exceptionally favorable circumstances, and comes to the conclusion, which I heartly endorse, that "the phenomena observed may all be accounted for as a result of the vicissitudes of aboriginal life and occupation within the last few hundred years as fully and as satisfactorily as by jumping thousands of years backward into the unknown"[1]

In 1857 was discovered near Düsseldorf the famous Neanderthal skull that occasioned such a flutter of excitement in the scientific world. Prof. Schaffhausen adjudged it to be "the most ancient memorial of the early inhabitants of Europe." Prof. Fuhlrott wrote a book on it in which he declared the age of the relic to be from two hundred to three hundred thousand years. But this estimate was soon proven to be as extravagant as it was unwarranted. Dr. Mayer, of Bonn, as the result of a critical examination of the "fossil" and the locality in which it was found, came to the conclusion that it was the skull of a Cossack killed in 1814!

Truly while examining some of the evidence presented by geolgists in favor of the antiquity of man one cannot help saying with Goethe: "The thing the most terrible to hear is the constantly reiterated assurance that geologists agree on a given point." For one who knows men it is easy to divine what this means. Persons of vivid and bold imaginations take possession of an idea and give it all the appearance of probability. They soon have followers and disciples, and

[1] "Glacial Man in the Trenton Gravels," in the *Journal of Geology*, vol. i., 1893, p. 32.

when these are somewhat numerous they are always looked upon as possessing special authority in science. Hundreds of educated men, occupied with other duties, are satisfied to leave to these adventurous explorers their chosen domain, and to give their approbation to all that does not affect them individually. This is what is called the unanimous consent of the learned.[1]

How applicable to the fantasies and idle babble, the seethings of brain and the vibrations of nerve of some of our modern scientists are the following lines of a contemporary versificator!—

> "Oh the thoughts, the revelations of our age that lie enshrined in the caldron of man's mind!
> How they seethe, how they simmer, how they swim, and how they swirl,
> How they wriggle, how they wrestle, how they whisk, and how they whirl!"

[1] Baumner's *Kreuzzeugen*, i. p. 70, "Goethe als Naturforscher."

CHAPTER IV.

THE ANTIQUITY OF MAN ACCORDING TO THE BIBLE.

BIBLICAL CHRONOLOGY UNDECIDED.

AFTER a long and tedious, but nevertheless necessary, excursion into the domains of history, astronomy, physical geography, and prehistoric archæology, we are at the long last prepared to discuss the question of scriptural chronology. This portion of our subject, however, although fully as important as that which precedes, can, fortunately for the reader, be disposed of much more briefly. But this is not because of any certainty respecting the data of biblical chronology, nor because the Church has rendered any decision regarding the question of the antiquity of our race. In some respects at least the chronology of the Bible is almost as vague and as uncertain as the various chronologies which we have been considering, while as regards the Church she is committed to no system of chronology and has defined nothing concerning the antiquity of man. As the learned and pious Abbé le Hir well observes, "Biblical chronology floats in an undecided state; it pertains to the human sciences to determine the date of the creation of our species. But let scientists await irrefragable proofs; let them avoid exaggerations and illusions, and let them not give as certain facts that are only probable or are no facts at all. When certitude in this respect shall have been acquired all discussion will be at an end, because all divergence shall have ceased."[1] Sylvester de Sacy, one of the ablest authorities on the subject, goes further and says: "There is no biblical chronology." Of substantially the same opinion are Hettinger, Valroger, and Lenormant, all of whom are noted for their learning and their devotion to Holy Church. Cardinal Manning, in his *Temporal Mission of the Holy Ghost*,[2] expresses the same view when he declares that "no system of chronology is laid down in the sacred books."

What may be said of biblical chronology may likewise, so far as the Scriptures are concerned, be affirmed of the vexed question of the antiquity of man. There is nothing certain about it, and scientists and apologists have therefore all the latitude in the discussion of the subjects which the certain facts and discoveries of profane science may demand. "It is an error to believe," as the erudite Mgr. Meignan truly remarks, "that the Catholic faith restricts the existence of man to a period that does not go beyond six thousand years. The Church has never pronounced on a question so delicate."[3]

The difficulties here suggested, contrary to what many suppose, are by no means new. They have been recognized from the earliest ages of the Church. St. Jerome was so impressed with their magnitude that he abandoned altogether the task of establishing a system of chronology for the Old Testament.[4] And the dif-

---

[1] *Études Réligieuses*, p. 511.   [2] P. 165.
[3] *Le Monde et l'Homme primitif selon la Bible*, p. 163.
[4] "Ejusmodi annorum," he tells us, "certum numerum difficile est invenire, propter librorum varietatem et errores

ficulties that beset all attempts at fixing the chronology of the Bible were acknowledged by other Fathers and commentators as well as by St. Jerome. More than a century and a half ago Des Vignoles in his learned work on the *Chronology of Sacred History* tells us that he collected upward of two hundred different calculations, the shortest of which gives but thirty-three hundred and eighty-three years from the creation of the world[1] to the birth of Christ, whilst the longest reckons sixty-nine hundred and eighty-four years. This makes a difference of thirty-five centuries. And Des Vignoles did not take account of all the chronological calculations which have been made, but only of the principal ones. D'Ortous de Mairan, a distinguished astronomer of the last century, arrived at a similar result. Having examined seventy-five distinct chronological systems, he found that the lowest estimate placed the date of the creation of the world at 3700 years B. C., while the highest fixed it at 7000 years. Since his time the number of systems of biblical chronology which have been excogitated and pro-

inolitos ; aut si invenimus magno studio et labore, nihil profutura cognoscas."

[1] The majority of chronologists until the present century confounded the time of the creation of the world with that of the creation of man, because they were of the opinion that the one was separated from the other by only six days of twenty-four hours each. According to Dr. John Lightfoot, Vice-chancellor of the University of Cambridge, and an eminent rabbinical scholar of the seventeenth century, "heaven and earth, centre and circumference, were created all together, in the same instant, and clouds full of water," and "this work took place and man was created by the Trinity on October 23, 4004 B. C., at nine o'clock in the morning."

mulgated has greatly augmented. During the past few decades especially scriptural scholars have been unusually active in their endeavors to clear up at least some of the difficulties that have so long puzzled chronologists. The discoveries of Assyriologists and Egyptologists have thrown a flood of light on many disputed points, but there are innumerable problems which are yet unsolved, and which will probably ever remain as much of an enigma as they are at present.

Indeed, no one who has not made a special study of questions like the one we are now discussing has the faintest conception of the countless obstacles encountered by the chronologist in his particular branch of science. A simple illustration is the colossal work of the Benedictines of Saint Maur, entitled *L'Art de Vérifier les Dates*. This remarkable monument of labor and erudition appeared in 1750 in a single quarto volume. In less than a century it was so augmented as to make no less than thirty-eight volumes.

Nature of Difficulties in Scriptural Chronology.

The causes of the difficulties and discrepancies occurring in scriptural chronology are manifold. In the first place, the Old Testament, as is well known, comes to us through three different channels—viz. the Hebrew text, the Samaritan text, and the Greek version of the Septuagint. In respect of their divers chronologies these three sources are hopelessly at variance with one another. Many attempts, it is true, have been made to reconcile them with each other, but they seem to be utterly irreconcilable.[1] Nor have we any intrinsic reason for preferring any one of them to the others. All have had and still have their defenders.

The chief if not the only difficulties worth mentioning here occur in the genealogical lists of the patriarchs from Adam to Noah and from Noah to Abraham. According to the Samaritan text, the interval between Adam and Noah and the Deluge amounted to 1307 years; according to the Hebrew, from which we obtain our Vulgate, it was 1656, while according to the Greek or the Septuagint version it was 2242 years. In like manner, the time that elapsed between the Deluge and the vocation of Abraham was, according to the Samaritan, Hebrew, and Greek sources, respectively, 1017, 367, and 1147 years. Thus the three texts in the order named would yield 2329, 2023, and 3389 years for the period intervening between the creation of Adam and the call of Abraham. But the Septuagint has a number of variants in the genealogies of both the antediluvian and postdiluvian patriarchs. For antediluvian times Eusebius gives a total of 2242 years; Julius Africanus, 2262; Clement of Alexandria, 2148; Josephus, 2156. From the Deluge to Abraham, Eusebius reckons 945 years; Theophilus of Antioch, 936; George Syncellus, 1070; Julius Africanus, 940; Clement of Alexandria, 1175; Josephus, 993. "These variants," as Darras well observes, "constitute for the general chronology of the first two epochs of history a difficulty which probably will never be solved." The figures,

---

[1] St. Augustine says anent this matter, *De quibus rationem aut nullam aut difficilimam reddunt*, and his words are as true to-day as when they were first penned.

however, which I have given are those ordinarily accepted.

As a consequence of these different elements and variants divers figures have been obtained by the supputations of chronologers for the period that elapsed between the creation of Adam and the beginning of our era. The modern Jews fix the date of creation at 3761 years B. C.; Scaliger, at 3950; the learned Jesuit Petavius, at 3983; Usher, at 4004; Clinton, at 4138; the new edition of the *Art of Verifying Dates*, at 4963; Hales, at 5411; Jackson, at 5426; the Church of Alexandria, at 5504; the Church of Constantinople, at 5510; Vossius, at 6004; Penvino, at 6311; the Alphonsine Tables, at 6984. The mean assumed by the earlier ecclesiastical writers fixes the date of the creation of the world at 5500 years before our era. Origen makes it 5000 years, while Eusebius places it at 5300, and Julius Africanus at 5562 years. Adding the highest of these numbers to 1894, the time since the coming of Christ, we have, as the age of our race, a period that embraces no less than 9000 years.

These figures, which are only a few of those which might be adduced, are amply sufficient to exhibit the total lack of certainty that obtains in the chronology of the earlier history of mankind.

Owing to the labors of Joseph Scaliger, who laid the foundations of modern chronological science, the chronology of the Hebrew text has generally prevailed since the sixteenth century. Before his time, however, the chronology of the Septuagint predominated. During the first six centuries of our era it was used by both Greek and Latin ecclesiastical writers. It is still employed by the Greek Church, and retained in the

Roman Martyrology, which places the date of the creation at 5199 years before the coming of Christ.

But, notwithstanding the efforts of Scaliger and his followers to give vogue to the Hebrew chronology, the Septuagint, even before the imperative demands of modern science were made, still counted many defenders among modern scholars. Among these were Isaac Vossius, Morin, Cappell, the learned religious of Citeaux, Father Pezron, and the erudite ecclesiastical historian, Cardinal Baronius. The latter, while fully recognizing all the difficulties of the question, avowed his preference for the chronology of the Septuagint as being more in accord with the traditions of the Church. Many of the earlier Fathers adopted it for a similar reason. They perceived, as we do to-day, the impossibility of reconciling the chronology of the Vulgate with the histories of Egypt and Chaldea. The most distinguished modern advocate of the Samaritan text is the celebrated German Egyptologist, Lepsius, who followed it in his learned work on the *Chronology of the Egyptians*.

For some unexplained reason, the chronological system of Usher, the Protestant archbishop of Armagh, has found its way into the English versions of the Bible, and many there are who believe that the dates given at the heads of some of the chapters belong to the original Scriptures, whereas all students of Holy Writ are well aware that the inspired authors of the Sacred Record gave no such dates.

The Church has always permitted her children full liberty of opinion regarding the much-controverted question of biblical chronology. The Council of Trent, which issued so many wise decrees respecting the Canonical Scriptures, left the subject of the number of generations of patriarchs, together with their respective ages, an open question to be settled, if possible, by historians and scientists. Biblical chronology, as such, has no bearing on dogma, and for this reason the Church has never given the matter any attention, and most likely never will.

It is perfectly manifest that the genealogical tables of but one of the three texts, Hebrew, Greek, and Samaritan, can be correct. The other two must therefore be erroneous. Which one is right and which are wrong will most likely ever remain a matter of dispute. "Some chronologists," says Bergier, "think that the Hebrews have shortened their chronology; others are of the opinion that the Seventy have lengthened the period of time from Adam to our Lord; while others, again, give their preference to the Samaritan text." But none of these three opinions are susceptible of demonstrative proof. The arguments advanced by critics in favor of any of these divers opinions are at best serious, never decisive.

But it is not certain that any of the three texts gives the exact figures contained in the original, authentic copy of Genesis. If two of the texts are manifestly erroneous in so far as they refer to the genealogical lists of the patriarchs, it is far from certain that the third is not likewise incorrect. It is impossible to prove that the original figures have not been altered by copyists, either intentionally or through inadvertence, and hence we have no warrant for concluding, as is so often done, that even the oldest copy of the Pentateuch in existence contains the exact numbers written by Moses. For this reason it is that Mgr.

Meignan does not hesitate to declare that "the precise date of the apparition of man on the earth cannot be determined with certitude."

If the alterations were but few and of but small moment, we should be justified in fixing the date of the creation of Adam somewhere between 4000 and 7000 years B. C.—a wide margin, it is true—and of placing the age of our race at between six thousand and nine thousand years. This we may assume until evidence is forthcoming to the contrary.

Lacunæ in Genealogical Lists.

But just here we are confronted with another and, if anything, a more serious difficulty. Are we sure that the lists of the antediluvian and postdiluvian patriarchs are complete? Have we any positive evidence that they are not fragmentary, and that there are no *lacunæ* in them? Far from it. On the contrary, there are grave reasons for believing that many links in the chain are lacking, and that the catalogue of the descendants of Adam in a direct line to Abraham is probably incomplete. It must be said, however, that there is no direct evidence in Genesis of such gaps. It is furnished rather by passages from other portions of the Old and New Testaments, and made more plausible by extrinsic considerations based on the declarations of science and history.

"The genealogies of the Bible," observes M. Wallon, "having for object to give us the filiation of men and not the succession of time, and being able therefore to suppress intermediaries, no calculation can, with any degree of certainty, go beyond Abraham."[1] In another place the same judicious writer asserts that "the chronology of the Bible can be established only by genealogical lists. But the Orientals in their genealogies have a care for only one thing—to follow the direct line, without attaching special importance to intermediaries. Thus, whole generations are suppressed, and as a consequence years, and even centuries, are taken from our calculations." Long ago, before the advance of science indicated the necessity of an extension of time for the patriarchal age, Father Lequien wrote as follows: "It is possible that Moses deemed it proper to make mention of only ten of the principal patriarchs who lived before the Deluge, and of ten others who lived between this epoch and Abraham, omitting the others for reasons to us unknown, as St. Matthew has done in the genealogy of our Lord, and as the authors of the book of Ruth and of the first book of Paralipomenon have done in that of David and in that of the high priests."[2]

To the instances adduced by Lequien, Vigouroux cites others. Thus, "even in the Pentateuch, Laban, the *grandson* of Nachor, is called his son, through the omission of the name of Bathuel, his father. Jochabed, the mother of Moses, is called the *daughter of Levi*, although Levi was certainly dead a long time before her birth. In the first book of Paralipomenon, Subael, a contemporary of David, is spoken of as the *son of Gerson*, who was the son of Moses and lived many ages before. In the third and fourth books

---

[1] *La Sainte Bible Résumée*, I. tome i. p. 435.

[2] Quoted by Vigouroux in the *Revue des Questions scientifiques*, October, 1886, p. 371.

of Kings, as well as in the second book of Paralipomenon, Jehu is named the *son of Namsi*, notwithstanding he was his grandson. In Esdras, Addo, who was the grandfather, is called the father, of Zachary. Our Saviour, as is well known, is often spoken of as the son of David. The Gospel of St. Luke according to the Septuagint contains in the genealogical tree of our Lord, as all are aware, a name—that of Cainan—which is wanting in the genealogical list of St. Matthew, and which is not found at all in the Hebrew and Samaritan texts."

A far more striking example of the existence of *lacunæ* in genealogical trees is afforded by St. Matthew. From the list of the ancestors of our Saviour he excludes, and to all appearances intentionally, three well-known royal names—Ochozias, Joas, and Amasias.[1] This suppression is the more especially deserving of attention inasmuch as it may enable us to detect the motive of the systematic omission of a number of links in the genealogical chain. It seems, indeed, to have been for mnemotechnic reasons. As the genealogical tables were learned by heart, numerous expedients were resorted to in order to facilitate the labor of the memory and to enable it to retain the dry lists of names. With this object in view, and indicating at the same time his method of procedure, the Evan-

---

[1] It is to be noted that in spite of this triple suppression the Evangelist uses the word *genuit—Joram genuit Oziam*—although Ozias was the son of Amasias. This proves that the Hebrews, like the Orientals generally, did not always employ this expression in its strict sense. The word is the consecrated term always employed in the genealogical lists, and may signify mediate as well as immediate filiation.

gelist has subdivided the entire series into three groups of fourteen members each. And because the second would have had seventeen in lieu of fourteen members, which would have destroyed the economy of distribution, he eliminates three of them. "We may suspect," continues Vigouroux, "an analogous mnemotechnic reason for the two patriarchal genealogies. They seem, indeed, to be based on even a more simple system. They each one reckon before and after the Deluge ten names, the number easiest to remember, the number which corresponds to the ten fingers of the two hands, and that, too, on which the decimal system is founded the world over."

In a word, the decimal number of the patriarchs before and after the Deluge, and the custom of the Orientals often to suppress intermediate members in their genealogical lists, all authorize us to admit the possibility of hiatuses in the enumeration which Moses makes of the direct descendants from Adam to Abraham. But if this be so, the date of the creation of man may go back much farther than has hitherto been believed, because it would then be necessary to extend it by the duration of the life of all those personages omitted in the catalogues of Genesis. The epoch, consequently, of the apparition of man on the earth is entirely uncertain, not only because we are ignorant of the true figures written by the author of the Pentateuch, as we have already seen, but also, and more especially, because we do not know what may be the number of hiatuses in the genealogical series. If the alteration of figures can affect the antiquity of man only to a limited extent, it is quite otherwise with the omission of whole generations, because if these omissions be numerous the date of the first man may be put back many centuries.

In consulting, therefore, only the Bible, we are left in a state of complete uncertainty regarding the antiquity of our race. It is possible that according to the actual Hebrew text it is but six thousand years; it is possible that it is eight thousand years, according to the Septuagint; it is also possible to suppose that it dates back much farther by reason of the lacunæ which we are justified in assuming to exist in the genealogical trees. Such is the final conclusion to which we are led by a critical study of the Sacred Text—uncertainty and ignorance.[1]

These views of the distinguished Sulpician are shared by many other modern exegetists whose erudition is as profound as their orthodoxy in matters of dogma is unquestionable. Among these may specially be mentioned the learned Jesuits, Fathers Bellynck,[2] Knabenbauer,[3] and Brucker.[4] Father Bellynck declares emphatically that "there does not exist any chronology in the Bible. The genealogies of our Sacred Books," he goes on to say, "from which a series of dates has been deduced, present occasional gaps. How many years are missing from this broken chain? We cannot tell. It is therefore permitted science to put back the Deluge as many years as science may judge necessary." Father Brucker main-

---

[1] Loc. cit., pp. 372 et seq.
[2] *Études religieuses*, art. "Anthropologie," April, 1868.
[3] *Stimmen aus Maria Laach*, art. "Bibel und Chronologie," 1874, pp. 362-372.
[4] *La Controverse*, art. "La Chronologie des Premiers Ages de l'Humanité," March, 1886, and "Quelques Éclaircissements sur la Chronologie biblique," September, 1886.

tains the existence of gaps in the list of postdiluvian patriarchs in order to account for the various ethnological and linguistic types of humanity that are known to have been formed during the interval between the Flood and the time of Abraham. Hence he does not hesitate to assert that "we are free to add to the vulgar date of the Deluge as many centuries as serious and scientific reasons may demand."

Scriptural Chronology and Church Teaching.

The learned Sulpician, the Abbé de Foville, gives in a nutshell the Catholic doctrine on the subject when he declares that "the Bible indicates in a measure which suffices for its divine scope the chronological order of the facts which it relates. But the Holy Spirit not having inspired it in order to found or cast light upon the science of chronology, we should not seek in it a detailed and precise chronology, a complete system of dates accurately indicated, methodically connected, and perfectly preserved."

The Abbé Bourgeois, the distinguished archæologist, and to the day of his death an ardent champion of Tertiary man, is not less positive when he affirms that "the text of the Bible is brief and obscure; geology and prehistoric archæology, notwithstanding some truths which have been acquired, are not less obscure in respect to many essential points. Why establish premature concordances, and not rather wait for light, with the well-founded confidence that scientific truth can never be opposed to religious truth?"[1]

[1] In our endeavors to explain biblico-scientific questions like the one we are now discussing we should always have before our minds the first paragraph of the admirable sum-

Modern science has certainly discovered nothing that should in the least change or weaken our faith or shake our confidence in any of those verities which mary of the Holy Father's recent encyclical on *The Study of the Sacred Scripture*. After laying down rules for the guidance of students of the Sacred Text, the Doctor of the Faithful writes: "Let them loyally hold that God, the Creator and Ruler of all things, is also the Author of the Scriptures, and that, therefore, nothing can be proved, either by physical science or archæology, which can really contradict the Scripture. If, then, apparent contradiction be met with, every effort should be made to remove it. Judicious theologians and commentators should be consulted as to what is the true or most probable meaning of the passage in discussion, and the hostile arguments should be carefully weighed. Even if the difficulty is, after all, not cleared up, and the discrepancy seems to remain, the contest must not be abandoned: truth cannot contradict truth, and we may be sure that some mistake has been made, either in the interpretation of the sacred words or in the polemical discussion itself; and if no such mistake can be detected, we must suspend judgment for the time being. There have been objections without number perseveringly directed against the Scripture for many a long year which have been proved to be futile, and are never heard of; and not unfrequently interpretations have been placed on certain passages of Scripture (not belonging to the rule of faith or morals) which have been rectified by more careful investigations. As time goes on, mistaken views die and disappear, but 'truth remaineth, and groweth stronger for ever and ever.' Wherefore, as no one should be so presumptuous as to think that he understands the whole of the Scripture, in which St. Augustine himself confessed that there was more that he did not know than that he knew, so, if he should come upon anything that seems incapable of solution, he must take to heart the cautious rule of the same holy Doctor: 'It is better even to be oppressed by unknown useful signs than to interpret them uselessly, and thus to throw off the yoke only to be caught in the trap of error.'"

the Church proposes for our belief. Only those who are ill-informed, or who take a one-sided view of the discussion which has engaged our attention in these pages, see in the question of the antiquity of man any cause for apprehension as to the ultimate results to which a thorough ventilation of the subject will lead. Learned archæologists and theologians like the Abbés Bourgeois and Delaunay and Valroger, who devoted the best years of their lives to the study and elucidation of this and cognate subjects, never came across anything in their investigations—and they were always in the front rank of the scientific movement—to discourage them or to cause them to think, even for a moment, that science and religion are irreconcilable. Far from it. The lives and the works of these pious and erudite advocates of our holy faith afford us a striking illustration of the liberty of thought permitted to the Catholic investigator in matters of science and speculation. When Abbé Bourgeois thought he had demonstrated the existence of Tertiary man by his discovery of the flint flakes at Thenay, he saw no reason for rejecting the scriptural chronology, and still less for impugning the authenticity and inspiration of the Bible as held by the Church. Granting that the flints discovered by him were fabricated by rational beings, might not such beings belong to a distinct species from that descended from Adam—a species extinct before the time of our first ancestor, and a species, consequently, about which the Scripture is silent? Nay, even, may there not have been many species of the genus *Homo*—Preadamites—who lived and died before the apparition of Adam and the race of which he is the father? Neither the Abbé Bourgeois nor the

Abbé Delaunay saw in this hypothesis anything contrary to the Catholic dogma. It is something that does not come within the purview of Scripture—which deals only with the Adamic species—and which does not in the least militate against any of the truths proposed by the Church for our acceptance. The Abbé Fabre d'Envieu and the Abbé Valroger, a distinguished member of the French Oratory, did not hesitate to advance as a conjectural hypothesis the existence of a race of rational beings—Preadamites[1]—distinct from our own, as a means of meeting the difficulty raised by the alleged discovery of Tertiary man.[2] But their theory was not needed, for Tertiary man, as we have seen, is a *chimæra*, and the concurrent testimony of the ablest geologists and archæologists of the day relegates his existence to the limbo of exploded hypotheses and fantastical speculations.[3]

Summary and Conclusion.

To resume. The evidence we have examined regarding the age of our race proves one thing, and

[1] It is scarcely necessary to observe that the Preadamites of Valroger and his confrères do not come under the category of the Preadamites of La Peyrère, whose doctrines in this matter were condemned by the Church. The theory of La Peyrère in a modified form was advocated by the late Prof. Winchell in his voluminous work, *Preadamites*.

[2] The hypothesis was favorably commented on by the eloquent Père Monsabré in his *Conferences de Notre Dame*, pp. 68, 69.

[3] See two letters of the Abbé Delaunay, the learned and zealous collaborator of the Abbé Bourgeois, on the flints of Thenay and their bearing on Tertiary man, in the appendix to vol. iii. of Vigouroux's *Les Livres Saints et la Critique rationaliste*.

proves it most conclusively, and that is, that the question we have been discussing is far from being definitively answered either by Scripture or science, and according to present indications it seems improbable that we shall ever have a certain answer regarding this much-controverted topic. The testimony of astronomy does not, as such, make either for or against the biblical chronology, because astronomy as a science was not cultivated until some thousands of years after the advent of man on the earth. The testimony of history, and especially the history which takes us back farthest —the history of Egypt, Assyria, Chaldea, and Babylonia—admirably corroborates the testimony of the Bible concerning the antiquity of man. The sciences of linguistics, ethnology, and physiology have discovered nothing which is incompatible with the acceptance of the chronology of Scripture as understood by our most competent apologists. The statements of geology and prehistoric archæology are so vague and conflicting and extravagant that nothing definite can be gathered from them beyond the apparently indisputable fact that the age of our species is greater than the advocates of the Hebrew and Samaritan texts of the Bible have been wont to admit. It may, however, be asserted positively that no certain geologic or archæologic evidence so far adduced is irreconcilable with a chronology which we are warranted in deducing from the known facts and genealogical records of the Book of books. Until other and more conclusive evidence is forthcoming, the chronology of the Septuagint, as read in the light of modern Catholic exegesis, is abundantly competent to meet all the real difficulties regarding the antiquity of man which have been proclaimed to the world with such pomp and circumstance by geologists and archæologists during the past few decades.

The late Abbé Moigno, who made an exhaustive study of all the evidence bearing on the question, gives it as his opinion that "the exact date of the creation of man, of his first appearance on the earth, remains entirely uncertain or unknown, but that there would be some rashness in carrying it back beyond eight thousand years."[1]

Canon Hamard, one of the most eminent archæologists of France, says in reference to this subject "that it is necessary to adopt the chronology of the Septuagint, as affording us notably more time, we are convinced, but we fail to see any reason for carrying this chronology beyond the eight or ten thousand years which it accords us as a maximum."[2] Father Hewit, C. S. P., writes: "Thus far, we have not seen any plausible reason to put back the beginnings of the human race to an earlier period than 10,000 years B. C. We are firmly convinced that a concurrence of proofs from all branches of science bearing on the subject, scriptural exegesis included, requires the admission of a date for the creation of the human species at least ten or twenty centuries earlier than the vulgar era of 4004 B. C.[3]

---

[1] *Splendeurs de la Foi*, tome ii. p. 612.
[2] *Les Science et l'Apologétique chretienne*, p. 31. Cf. the article by the same writer on "Adam," in the *Dictionnaire de la Bible*, publié par F. Vigouroux, fascicule i., as also his articles on *L'Antiquité de l'Homme*, published in 1886–87 in *La Controverse et lé Contemporain*.
[2] *The Catholic World*, January, 1885, p. 451.

Abbé Vigouroux, who, although conservative, never flinches before a difficulty, says: "We maintain, it is true, that the progress of the civilizations which flourished in Egypt and Chaldea from the times of the most ancient kings whose names are known to us, as well as the discoveries of geologists and palæontologists, demand a longer time than the chronology of the Septuagint allows us; but here all calculation becomes impossible, and we can but say to the archæologists and savants, Establish by irrefragable proofs the antiquity of man and of the people of the earlier ages, and the Bible will not contradict it. Does it not give us to understand that it leaves these questions to the discussion of men, provided they keep within the bounds of sound criticism, when it declares through Ecclesiasticus, *Arenam maris et pluviæ guttas et dies sæculi, quis dinumeravit?*[1]— "Who hath numbered the sand of the sea and the drops of rain and the days of the world?"

As to myself, I incline to a liberal but legitimate interpretation of the version of the Septuagint, and am disposed to attribute to man an antiquity of about ten thousand years. It may be a little more or it may be a little less. Certain it is that there is not as yet a single known *fact* which necessitates an extension of this period. Future research may indeed raise the figure to twelve or fifteen thousand, or even to twenty thousand, years, but, judging from the evidence now available, and bearing in mind the disposition of many of our most eminent scientists to shorten rather

---

[1] *Revue des Questions scientifiques*, October, 1886, p. 407. Cf. *Manuel biblique*, tome i. p. 568, and *Les Livres Saints et la Critique rationaliste*, vol. iii. p. 547.

than prolong the age of our species, it seems more
likely that the general consensus of chronologists will
ultimately fix on a number which shall be below rather
than above ten thousand years as the nearest approximation to the age of our race.[1]

[1] Nearly a year after the preceding paragraph was written I
was gratified to find that both Mgr. d'Hulst and M. le Marquis de Nadaillac entertain similar views to my own in respect
to the age of the human race. Mgr. d'Hulst, the distinguished rector of the Catholic University of Paris and the
eloquent preacher of Notre Dame, in his admirable brochure, *La Question biblique*, is disposed to put the antiquity
of man at about ten thousand years. In a learned paper in
Le Correspondant for Nov. 10 and 25, 1893, the Marquis de Nadaillac, who is recognized as one of the ablest archæologists of
Europe, sums up the evidence for the age of our species as follows: "Il est impossible de ne pas être frappé de la concordance des calculs géologiques avec les données que nous avons
empruntées à l'histoire et à l'archéologie. Appuyés sur des faits
indéniables, sur tous ceux actuellement connus, nous répéterons que la limite extrême qui l'on peut assigner à l'humanité, depuis la creation, ne saurait guère depasser 10,000 ans."

Views essentially identical are expressed by Padre Mir, S. J.,
in his erudite work, *La Creacion*, and by Cardinal Gonzales in
La Biblia y la Ciencia. In closing his thoughtful chapter on
the antiquity of man, his Eminence thus observes: "En todo
caso, lo que aqui no debe perderse de vista, y lo que en realidad
representa el pensamiento cristiano con relación á este problema, es que ni la Biblia ni la Iglesia enseñan nada concreto y
fijo acerca del tiempo transcurrido desde Adam hasta nosotros,
y que, por consiguiente, hoy por hoy la ciencia, por este lado,
tiene el camino expedito para entregarse á sus investigaciones
propias, formular hipótesis, y, sobre todo, acumular hechos y
datos que puedan conducirla á la solución definitiva del problema. Entretanto, es prudencia, no sólo cristiana, sino cientifica, suspender el juicio en cosa tan dudosa, de conformidad
con el conseje de San Augustin: *Servata semper moderatione
piæ gravitatis, nihil credere de re obscura temere debemus.*"

The question, in reality, is one which is to be settled by history rather than by natural science, whatever geologists and archæologists may say to the contrary. It is precisely in questions like this that history, to use the happy expression of Cicero, is not only the *nuntia vetustatis*—"the messenger of antiquity"— but also the *lux veritatis*—"the torch of truth"— without which we must for ever hopelessly grope in darkness. Science may adduce facts regarding the age of our race, but history, and history alone, must be their chief and, ofttimes, their sole interpreter. Thus far, the conclusions of authentic history and the teachings of Holy Writ respecting the age of the human race are so marvellously concordant that they may be considered as giving testimony which is identical. Aside from certain apparent discrepancies, resulting from lack of information or misinterpretation of fact, there has never been any serious conflict between the two; there is no conflict now, and I am firmly convinced there will be none in the future, because, from the Catholic point of view, a conflict is from the very nature of the case impossible. And I make this declaration, not in the spirit of special pleading, not because I love science less and the Bible more, not because I assume that there is or can be an attitude of hostility on the part of science—I do not mean theory—toward religion; not because I ignore facts or minimize logical deductions from facts observed, but because I am as firmly convinced as I can be of anything that God is the Lord of science, that science is the handmaid of religion, that the two, speaking of the same Author, although in different tongues, must voice the same testimony, and that this

THE AGE OF THE HUMAN RACE. 315

testimony must be not only unequivocally true, but also unequivocally one. I fear not facts—I have been searching for them all my life—but experience has led me to distrust theories which are prematurely formulated. I welcome now all facts, as I always have welcomed them, bearing on the age of our race, and I am certain that in the long run, when all the necessary facts are reported and co-ordinated, the results will be as harmonious as a certain school would now have us believe they are discordant.

We could not have a more striking illustration of the vagaries to which the unguided human intellect is subject than is afforded by the vacillating and extravagant notions it has entertained regarding the antiquity of man. It has been willing to believe everything as possible, and to accept the most manifest absurdities as tenable. For more than a generation past we have been asked to accept as veritable science what was obviously nothing more than a tissue of arrogant and threadbare conceits—a reflection of individual fancy and not a mirror of the facts of nature. Like the spectre of the Brocken, the science of many of our "advanced thinkers" is but an empty shadow of their own mind's throwing—a magnified, intangible, evanescent phantom projected on a background of cloud and mist. The theories are, indeed, made plausible to an unsuspecting public, because they are presented with all the enchantments of persuasive speech. For their authors, truth to tell, often possess what St. Augustine characterizes as the *illecebræ suaviloquentiæ*—what Renan happily designates as *une certaine habilité dans l'art d'amener les cliquetis des mots, et des idées;* but all this is but a specious cloak for uncertainty and ignorance. The inductions from false premises which we are bidden to regard as the last word of science are frequently as hypothetical as the *chimæra bombinans in vacuo* of the mediæval metaphysicians. But such is the vogue of much that passes under the name of modern science, not in any one particular part of the earth, but the world over from Copenhagen to Lisbon,

> "a Gadibus usque
> Auroram et Gangen."

We must, however, regard it as one of the manifestations of the *zeitgeist* of our generation. For, be it known, the zeitgeist is a capricious being and more changeable than Proteus. It knows how to satisfy its votaries, who, like the Athenians and the strangers whom St. Paul addressed on the Areopagus, "employed themselves in nothing else but either in telling or in hearing some new thing."[1] But recent events and revelations in every department of science seem to betoken a speedy return to a more serious and a more conservative *régime*. The fin-de-siècle, dilettante man of science is fast losing the prestige he once had, and scientists generally, who have long been travelling in an orbit of great eccentricity, are rapidly returning to perihelion—to the centre of light and truth where flames for all earnest seekers after knowledge the light of science and wisdom.

[1] Acts of the Apostles xvii. 21.

www.ingramcontent.com/pod-product-compliance
Lightning Source LLC
Chambersburg PA
CBHW030019240426
43672CB00007B/1011